SUSTAINABILITY FOR BEGINNERS

INTRODUCTION AND BUSINESS PROSPECTS

Other World Scientific Titles by the Author

An Introduction to Electrospinning and Nanofibers
ISBN: 978-981-256-415-3
ISBN: 978-981-256-454-2 (pbk)

An Introduction to Biocomposites
ISBN: 978-1-86094-425-3
ISBN: 978-1-86094-426-0 (pbk)

Polymer Membranes in Biotechnology: Preparation, Functionalization and Application
ISBN: 978-1-84816-379-9
ISBN: 978-1-84816-380-5 (pbk)

The Changing Face of Innovation: Is it Shifting to Asia?
ISBN: 978-981-4291-58-3 (pbk)

Additive Manufacturing: Foundation Knowledge for the Beginners
ISBN: 978-981-122-481-2
ISBN: 978-981-122-624-3 (pbk)

An Introduction to Biomaterials Science and Engineering
ISBN: 978-981-122-817-9
ISBN: 978-981-124-196-3 (pbk)

SUSTAINABILITY FOR BEGINNERS

INTRODUCTION AND BUSINESS PROSPECTS

RAMADOSS TAMIL SELVAN
SEERAM RAMAKRISHNA

National University of Singapore, Singapore

 **World Scientific**

NEW JERSEY · LONDON · SINGAPORE · BEIJING · SHANGHAI · HONG KONG · TAIPEI · CHENNAI · TOKYO

Published by

World Scientific Publishing Co. Pte. Ltd.

5 Toh Tuck Link, Singapore 596224

USA office: 27 Warren Street, Suite 401-402, Hackensack, NJ 07601

UK office: 57 Shelton Street, Covent Garden, London WC2H 9HE

Library of Congress Cataloging-in-Publication Data
Names: Tamil Selvan, Ramadoss, author. | Ramakrishna, Seeram, author.
Title: Sustainability for beginners : introduction and business prospects /
    Ramadoss Tamil Selvan, Seeram Ramakrishna, National University of Singapore, Singapore.
Description: 1st Edition. | Hackensack, NJ : World Scientific, 2022. |
    Includes bibliographical references and index.
Identifiers: LCCN 2021024471 | ISBN 9789811241932 (hardcover) |
    ISBN 9789811241949 (ebook) | ISBN 9789811241956 (ebook other)
Subjects: LCSH: Entrepreneurship. | Business enterprises--Environmental aspects. |
    Sustainable development.
Classification: LCC HB615 .T36 2022 | DDC 658.4/21--dc23
LC record available at https://lccn.loc.gov/2021024471

British Library Cataloguing-in-Publication Data
A catalogue record for this book is available from the British Library.

For any available supplementary material, please visit
https://www.worldscientific.com/worldscibooks/10.1142/12413#t=suppl

Desk Editor: Shaun Tan Yi Jie

Typeset by Stallion Press
Email: enquiries@stallionpress.com

To innocent people who lost their lives to the Covid-19 virus, with the expectation that scientific developments could avert such a devastating outbreak in the future

PREFACE

The Covid-19 crisis has revealed the uncertainty of our current economic model. It has significantly impacted our global supply and distribution chains, making them more vulnerable. This circumstance has caused us to recognize that our present economic paradigm, the Linear Economy (take, make, use, dispose), is losing its integrity. As a result, emissions, resource scarcity, and massive waste generation have become prevalent, leading to climate change, sea-level rise, and adverse effects on humans and other beings on the planet.

Researchers, practitioners, industrialists, and policymakers are investigating the usefulness of the Circular Economy (reduce, reuse, recycle) to overcome the impacts created by Linear Economy. Sustainability (people, planet, profit) and Sustainable developments, on the other hand, is a holistic idea, integrating Circular Economy, Corporate Social Responsibility (CSR), Sustainable Investments, Sustainable business practices, etc., and have become widespread among industries and scholars. In this direction, the United Nations has developed 17 Sustainable Development Goals to promote a sustainable economy, environment, and society.

This book is a nexus between sustainable engineering, businesses, and investments. Chapters 1, 2, and 3 provide an overview of the linear economy, circular economy, sustainability, and sustainable development. These chapters assist students from all backgrounds and programs, as well as emerging entrepreneurs interested in sustainability to gain a better understanding of current circumstances.

Chapters 4 and 5 will discuss engineering viewpoints on sustainability. These chapters will take you through the framework for achieving long-term sustainability created by academics and governments. Then, using examples and equations, subsets of the sustainability framework (indicators and assessment) are addressed. Following that, a life cycle assessment of coal-fired power plant and solar panels production is conducted using a 100 MW electricity generation scenario. These chapters would demonstrate how to apply sustainable thinking using open-source software such as openLCA and gain a fundamental understanding of environmental impacts.

Chapters 6 and 7 will provide a basic introduction to Environmental, Social, and Corporate Governance (ESG) evolution with a timeline. The term ESG reporting, Sustainable reporting, or CSR are synonymous. These chapters would explain the importance of ESG reporting and how investors use these criteria to assess businesses to invest in with the aid of rating companies such as Refinitiv. The basics of ESG reporting are addressed, using a framework and case studies from Singapore Airlines, Microsoft Corporation, and Samsung Electronics.

Chapters 8 and 9 are geared toward entrepreneurs and explore the fundamentals of Osterwalder's commonly known business model canvas. Following that, these chapters draw inspiration from Osterwalder's business model canvas and suggest a sustainable business model canvas and sustainable innovation cycle, offering a deeper explanation for entrepreneurs focused on sustainable businesses. Singapore-based sustainable start-up Tria is also discussed as a local case study, presenting the sustainable business model canvas to facilitate entrepreneurs fostering sustainability.

Chapter 10 addresses the relationship between engineering, business, and society through a sustainability lens. We identify five critical areas that need urgent attention from academia and companies to mitigate ongoing global problems from a sustainable and prospective standpoint. Subsequently, a pathway towards a zero-carbon planet is proposed from the authors' perspective.

This first version of the book was written with great caution. However, there may be several unintentional mistakes and some topics that are left unattended or overlooked. We appreciate feedback and criticisms, which would be addressed suitably in the second edition of this book.

We thank Canva for facilitating the front cover design with an image.

Ramadoss Tamil Selvan
Seeram Ramakrishna

ACKNOWLEDGEMENTS

First and foremost, I want to show my thankfulness to my wife, Saranya, for her compassion and emotional support. Regardless of our split due to travel constraints during the global Covid-19 crisis, she is still by my side and tends to embrace me warmly. She is always at the forefront of my achievements, adding values and rendering meaning to my life. Additionally, our adored one-and-a-half-year-old daughter, Tharagai, catalyses our difficult days with her cute expressions, infusing our life with purpose.

Secondly, I would like to express my gratitude to Dr Pankaj Pathak of SRM University in India for her assistance with Chapter 5. I am fond of her kindness and friendliness, which are sorely missing these days.

Finally, I am at a loss for words to describe such a towering person in the universe. Prof. Seeram Ramakrishna FREng, an exceptional intellectual mind with heaps of recognition, a person with infinite positive attributes, and an unmatched human being. I have been blessed to work with him for several years and am genuinely awestruck by his unparalleled love. From the bottom of my heart, I wish him a healthy life and hope that his scholarly efforts would continue to benefit humanity.

Ramadoss Tamil Selvan

ABOUT THE AUTHORS

Mr Ramadoss Tamil Selvan is a Research Engineer at the National University of Singapore, Singapore. Before this appointment, he was working as a Chief Technical Officer in startup companies. He has been actively involved in sustainability business development and prospects by working with startup companies. He is a keen entrepreneur, innovator, speaker, and developed sustainability/circularity software tools for industries and academics. He received an MSc from the University of Nottingham, UK, and a BEng from the Anna University, India. He also received a Nottingham Business School scholarship to pursue an MBA.

Professor Seeram Ramakrishna, FREng is the Chair of Circular Economy Taskforce at the National University of Singapore (NUS). Microsoft Academic ranked him among the top 36 salient authors out of three million materials researchers worldwide. He is the Editor-in-Chief of the Springer NATURE Journal *Materials Circular Economy — Sustainability*. He is a member of Enterprise Singapore's and International Standards Organization's Committees on ISO/ TC323 Circular Economy and Circularity. He teaches ME6501 Materials and Sustainability module, and also mentors Integrated Sustainable Design

ISD5102 course projects on reimagining and enhancing circularity of Industrial Estates. He is an opinion contributor to the Springer Nature Sustainability Community. He is an advisor to the National Environmental Agency's CESS events. He is an Impact Speaker at University of Toronto, Canada's Low Carbon Renewable Materials Center. He is a judge for the Mohammed Bin Rashid Initiative for the Global Prosperity. He is an advisor to the Singapore company TRIA which specializes in zero waste packaging.

Professor Seeram, with a h-index of 161 as of May 2021, is named among the World's Most Influential Minds (Thomson Reuters), and the Top 1% Highly Cited Researchers (Clarivate Analytics). He is an elected Fellow of UK Royal Academy of Engineering (FREng); Singapore Academy of Engineering; Indian National Academy of Engineering; and ASEAN Academy of Engineering & Technology. He is appointed as the Honorary Everest Chair of MBUST, Nepal. His senior academic leadership roles include NUS University Vice-President (Research Strategy); Dean of NUS Faculty of Engineering; Director of NUS Enterprise; and Founding Chairman of Solar Energy Institute of Singapore. He received PhD from the University of Cambridge, UK; and TGMP from the Harvard University, USA.

CONTENTS

CHAPTER ONE
LINEAR ECONOMY AND ITS CONSTRAINTS

Introduction

Early human beings used tamed animals, efficient farming techniques, and reliable sheltering methods for ideal settlement across the untouched lands. As a result of evolution, the curious brain began to harness natural energies from the sun, wind, and water for the good of humans. Metalworking, beginning with copper around 6000 BCE, was the first nature material utilized for tools and decorations.[1] Gold quickly followed, with its primary use for adornments and transaction purposes. The requirement for metal minerals invigorated trade across the vast human establishments.

Historically, the characteristic way of life of living beings permitted resources to return to the ecosystem through a complex network of energy streams and nutrient cycles. However, we started to move away from the sustainable way of life with the rise of industrialization.[2] During the Industrial Revolution, which started around 1750, all changed. People discovered additional energy supplies from fossil fuels — coal, oil, and natural gas, with great potential to function.

A Scottish instrument builder, James Watt, invented a coal-powered engine at the beginning of the 18th century that drove a piston aided by a partial vacuum using steam. A century later, cotton mills driven by steam engines attracted popularity to manufacture fabrics.[3] Subsequently, steam-powered locomotives and ships modernized transportation early in the

19th century. Other nations subsequently picked up the trend, and the expansion of the Industrial Revolution took place swiftly across continents.

The planet had a population of 670 million inhabitants in the 18th century before the Industrial Revolution began. The global population has now hit 7.8 billion in 2020, an 11-fold surge in just 300 years. In the 20th century alone, the global economy expanded 14-fold, per capita income increased almost four-fold, and the consumption of energy rose at least 13-fold.[3]

The rapid population growth implies 1) resource consumption — depletion of non-renewable resources, and 2) waste generation — polluting the environment and affecting the well-being of humans and biodiversity. As shown in Figure 1.1, within the last three centuries, there has been a remarkable transformation that has impacted our lives both positively and negatively. For instance, there were countless beneficial outcomes of the Industrial Revolution, such as a rise in individual wealth, production of cheaper goods, improved quality of life, healthy foods, and decent accommodation. On the other hand, the Industrial Revolution has transformed the landscape from rural to urban-centric, meaning small towns and cities have a concentrated population that contributes to poor living conditions. Factories, using coal as fuel for steam engines, generated vast quantities of air pollution during the 19th century resulting in a contaminated atmosphere. Many great inventions and transformations that occurred throughout the 20th century, such as automation using state-of-the-art electronics and computers, have contributed to mass/rapid production resulting in increased global consumption and generating more waste than before. These industrial advancements heavily relied upon non-renewable resources implying resource depletion, population expansion, and major environmental consequences (e.g., ozone holes).

Likewise, 21st-century residents pursued the same direction as the preceding generation, and the Industrial Revolution 4.0 took effect promptly. As a result, this ultra-modern society has greatly benefitted from the internet, transportation, and technology contributing to accelerated natural resource consumption and generating unprecedented levels of wastes (e.g., plastic and electronic wastes). Meanwhile, the total global volume of Municipal Solid Waste (MSW) production is estimated at 2.01 billion tonnes in 2020 by the World Bank. Waste produced per person

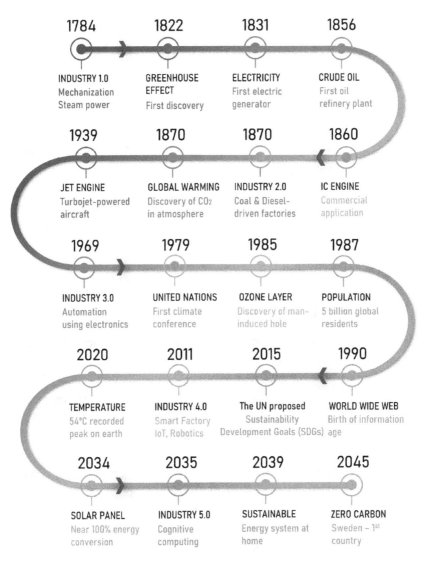

Figure 1.1. Timeline of the Industrial Revolution, consequences, and major efforts over three centuries.

per day averages 740 g worldwide, but varies greatly, from 0.11 to 4.54 kg. Global waste is estimated to reach 3.40 billion tonnes by 2050, with population growth more than doubling over the same period.[4] Likewise, as per the report — The Global E-waste Monitor 2020, the world generated a staggering 55.5 million tonnes of e-waste, an average of 7.5 kg per capita, and is expected to reach 74.4 million tonnes by 2030.[5] The estimates representing the results of global industrialization are alarming. These pieces of evidence have shown that humankind has already begun the sixth mass extinction event if the current pace of resource consumption and waste generation is continued.[6]

On the other hand, as shown in Figure 1.1, governments, businesses, and academics are making attempts to limit resource consumption through policies, sustainable business practices, and research to improve sustainability in the 21st century. As a result, the United Nations Sustainable Development Goals, Carbon Neutrality policies, and Zero-Carbon countries were born. In this chapter, we will explore the availability of critical natural resources and their continuation. Subsequently, we discuss the Linear Economy model and its limitation with examples.

1.1. Current Global Situation

Since the advent of the Industrial Revolution, the manufacturing of commodities has been made possible by revolutionary techniques resulting in high demands and low-cost products. In parallel, this accelerated economic and industrial development catalyzed global population growth and consumer expansion also contributed to high quantities of solid and gaseous wastes being produced and passed on to the atmosphere.[7]

Currently, the threat of environmental degradation is not the only one that needs to be resolved immediately, but also the lack of global resources.[8] During the 21st century, energy use has steadily risen. By consuming fossil fuels containing oil, gas, and coal, about 80% of global energy demand is maintained. The resource extraction industries are responsible for half of the global CO_2 pollution and more than 90% of biodiversity depletion, according to Global Resources Outlook.[10] During the last five decades, natural resource loss has more than tripled, including crude, gas, and coal production, increasing from 6 to 15 billion tonnes, biomass harvests from 9 to 24 billion tonnes, and other mineral supplies growing five-fold.[11] Manufacturing firms would thus find themselves in an unpredictable position soon, with intensified rivalry for access to limited or essential resources. In the modern global context, it appears that the fundamental principles of the linear paradigm are no longer valid and many major developments challenge its sustainable growth, increasing the need for an alternative economic model.[9]

1.2. Critical Non-Renewable Resources

Conceivably, there would be an unavoidable rise in demand for the Earth's natural resources with 7.8 billion humans on the globe now. There are good arguments for questioning the idea that fossil resources are going to run out. For over a century, scientists and engineers have been forecasting the depletion of non-renewable natural resources, as depicted in Figure 1.2.

1.2.1. *Oil*

The Petroleum Exporting Countries Association reports that the planet has 1.49 trillion barrels of crude oil reserves left as of 2020.[12] However, the speculation is somewhat debatable since we lack a reliable tool for

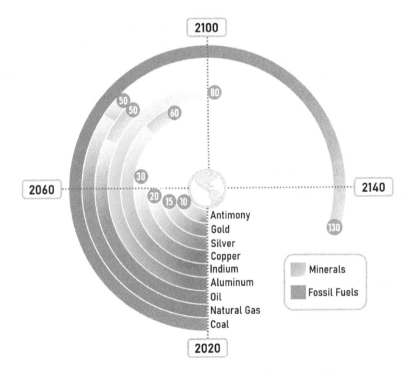

Figure 1.2.   Estimated remaining world supplies of non-renewable resources.

estimating the world's usable oil supplies. Nevertheless, various scientists and consulting companies have decided on one thing: we are running out of crude oil. According to the International Energy Agency, 34 billion barrels of crude oil are consumed annually across the globe, and we all realize that crude oil cannot be replenished.

For the time being, based on Worldometer estimates 2020, we shall account only for proven oil reserves and current consumption rate; thus we might expect that the crude oil period will end anywhere between 2060 and 2070.[13] Indeed, while other considerations, such as the discovery of new deposits, adjustments in annual demand/supply, international policy, etc., should be taken into account, the fact is very evident that the availability of crude oil is declining more and more every day.

1.2.2. *Coal*

Now, let us look at coal, the next critical non-renewable energy source that drives our electricity generation and manufacturing industries. There are approximately 1.1 trillion tonnes of proven coal reserves across the globe, and at current usage rates, this inventory may last us until 2150.[14] Coal is a primary fuel source that supplies 40% of the world's electricity and accounts for 39% of global greenhouse gas emissions.[15] Coal usage represents a key source of our present global warming, health hazards, and environmental pollutions. However, global growth in coal demand has declined in recent years owing to social policy interventions, gas-fired, and renewable-based power generation.[16] The bottom line is that coal has had a significant impact on our economies and would undoubtedly be phased out.

1.2.3. *Natural Gas*

Natural gas, accounting for 23% of the global energy market, is the fastest-rising fossil fuel. As the cleanest fossil fuel, natural gas is responsible for approximately a quarter of our electricity generation, offering a range of environmental advantages, especially in terms of air quality and carbon emissions.[17] According to Global Energy Review, there are 6,556 trillion cubic feet, or 1,092,792 million barrels, of proven gas reserves in the world as of 2020. Looking at the current pace of natural gas production and known reserves, we have about 47 years remaining of natural gas supplies, which will last us till sometime between 2065 and 2070.[18]

1.2.4. *Minerals*

1.2.4.1. *Aluminum*

Bauxite ore is the world's primary aluminum source. First, the ore must be chemically treated to manufacture aluminum oxide (alumina). Subsequently, using electrolysis, pure aluminum metal is created by smelting alumina. With an estimated 8% accumulation of planetary crust, aluminum is 100% recyclable material and maintains its properties forever. Aluminum is predicted at 40–75 billion tonnes of proven reserves,[19] which would last us until at least 2100.

1.2.4.2. *Copper*

Copper still plays a vital role in human growth owing to geological abundance, new technology, and business development. It is estimated that global copper reserves are 870 million tonnes (United States Geological Survey 2020),[20] and the annual demand for copper is 28 million tonnes. Without recycling, our copper reserves will be exhausted in just over 30 years at current use rates.

1.2.4.3. *Gold*

The best figures indicate that roughly 197,576 tonnes of gold have been mined, of which about two-thirds have been extracted since 1950. The world has 50,000 tonnes of proven gold deposits, according to the US Geological Survey (USGS) in 2020.[21] Each year, we consume approximately 4,000–5,000 tonnes of gold for many purposes, such as jewelry making, investments, official holdings, etc. We foresee more gold mining explorations happening across the globe; however, our proven reserves could last conservatively until only 2035 based on the current consumption pace.

1.2.4.4. *Silver*

Silver is found much more commonly on the planet and has numerous manufacturing, consumer, and medical applications. According to the United States Currency Reserve, 1.74 million metric tonnes of silver have been extracted around the world, as of 2020.[22] The USGS estimates that about 560,000 metric tonnes of silver reserves remain globally. The global silver demand was measured at 27,000 tonnes in 2019,[23] so our silver reserves would be wiped out completely by 2040 at this present rate of consumption without considering recycling.

1.2.4.5. *Indium*

Most of the world's indium supply is alloyed with tin and oxygen to form ITO (indium-tin-oxide), which acts as a translucent conductor Liquid Crystal Display (LCD) for smartphones and TV applications. Because of the LCD market's tremendous growth over the past decade, many analysts doubt indium metal's potential supply. Indium is a by-product of zinc mining, and forecasting the future is difficult since it is not specifically extracted. However, we shall take baseline estimation; a broader estimate, including reserves and resources, from the Indium Corporation of America projected gross reserves and resources of about 50,000 tonnes.[24] In 2019, global indium refinery output surpassed 760 metric tonnes as recorded by Statista.[25] While indium has a strong recycling potential, based on current production and reserves, we can infer that indium will be extracted for another 50–60 years. The annual consumption growth rate, however, is not considered in this estimation.

1.2.4.6. *Antimony*

Antimony is mainly used for flame retardants (35%), batteries (29%), and chemicals (16%). According to the Statista 2020 report, China has the world's largest antimony reserves totaling 480,000 tonnes.[26] In 2020, USGS reported that the world has 1.5 million tonnes of antimony reserves. Global consumption for 2019 remains unclear; however, it was estimated to be about 184,000 tonnes in 2015 by the USGS.[27] Also, markets projected a compound annual growth rate of 6.0% between 2018 and 2023.[28] Thus, in 2019, annual antimony consumption would have been nearly 195,000 tonnes. With this data, we can say our antimony reserves would last a decade from now.

The annual consumption rate and resource depletion was calculated as a benchmark based on the year 2019 due to a stable economic stature. While writing this book, the world was engulfed in the Covid-19 pandemic situation in 2020; production and buying capacity was severely impaired. Nonetheless, after a few years or so, the condition will likely return to normal. In general, the available data show that non-renewable reserves will not last a few centuries. It will be more challenging for financial companies or qualified analysts to forecast the supply of non-renewable resources in the coming years with declining supplies and increasing demands. We have to extend their lifetime by recycling, mining exploration, and alternative material findings.

1.3. Linear Economy

What does this natural resource depletion tell us? What are the consequences? To answer these questions, we must agree upon one thing from the two sections discussed earlier. Industrial evolution has enabled humankind to advance by harnessing non-renewable resources and equipping us with extra-human abilities. We transformed ourselves from survival to sophistication mode and spent a lot of time finding new resources by conquering lands and seas. Simultaneously science and technology added their flavour into the system and massively transformed our lives by benefitting from naturally available resources. Hence, our current whole socio-economic system relies heavily upon non-renewable resources for humanity progression.

The advantages of the Industrial Revolution are felt by many people across the world today. Many of us continue to do far less physically demanding work than in past decades, with so much more resources going into human societies than ever before. The Industrial Revolution of the 18th century fundamentally altered the interaction and principles between people and the natural environment. Technological advances related to the economic demands of developing and sustaining economies have culminated in product manufacturing, governed by a Linear Economy (LE) model of production in which products are made from raw materials, distributed, consumed, and either landfilled or incinerated as waste as depicted in Figure 1.3. This drives the modern era of business, which allows the mind to discard the products after use — a practice that is recognized as linear consumption.[29]

1.3.1. *An Example of a Linear Economy Model*

Undoubtedly, the LE model that resulted in the Industrial Revolution has improved economic status and contributed to our society's incredible success through technological advancements. The LE structure has offered opportunities to maximize revenue and mimic economies of scale to expand globally, contributing to the growing consumption of products and services in the marketplace.[30]

However, at what cost are we pursuing the LE model? For starters, let us understand the LE production model and its consequences. For instance, let us consider the plastic manufacturing industry, which is a good example of the LE model, and investigate the associated waste generated by the system. Indeed, plastic bags serve incredible usage purposes, yet the service life is usually only a few hours. Raw materials used to manufacture plastic bags are derived from natural materials such as crude oil or gas that took millions of years to form. We somehow managed to modify the internal structure of the natural materials and transformed them into useful items for our consumption using state-of-art manufacturing technology. Subsequently, the plastic bags are shipped to the marketplace, used, and disposed of by consumers.

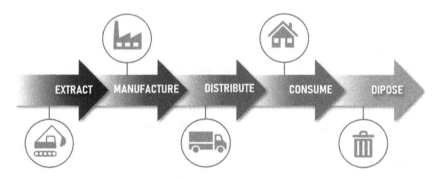

Figure 1.3. The LE model.

This whole supply chain represents the LE or cradle-to-grave model. As customers, most of us will not care about how plastic is being disposed of or recycled. The LE paradigm has been ingrained into our mindset and it is impossible to alter people's behaviors and throw away the LE model in a short period of time. Creating social knowledge to change social behavior is an ongoing process that requires time. But this is crucial when it comes to plastic usage reduction, considering the impact we create on natural systems. From 2016 to 2040, if we do not respond, more than 1.3 billion tonnes of plastics will be discarded on land and seas, claims a team of 17 global experts who have built a computer model to map plastic waste accumulation and flows across the world.[31]

In 2020, as depicted in Figure 1.4, the global production of virgin plastic resins and fibers amounted to approximately 334.83 million tonnes, according to a recent report by Grand View Research Inc, of which 79% of plastic waste was dumped on land and just 9% recycled and 12% incinerated.[32] The bulk of this plastic waste discarded on the ground is then swept into seas via water channels. These plastic materials are divided into smaller pieces by degradation and fragmentation, releasing toxic chemicals in the process. Marine animals often consume a huge volume of

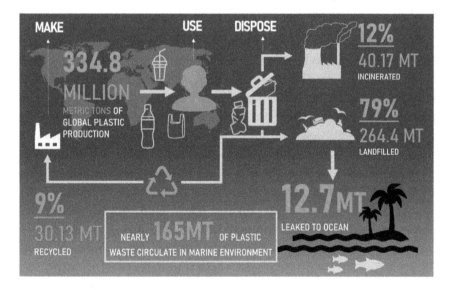

Figure 1.4.　Life cycle of plastic waste scenario in 2020.

plastics as food; these ingested plastic contaminants destroy their digestive organs and weaken their immune systems, resulting in death. People could unknowingly take in 5 g of micro/nano plastics a week via this food chain. Thus, plastic waste disrupts the food chain of aquatic animals, and may also harm our well-being as a result of the LE model.[33]

About 165 million tonnes of plastic waste is projected to remain in the ocean currently, and we can expect somewhere around 710 million tonnes of plastic to be dumped into the environment by 2040, according to a new report "Breaking the Plastic Wave".[34] Such alarming statistics and evidence send a strong warning to society, that our LE paradigm will quickly become outdated, and the damage to the environment is at its maximum. From the plastic waste management situation, we can easily grasp that our LE model assumes that our resources are limitless and will provide consumer goods to a rising population, and that nature is extremely capable of rebuilding itself despite all these pollutants entering the environment. Unfortunately, our natural eco-system is unable to manage this tremendous disruption and does not support a take-make-waste approach.

1.4. Constraints of the Linear Economy

1.4.1. *The LE Framework*

Before investigating the constraints of the LE model, we must consider the conceptual explanation behind the prevailing LE model, which motivates the LE framework to evolve into such a devastating paradigm. Specifically, growing product demand has highly motivated First World nations to procure raw materials from the global marketplace at lower prices. As a result, these developed nations witness surplus materials supplies and energy sources. Manufacturing firms, because of their continuous flow of resources and energy, are embracing business models that rely on widespread materials use; developing countries such as India, China, and Southeast Asian nations, on the other hand, supply inexpensive human resources. Hence, multinational manufacturing companies set up production facilities in and outsource product development to labor-intensive countries under this structure. The inevitable effect of inexpensive material and proximity to low-cost labor markets is the widespread lack of **recycling** and **reuse** mentality that has resulted in massive waste generation.

In the process, lawmakers and regulatory agencies were lenient to charge manufacturing firms with the wastage, and there were no manufacturing guidelines in effect.[35] As a result, by pursuing illusionary development without considering the negative effects, these conditions intensified our LE model to become unsustainable. There is no question that the population is increasing, and essential human needs such as food, accommodation, and transportation have to be addressed immediately. Let us explore our LE paradigm in this direction and its limitations towards our basic needs.

1.4.2. *Food Production*

Let us aim to understand the intricate relationship between the LE food production model and the growing population. According to a recent UN survey, the present global population in 2020 is about 7.8 billion, and it is estimated to grow by about one billion by 2025 and exceed 9.7 billion by 2050.[36] A significant consequence of this trend is growing demand for food and freshwater, consumer products, and energy resources. This places more strain on our economic, environmental, and social facets of the planet. At the fundamental level, to maintain our existence, extreme levels of energy sources are needed to support food production. In this context, let us look at our current LE-related food production paradigm and how our established LE framework is deteriorating against the rising population.

Figure 1.5 indicates the alarming statistics of the growing population against our current food production. We lose approximately 15% (1.1 billion tonnes) of the food we generate every year, according to the Ellen MacArthur Foundation,[37] owing to a lack of storage and expertise to keep food fresh and inadequate logistics.

Urbanites (4.3 billion residents) occupy nearly 56.2% of the global habitable space. Almost 2.4 billion tonnes of food were consumed in 2020; and 0.55 billion tonnes wasted, which is about 1/4th of food entering cities or the potential to feed around 1 billion people. By 2050,[38] 68% of the world's residents would reside in metropolitan cities and be capable of generating 0.85 billion tonnes of food waste, if the current trend continues. High-income city dwellers waste more food attributed to low food prices, and lack of awareness of food production leads to an excessive amount of food demand.

Figure 1.5.   The LE food system. (Source: Data collected from Ellen MacArthur Foundation and projected for 2020 and 2050.)

Urbanization is inevitable but the food we produce today rely on non-renewable resources including phosphorus, potassium, and crude oil.[39] With 80% of all food projected to be consumed by urbanites by 2050, the planet would need to raise food production by 70%.[40] This rising demand for food would pose a major burden on the Earth's environment, for example, higher CO_2 emissions, deforestation, excessive usage of freshwater, etc. Our existing LE food production is highly dubious concerning the increasing population, considering the overwhelming impact that the LE food production paradigm has on the environment. Today, our LE food production model extracts resources heavily, but loses/wastes much of them and supplies <2% of essential nutrients (organic waste) back into the system.[39]

1.4.3. Construction Industry

Our next vital necessity to sustain our lives on the planet is housing. As the city population increases, a vast landscape is continuously being used for constructing our living and working spaces. In this line, globally, the construction industry accounts for over 30% of natural resource extraction and 25% of solid waste generation.[41] This arises since the construction industry typically implements a linear "take, make, dispose" business practice. The construction sector relies on the use of depleting natural resources and minerals to build structures with limited life expectancy or reuse capacity, producing significant waste during demolition which ends up in a landfill.

In the past two decades, opportunities for recycling, reuse, and waste reduction are continually gaining momentum. The need for modern building developments, however, ensures that non-renewable natural resources are rapidly harvested, incurring significant energy usage. Indeed, the industry accounts for 40% of the world's total energy[42] consumption for excavation, transportation, and construction. With the construction industry undergoing development transformation, massive direct and indirect environmental impacts ensued, such as greenhouse gas emissions, deforestation, desertification, acidification, eutrophication, and depletion of the stratospheric ozone layer.[43]

Among these effects, carbon dioxide (CO_2) is a crucial anthropogenic greenhouse gas owing to its contribution to global warming and adverse effects on human beings. Building materials, construction, and operations contribute nearly 39% of global CO_2 emissions[44] compared to other industries, as shown in Figure 1.7. Moreover, new buildings have an estimated lifetime of 100 years, and are being designed and developed without recognizing ecological standards, meaning that they remain a life-long source of emissions (refer to Figure 1.6: operations represent 28% of CO_2 emissions). These erected buildings continue to emit CO_2 during their service life due to inefficient heating and cooling systems.

Undoubtedly, recycling construction materials is a widespread practice, especially in First World nations. More than 90% of construction and demolition waste are sent to recycling facilities to recover valuable materials such as ferrous metals, non-metallic minerals, plastics, and wood. However, developing nations often suffer inadequate management of construction and demolition waste or recycled materials, resulting mainly in landfills. We cannot ignore that a considerable amount of energy is being used for recycling materials such as crushing concrete to recover gravels, smelting metals, shredding woods, etc. Thus, holistically, we cannot

Figure 1.6.   Representation of the LE construction industry (data collected based on 2019 statistics).

assume that recycling is 100% sustainable, and we should think about how to deconstruct the buildings and recover materials without spending much energy. Therefore, we may infer that our construction industry still follows the LE paradigm, which needs a significant change towards sustainability.

1.4.4. *Transportation*

Transportation nowadays is unavoidable and inseparable from us. On the other hand, transport activities are known to be highly detrimental to the environment, generating 23% of global CO_2 emissions as shown in Figure 1.7. Our modern transport infrastructure is mainly classified into land, air, and water and their corresponding CO_2 emissions breakdown are presented in Figure 1.7. For convenience, in this section, we shall consider land (road) transport and the aviation industry, which are our primary modes of travel. Counting land-based vehicles such as cars, buses, and commercial vehicles is very difficult due to data insufficiency. It is projected that more than 1.5 billion vehicles are being built and operated on Earth today and are continuing to expand at an extraordinary pace. If the impressive growth rate persists, some 2.8 billion vehicles will be seen on the Earth in 2036.[45]

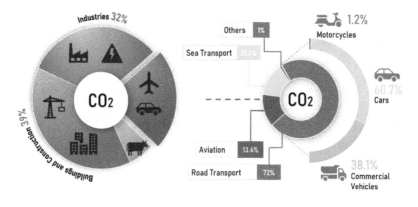

Figure 1.7. (Left) Overall CO_2 emissions by industries and (Right) CO_2 emissions breakdown of the transport industry.

These billions of vehicles are responsible for injecting enormous amounts of greenhouse gases into the atmosphere and draining massive petroleum reserves from the planet. The world consumed 100.1 million barrels per day in 2019 and the demand is projected to hit 120 million barrels per day by 2030.[46] Meanwhile, these 1.5 billion automobiles on the road will emit 2.32 billion metric tonnes of CO_2 into the atmosphere in 2021.[45] To put that into perspective, that is equivalent to 7,000 Empire State Buildings (refer to Figure 1.8).

Greater advancements are being explored in the quest for alternative fuels (biofuels), electricity, and hydrogen-powered vehicles. Nonetheless, today, over 98% of the vehicles on the road are either driven by petrol or diesel. The 20th century can be said to be characterized by readily available and comparatively inexpensive oil that encouraged our society to consume more and think less about the consequences.

Air travel is our next mode of transportation; we use commercial aircraft and charter flights to cover long, medium, and short distance traveling in a short period of time. In 2019, the worldwide commercial air travel fleet stood at around 25,900 planes. The global commercial fleet will expand by an average of 3.8% annually over the next decade, which will increase the fleet size to 48,400 by 2039.[47] The global aviation industry carried 4.5 billion passengers across the globe and produced 915 million tonnes of CO_2 in 2019.[48] To put that into perspective, that is equivalent to nearly 2,765 Empire State Buildings. Meanwhile, new developments such

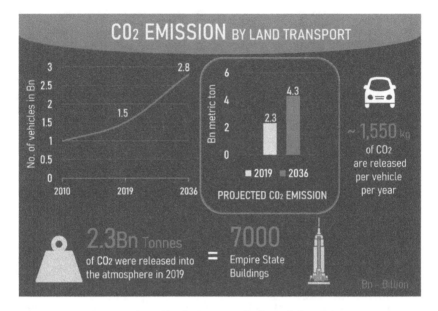

Figure 1.8.   Growing number of land transport vehicles and their CO_2 emission statistics.

as electric planes and hybrid fuels are underway to mitigate greenhouse emissions. The aviation industry claims that about 80–85% of an aircraft by weight can be recycled, while 15% of aircraft material waste are sent to landfills.[49] As mentioned in the previous section, recycling is strongly promoted, but at what cost? For example, the recovery of nickel and cobalt from engine parts involves costly machinery and an immense amount of energy is required to disintegrate aircrafts to collect metal parts. Unfortunately, aircrafts manufactured today have not generally taken into account their end-of-life or cost-effective recycling. If the current trend continues, the aircraft manufacturing industry requires a massive transformation to achieve sustainability.

Concluding Remarks

From this chapter, we can infer that our current linear paradigm would certainly collapse at one point; we would no longer be able to rely on our existing infrastructure to satisfy the global supply and demand. For instance, generating massive unhealthy waste and rising CO_2 emissions pose threats to the planet, humans, and biodiversity. A lack of essential industry resources, on the other hand, will result in business discontinuity and unemployment. Governments, organizations and business entities are recognizing the vulnerability and uncertainty of the current LE model. Furthermore, these restrictions and limitations present entrepreneurs and researchers with new opportunities and challenges. To maintain our sustainability and limit our reliance on non-renewable resources, a new framework and strategy are required. In this direction, the transition from the current LE (take, make, waste) to a circular model is necessitated. We need an economic system that is sustainable, reusable, recyclable, and environmentally friendly to stimulate new business opportunities and research directions. These action items take us to the second chapter of the book.

References

1. The ancient history of copper. https://www.thoughtco.com/copper-history-pt-i-2340112.
2. Tan, B., Way, K., Ong, M. & Kai, J. Is your waste a waste? Rethinking the linear economy. *Asian Manag. Insights* **3**, 1–4 (2017).
3. The Industrial Revolution (article) | Khan Academy. https://www.khanacademy.org/humanities/big-history-project/acceleration/bhp-acceleration/a/the-industrial-revolution.
4. Trends in solid waste management. https://datatopics.worldbank.org/what-a-waste/trends_in_solid_waste_management.html.
5. Forti, V., Baldé, C. P., Kuehr, R. & Bel, G. *The Global E-waste Monitor 2020: Quantities, Flows, and the Circular Economy Potential.* United Nations University/United Nations Institute for Training and Research (2020).
6. Earth's sixth mass extinction event under way, scientists warn | Environment | The Guardian. https://www.theguardian.com/environment/2017/jul/10/earths-sixth-mass-extinction-event-already-underway-scientists-warn.
7. Wautelet, T. Exploring the role of independent retailers in the circular economy: A case study approach (Master's Thesis). doi:10.13140/RG.2.2.17085.15847 (2018).
8. Kirsch, S. The extractive industries and society running out? Rethinking resource depletion. *Extr. Ind. Soc.* **7**, 838–840 (2020).
9. Torres, A. S. & Parini, F. P. Circular Economy: Perspective of Changes in Entrepreneurial Dynamics. In: L. C. Carvalho, C. Rego, M. R. Lucas, M. I.

Sánchez-Hernández & A. Noronha (eds.), *New Paths of Entrepreneurship Development*, pp. 315–349, Springer (2019).

10. Oberle, B. *et al. Global Resources Outlook 2019: Natural Resources for the Future We Want.* International Resource Panel, United Nations Environment Programme (2019).

11. Hussain, J., Khan, A. & Zhou, K. The impact of natural resource depletion on energy use and CO_2 emission in Belt & Road Initiative countries: A cross-country analysis. *Energy* **199**, 117409 (2020).

12. How much oil is left on earth? | Seeker. https://www.seeker.com/how-much-oil-is-left-on-earth-1792718444.html.

13. World Oil Statistics | Worldometer. https://www.worldometers.info/oil/.

14. Coal | World Coal Association. https://www.worldcoal.org/coal.

15. A cheap but dirty fuel source. https://www.theworldcounts.com/stories/negative-effects-of-coal-mining.

16. Consumption of coal and lignite | World Coal consumption | Enerdata. https://yearbook.enerdata.net/coal-lignite/coal-world-consumption-data.html.

17. Gas — Fuels & Technologies | IEA. https://www.iea.org/fuels-and-technologies/gas.

18. World Natural Gas Statistics | Worldometer. https://www.worldometers.info/gas/.

19. Bauxite | The Aluminum Association. https://www.aluminum.org/industries/production/bauxite.

20. Johnson, K. M., Hammarstrom, J. M., Zientek, M. L. & Dicken, C. L. Estimate of undiscovered copper resources of the world, 2013. doi:10.3133/fs20143004 (2014).

21. U.S. Geological Survey. Mineral Commodity Summaries 2020. doi:10.3133/mcs2020 (2020).

22. How much silver is in the world? | U.S. Money Reserve. https://www.usmoneyreserve.com/blog/how-much-silver-is-in-the-world/.

23. See Ref. 21.

24. Indium Corporation. *Indium Sources and Applications.* Malcolm Harrower, Minor Metals Conference (2012).

25. Indium production globally by country 2019 | Statista. https://www.statista.com/statistics/1060401/global-refinery-production-of-indium-by-country/.

26. Antimony reserves by country 2019 | Statista. https://www.statista.com/statistics/264625/countries-with-the-largest-antimony-reserves/.

27. See Ref. 21.

28. Antimony market global forecast to 2023 | MarketsandMarkets™. https://www.marketsandmarkets.com/Market-Reports/antimony-market-105828834.html.

29. Linear vs. circular, History and context | EDMIRE. https://edmire.design/blog-x/circular-economy-history-and-context.

30. Popkova, E. G., Ragulina, J. V. & Bogoviz, A. V. *Industry 4.0: Industrial Revolution of the 21st Century*. Springer (2019).

31. A world drowning in plastic pollution. https://phys.org/news/2020-07-world-plastic-pollution.html.

32. Plastics market worth $654.38 Billion by 2020: Grand View Research, Inc. https://www.prnewswire.com/news-releases/plastics-market-worth-65438-billion-by-2020-grand-view-research-inc-511720541.html.

33. Ramakrishna, S. Sustainable plastics engineering. https://www.tplas.com/pdf/Sustainable-Plastics-Engineering.pdf.

34. Enormous amount of plastic will fill oceans and land by 2040: Report. https://www.cnbc.com/2020/07/23/enormous-amount-of-plastic-will-fill-oceans-and-land-by-2040-report.html.

35. Sariatli, F. Linear economy versus circular economy: a comparative and analyzer study for optimization of economy for sustainability. *Visegr. J. Bioeconomy Sustain. Dev.* **6**, 31–34 (2017).

36. Growing at a slower pace, world population is expected to reach 9.7 billion in 2050 and could peak at nearly 11 billion around 2100 | UN DESA | United Nations Department of Economic and Social Affairs. https://www.un.org/development/desa/en/news/population/world-population-prospects-2019.html.

37. Food and the circular economy. https://www.ellenmacarthurfoundation.org/explore/food-cities-the-circular-economy.

38. 68% of the world population projected to live in urban areas by 2050, says UN | UN DESA | United Nations Department of Economic and Social Affairs. https://www.un.org/development/desa/en/news/population/2018-revision-of-world-urbanization-prospects.html.

39. Our food system is no longer fit for the 21st century. Here are three ways to fix it — The European Sting — Critical News & Insights on European Politics, Economy, Foreign Affairs, Business & Technology | europeansting.com. https://europeansting.com/2019/01/27/our-food-system-is-no-longer-fit-for-the-21st-century-here-are-three-ways-to-fix-it/.

40. Creating a sustainable food future: interim findings | World Resources Institute. https://www.wri.org/publication/creating-sustainable-food-future-interim-findings.

41. Enhancing the circular economy in building with functional, green and sustainable construction | Frontiers Research Topic. https://www.frontiersin.org/research-topics/15788/enhancing-the-circular-economy-in-building-with-functional-green-and-sustainable-construction.

42. Devi, L. P. & Palaniappan, S. A study on energy use for excavation and transport of soil during building construction. *J. Clean. Prod.* **164**, 543–556 (2017).

43. Raw materials use to double by 2060 with severe environmental consequences — OECD. https://www.oecd.org/environment/raw-materials-use-to-double-by-2060-with-severe-environmental-consequences.htm.

44. Ali, K. A., Ahmad, M. I. & Yusup, Y. Issues, impacts, and mitigations of carbon dioxide emissions in the building sector. *Sustain.* **12**, 7427 (2020).

45. How many cars are there in the world? | CarsGuide. https://www.carsguide.com.au/car-advice/how-many-cars-are-there-in-the-world-70629.

46. Sperling, D. & Gordon, D. Two billion cars transforming a culture. *TR News* **259**, 3–9 (2008).

47. Size of aircraft fleets worldwide 2019–2039 | Statista. https://www.statista.com/statistics/262971/aircraft-fleets-by-region-worldwide/.

48. Facts & figures | Air Transport Action Group. https://www.atag.org/facts-figures.html.

49. Aircraft recycling — the life and times of an aircraft | Airlines. https://airlines.iata.org/analysis/aircraft-recycling-the-life-and-times-of-an-aircraft.

Exercises

1) In addition to economic and industrial development, what other causes led to the high volume of solid and gaseous wastes?
   (A) Population growth and consumer expansion
   (B) Population growth and deforestation
   (C) Consumer expansion and buying behavior
   (D) Consumer sales and automobiles upsurge
2) Along with environmental degradation, what other critical issues should be addressed immediately in the 21st century?
   (A) Conflict between national borders
   (B) Rising commodity prices
   (C) Lack of global natural resources
   (D) Education in the developing nations
3) Which fossil fuel energy source is regarded to be the cleanest and least polluting?
   (A) Crude oil

(B) Coal

(C) Natural gas

(D) Wood

4) How many grams of plastic do we consume each week through the marine animal food chain?

    (A) 2 g

    (B) 3 g

    (C) 4 g

    (D) 5 g

5) Which ideology underpins the Linear Economy model?

    (A) Take, make, and dispose

    (B) Take, make, and recycle

    (C) Take, make, and refurbish

    (D) Take, make, and reclaim

6) What factors lead to the urban population producing a large amount of food waste?

    (A) Food is readily available and reasonably priced

    (B) Lack of awareness of food production process and low food prices

    (C) High income and low food prices

    (D) Accessible to fast and easy supply of food

7) Among anthropogenic greenhouse gases, which causes the most damage to the environment and harm to humans?

    (A) Methane

    (B) Nitrous oxide

    (C) Carbon dioxide

    (D) Fluorinated gases

8) Which industry is responsible for more than 30% of natural resource exploitation and 25% of solid waste generation?

    (A) Food and agricultural industry

    (B) Shipping industry

    (C) Manufacturing industry

    (D) Construction industry

9) On average, how many kilograms of carbon dioxide does a car release into the atmosphere each year?

    (A) 1,550 kg

    (B) 1,250 kg

    (C) 1,000 kg

    (D) 950 kg

10) What are the critical components in the aviation industry that involve huge costs and energy during recycling?
    (A) Nickel and Copper
    (B) Copper and Magnesium
    (C) Nickel and Iron
    (D) Nickel and Cobalt

CHAPTER TWO
INTRODUCTION TO CIRCULAR ECONOMY

Introduction

In the coming years, the human footprint could transcend the physical limits of the Earth. As a result, demand for food, access to clean water and air, global warming, depletion of natural resources, biodiversity loss, deforestation, sea-level rise, marine pollution, greenhouse gas emissions, and waste (plastic, electronic, municipal) generation would become major issues. Our global economy might crumble, and livability will be difficult if these issues remain overlooked.

We discussed the direct consequence of the growing population and increasing natural resource depletion in the first chapter. To ensure future prosperity, we must bring a drastic adjustment to how we cope with waste disposal and greenhouse gas pollution. In this path, significant yet commercially feasible reform needs to be embraced and enforced by governments and businesses.

What ideas and frameworks will contribute towards an environmentally friendly or relatively sustainable economy in the future? A new economic model — the Circular Economy (CE), a systemic strategy or process to restructure our existing linear economy, is the solution to this challenge. *A CE is a closed-loop mechanism where raw materials, components, and products are reused and recycled continuously within the system unless the product or component lacks sustainability and reusability.*[1]

The CE principle implies: 1) **Closed cycles** — continuous cycles of input and output, e.g., biowaste used for food production; 2) **System thinking** — interdependence among participants such as people, ecosystem, and businesses; 3) **Renewable energy** — the energy required to fuel the CE should be renewable by nature, e.g., solar, wind, and hydroelectricity.[2] The CE increases the utility and value of the products by maximizing the material resource, converting it into a high-value product and ensuring that material and energy continue to circulate across the system, thereby reducing waste generation.[3]

To begin with, let us understand the origin and evolution of the CE concept, what are the different schools of thought and how they came together to construct the CE foundations, and what are the principles and commonalities behind these different viewpoints. Subsequently, we study the CE definitions, framework, systems, subsystems, characteristics, advantages and opportunities, challenges and limitations, and the missing social dimension in line with sustainability.

2.1. Circular Economy

2.1.1. *Origin and Evolution of Concept*

CE is attracting growing attention among industrial sectors and research groups. The CE description has been around for many years; however, there is no single root or date to pinpoint its creation. Based on the literature, the CE scientific paradigm began in the 1960s. In 1966, Kenneth Boulding, an economist, defined the Earth as a resource-limited spaceship and ideated the relationship between economic and environmental systems. Subsequently, U.S. professor John Lyle; his student William McDonough; the German chemist Michael Braungart; architect and economist Walter Stahel further improvised the concept of the CE. Recently, Ellen MacArthur's Foundation rendered a substantial contribution to the CE concept.[4]

Extensive research papers have been published to clarify how the CE idea came to be. For instance, Alvair *et al.*[3] presented the main movements, origin, and evolution of concepts that arise from the process of "circularity thinking". Several academic findings justify that CE has been commonly used in many sectors over the last two decades as a sustainable model. With the emergence of CE practice and implementation, literature has shown that the CE concept is largely embedded in ecological as well as environmental economics, focusing on the interdependence between nature and humans.[5]

The study on the features of the CE has become more advanced since its inception. In the transformation from industrial to post-industrial societies, competing viewpoints like industrial ecology, cradle-to-cradle, biomimicry, performance economy, and blue economy were implemented to shape the new CE system.[6] Due to the various facets of the idea, the CE can be seen from many perspectives. For example, one of the CE pioneers, Walter Stahel, suggests that the CE is a generalized notion that can be interpreted as a structure that draws multiple viewpoints from different strategies.[7] Figure 2.1 reflects the various principles originating from different sets of ideas relating to the CE.

Despite varying points of view, they agree upon one thing: all these schools of thought advocate that our modern industrial economic structure is increasingly losing its effectiveness. A better understanding of the environment and social systems is needed to accommodate human and

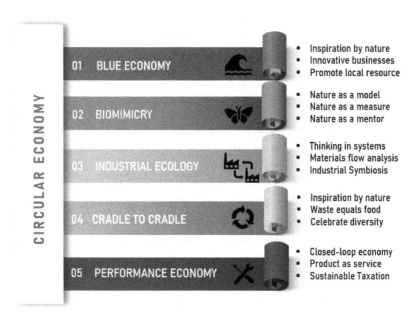

Figure 2.1.   A summary of the CE concept based on different schools of thought and principles.

eco-needs in the future.[8] In this regard, these different schools of thought have suggested strategies to use our resources more beneficially and sustainably, as well as minimize our negative effect on our environment. In this way, industrial ecology and cradle-to-cradle approaches primarily focus on the environmental impact. Performance economy and blue economy focus on the innovative business model, and biomimicry on the product design inspired by nature.[8]

Recently, the performance economy-based business model is gaining momentum due to its innovative product as a service business model; in other words, the product is leased rather than purchased. These diverse schools of thought, regardless of their principles, agree to the significance of "system thinking" when discussing problems correlated with our modern neoliberal economic structure. The idea of the CE incorporates multiple viewpoints to reinforce a sustainable future regardless of varied debates.[7]

2.1.2. *Integration and Commonality of Different Principles of Circular Economy*

As discussed in Table 2.1, in 2013, the Ellen MacArthur Foundation utilized various schools of thought and principles to describe the group and proposed an outline to classify and identify the commonality between ideas.

2.1.2.1. *The First Principle — Clean Materials*

When goods or products are successfully developed and assembled to work within the biological and technological materials process with simple removal and replacement options, waste becomes insignificant as shown in Figure 2.3. Biological materials are non-toxic and can be easily recycled into the atmosphere, whereas technological materials are built to be reused with little resources and optimum content preservation. In this way, waste is minimized, and recycling becomes more efficient.[9]

2.1.2.2. *The Second Principle — Resilience*

Resilience advocates modular design, flexibility, and adaptability. With the help of diversity, natural habitats and mechanisms have adapted, rendering

Table 2.1.   Integration of the CE ideas and commonality of different school of thoughts.

PRINCIPLES OF CIRCULAR ECONOMY	1 BLUE ECONOMY	2 BIOMIMICRY	3 INDUSTRIAL ECOLOGY	4 CRADLE TO CRADLE	5 PERFORMANCE ECONOMY
1. CLEAN MATERIALS		Life-friendly chemistry	Reduce loss	Waste is food	
2. RESILIENCE	Be abundant – satisfy basic needs	Evolve to survive and adapt to change		Celebrate diversity	
3. RENEWABLE ENERGY			Energy from fossil hydrocarbon	Solar energy	
4. SYSTEM THINKING	Be systemic				
5. RESOURCE EFFICIENCY	Be efficient	Be resource-efficient	Waste must be valorised	Waste is food	Optimisation of existing stock
6. CASCADING	Be profitable				
7. PROCURE LOCALLY	Be local	Be local			
8. PERFORMANCE	Be innovative		Economy must be dematerialised		Sell goods as service

them more robust to shocks and stresses.[10] The second principle seeks to achieve the ideal balance between durability and performance, while finding efficacy.

2.1.2.3. *The Third Principle — Renewable Energy*

This principle relates to fossil energy and promoting new means of control. Traditional economies usually depend on fossil fuel-derived resources. Substituting renewable energy for fossil fuels would create a sustainable and CE-compatible environment.[11] This principle implies that the utilization of natural and green energy sources is an essential aspect of CE adoption. It should be remembered that dependence on green energies can only be accomplished by reducing energy use.

2.1.2.4. *The Fourth Principle — System Thinking*

System thinking is more critical when concerned with integrating and developing CE; it describes the interaction between the parts/subsystem and whole/system, and how subsystem influences system and vice versa.[10] Using this approach, we can analyze elements concerning their infrastructure, environment, and social setting. We also consider the stock and flow of products impacted by each decision.[12]

2.1.2.5. *The Fifth Principle — Resource Efficiency*

At the end of the product's service life, the product retains little value; thus, the product becomes obsolete and ends up in the landfill. However, with appropriate engineering, the waste product which holds less intrinsic worth can be transformed into a valuable resource to other industries. Product upcycling and industrial symbiosis are the fundamental facets of resource efficiency.[13] Product upcycling implies reusing an old product and enhancing its appeal by the incorporation of creative and environmental features. On the other hand, industrial symbiosis implies the flow of materials/waste within a network of industrial businesses.

2.1.2.6. *The Sixth Principle — Cascading*

The cascading principle resembles resource efficiency. This hypothesis posits that the utility of materials or products resides in the potential to derive value by either rendering the product more valuable or by using up part of the resource (cascading with other materials) and then getting more value out of it.[14] Overall, it makes practical sense to utilize products for something other than their initial intent at the end of their existence. The solution is also more cost-effective since it is not technically possible to restore the exhausted product or materials without investing money.

2.1.2.7. *The Seventh Principle — Procure Locally*

For an ecosystem to thrive, it should consider the available resources within the community rather than importing. Also, if the business wishes to expand, it must make sure it is viable and procure locally. This includes looking at local services and those that are "underused" and evaluating all output productions, both planned and unintentional. The key objective is to include some customized solutions to the local community and integrate the local people in deciding how best to adjust and react to local settings.[13]

2.1.2.8. *The Eighth Principle — Performance*

The performance principle refers to efficiently leveraging values, new jobs, and being less reliant on resource consumption. This principle sets out novel business models by selling performance rather than products. During the lifespan of the products, the manufacturer maintains control over the products! Manufacturers incentivize companies to monitor their product consistency and efficiency in the interests of sustainability. Thus, it promotes more people to develop or establish new businesses and build creative job options.[7]

In summary, independent of various ideas or schools of thinking, the CE aims to maintain our existence and promote sustainability, keeping it theoretically viable in the long run by enabling a closed-loop mechanism where materials and products can be repaired, reconditioned, recycled, and reused.

2.2. Definition

A proper definition for the CE concept has yet to be established. We have seen different schools of thought and their interlinked principles related to the CE; in the last few years, academia has established different ways to explain the CE concept. In addition, policymakers and consulting firms have often sought to implement the CE definition. In this regard, London-based consulting firm, Ellen MacArthur Foundation, defined the CE concept as follows[15]:

"The circular economy refers to an industrial economy that is restorative by intention; aims to rely on renewable energy; minimizes, tracks, and eliminates the use of toxic chemicals; and eradicates waste through careful design."

This definition has been generally recognized and widely quoted by many academics, individuals, and professionals.

Likewise, the CE definition with an economic aspect has been established by the European Commission[16]:

"Circular economy represents a development strategy that entails economic growth without increasing consumption of resources, deeply transform production chains and consumption habits and redesign industrial systems at the system level."

The CE seeks to optimize resource efficiency, which implies less waste generation and less reliance on virgin materials. This approach introduces a new paradigm in the way that resources are handled; for example, waste produced by one industry may be used as feedstock for others. **Repair, Recycle** and **Reuse** are the key foundational rules of the CE concept, in which materials/products are used in such a way as to capture more value instead of getting tossed out.[17]

Figure 2.2 demonstrates in a simple way how an economy can function through a circular model. We know that the linear economy model operates simply by taking, making, and disposing, whereas the CE model has intuitively an environment-benefitting aspect. As a result, residual waste produced from the CE approach is limited, which means resources are continuously used in the entire process. Therefore, minimizing emissions and waste production is assured.

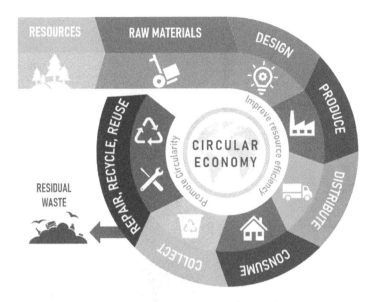

Figure 2.2.   Conceptual representation of CE.

Figure 2.3, proposed by the Ellen MacArthur Foundation,[15] offers a complete graphic description of the CE with different stages. We have previously discussed the eight different principles in Section 2.2 and identified the interconnections from Table 2.1. Now, let us understand how these principles are found in agreement with Figure 2.3.

There are two clusters in the diagram: (1) Biological materials, and (2) Technical materials. Biological materials are engineered to be biologically stable **(clean materials)** and processed to the maximum eco-efficiency. The whole system implies the repetition of biological cycles, whereby foods and bioproducts such as cotton or wood enter for consumption, and the consumed products return at the end of their service life to the cycle by mechanisms such as composting and anaerobic digestion. Hence, by injecting valuable nutrients, these cyclical processes restore the sustainability of living environments and the ecosystem.[18]

On the other hand, technical materials such as metals and plastics are meant to flow at high quality, thus they are engineered to endure and maintain their economic benefit. Like the biological cycles, used technical materials are retrieved and repaired by continuous technological processes utilizing the reuse, repair, and remanufacturing principle. This can be

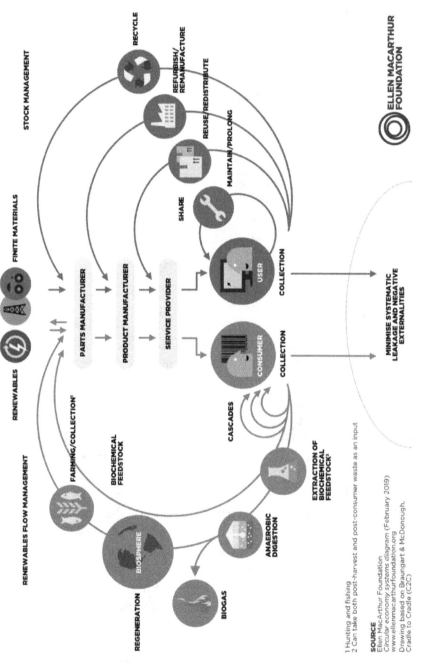

Figure 2.3.   CE system diagram with different stages. (Source: Ellen MacArthur Foundation.)

attributed to "**resource efficiency**": at the end of the product's service life, the product retains little value; however, with appropriate engineering, it can be used for other industries via industrial symbiosis.[19]

For the technical materials cycle, CE improves the utility of products by transforming them into high-value products. Hence, the continuous flow of materials/products within the system is ensured, and waste is limited. The technical material aspect erases the idea of ownership and replaces it with access and efficiency. For instance, we typically procure products for our personal use such as smartphones, and the usage cycles of these products are limited. We can thus consider that such an asset is rented for its usage rather than owned; when we dispose of it, it goes back into the cycle. In this way, optimum utilization cycles could be accomplished. Therefore, product value and "**performance**" have been sustained throughout the system.[7]

Product upcycling requires energy. Hence, depending on fossil fuels to transform the least significant goods into valuable products would not be commercially viable. It indicates that the CE paradigm promotes the utilization of "**renewable energy**" sources and discourages the use of fossil fuels.

The technical cycle promotes "**system thinking**" (interdependence among participants), in which products are designed to be easily dissembled, refurbished, remanufactured, and thereafter enter the cycle. The interaction of each stakeholder is quite significant; in reality, everyone has a big impact on everyone else.[20]

2.3. Advantages and Opportunities of the Circular Economy

The CE has several advantages and opportunities, as shown in Figure 2.4, over the current linear economy. The CE initiative has benefits that are operational, strategic, and adds value to the economy and environment. Thus, businesses and communities will flourish. Despite the reality that we are far from reaching maximum circularity, Accenture forecasts that CE will produce $4.5 trillion in increased economic output by 2030.[21] The tangible outcome of CE's global acceptance has been recognized widely, and a shift to a resource-efficient society is growing. In this direction, let us evaluate the potential advantages of CE in economic and environment aspects.

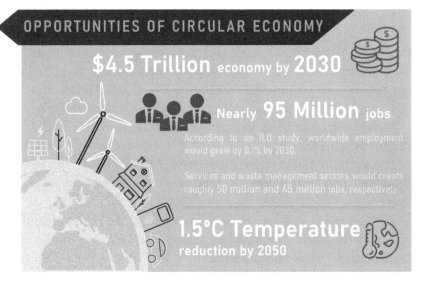

Figure 2.4.   (Top) Advantages of CE. (Bottom) Opportunities of CE.

A: Resource extraction

The CE aims to have a beneficial impact on the ecosystems and to create a resilient community. It ensures effective resource utilization by improving the recycling process and encouraging continuous usage of resources within the closed-loop system. Therefore, the requirement for new virgin raw materials is limited, and less reliance on natural resources is assured.

B: Economic growth

CE implies that economic growth should not directly be related to the consumption of resources. Hence, the economy becomes less dependent on natural resources, and is not hindered by the scarcity of raw materials to expand. Increasing income from modern circular operations, coupled with inexpensive manufacturing processes, rendering goods and materials more usable and simpler to refurbish and reuse, have the potential to raise GDP.[22]

C: Stimulate innovation
Productivity is the priority of the traditional linear economy, and thus the value of creativity has become trivial. On the other hand, the CE embraces innovation; it implements system thinking, aligning architects, engineers, entrepreneurs, and other stakeholders to identify sustainable solutions through creative business models.[3]

D: Reduce emissions
Indeed, the idea of CE is to minimize environmental damages by promoting sustainability. It is anticipated that carbon emissions would be minimized by limiting linear practices and adopting the CE concept. Industries such as power plants and manufacturing industries depend mainly on fossil energy, responsible for 32% of global greenhouse gas emissions.[23] Renewable energy is at the forefront of the CE ideology; it will dramatically mitigate pollution by encouraging renewable energy for the manufacturing and recycling processes.

By 2050, along with existing mitigation plans, emissions are projected to exceed 60 billion tonnes. Climate researchers and professionals are continuously looking out for novel and creative methods to combat climate change and it is suggested that the CE will have the ability to minimize global warming to 1.5°C.[24] However, attaining this goal would require accelerated, far-reaching and unparalleled transformation in all facets of society.

E: Employment growth
A CE will generate more employment than the linear model because of the aggregation of multiple stakeholders. Instead of building a new one, it seeks to restore, refurbish, and reuse, which suggests the intention is to preserve the environment already accessible. The CE has given rise to creativity, which would result in numerous innovative market concepts for diverse client groups and revenue streams. It embraces innovations, widens the business boundaries, and creates new jobs. According to the International Labor Organization (ILO), global employment will increase by 0.1% by 2030 relative to business-as-usual, and the workforce in the services and waste management industries would increase by approximately 50 million and 45 million jobs, respectively.[25]

2.4. Challenges and Limitations of the Circular Economy

Although CE aims to transform the existing industrial paradigm for the better and work towards sustainability, there are issues with complete adoption. To achieve sustainability, the three facets of environment, economy, and society are needed. We have discussed the advantages of the CE related to the environment and economy in the previous section. However, CE fails to address the social dimension, and we shall explore the causes in the next chapter. It seems that the research community is still examining the implications of CE towards *social* and *economic* aspects. On the other hand, J. Korhonen[26] has identified key unanswered questions related to *environmental* sustainability, listing six fundamental challenges faced by the existing CE framework (as shown in Figure 2.5). They are discussed as follows.

Thermodynamic limits in the CE refer to entropy, which means the material loop is theoretically impractical for an infinite period; in other words, 100% recycling is impossible. In a system, entropy is an indicator of the condition

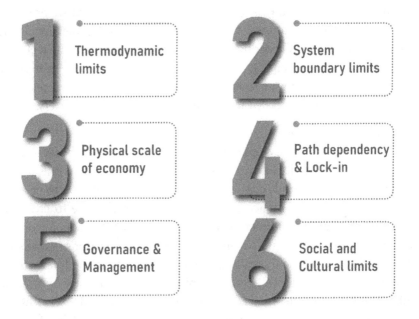

Figure 2.5.   Limitations of CE.

of disorder, which is said to increase as the system continuously functions. Applying the same principle in the CE recycling process indicates that recycling will still require energy and generating waste and side products are inevitable (increasing entropy).[26]

In the current scenario, attempting to achieve 100% recyclability would be ineffective if the recovery price stays higher than the value of materials recycled. Earlier, we discussed that the CE uses renewable energies for materials recovery and recycling; indeed, it is a good option and certainly would be possible. However, another set of arguments is that constructing renewable energy sources (solar panels, windmills) require non-renewable sources, leaving CE unsustainable. Nevertheless, recycling is preferred when fossil fuel is used insignificantly.[27]

System boundary limits can be assessed in two aspects: a) spatial and b) temporal. *Spatial* boundary limits refer to problems that are shifted along the product life cycle. For instance, less developed nations import products that need to be recycled from First World nations to realize economic growth by creating more opportunities.[28] On the other hand, recycling often damages the environment by releasing hazardous waste. We can infer that First World countries are fully aware of environmental degradation and thus transport recyclable goods to other parts of the world to preserve their own environment. Holistically, as a community, we are shifting the problem from one place to another and still impacting the ecosystem rather than addressing it.

Temporal limitation — CE advocates limiting mining activity to rejuvenate the biosphere and proposes recycling, reuse, and refurbishment. However, increased material cycles and recycling require facilities, infrastructure for transportation and eco-friendly transports, etc. Hence, this scenario poses a new set of challenges and limitations to realize fully sustainable recycling methods.

Physical economic growth — CE consumes resources, increases entropy, and decreases energy. Therefore, CE programs and projects, irrespective of their sustainable foundation, would influence the environment and resource consumption.[26] CE foundations seem to be regionally specific, and the effectiveness of the theory can be realized within the limited boundaries (e.g., within the nation). When the physical economy grows across the borders, the implications tend to rise, and thus, the CE structure requires additional reinforcement regarding physical expansion.[29]

Path dependencies and Lock-in states that new products fabricated via the LE model receive vast reception and awareness in the marketplace, whereas CE recommends reused and refurbished products. We know that CE has compelling reasons to promote sustainable products, but market penetration would be challenging when compared with existing LE products due to strong market occupancy. This phenomenon is called path dependency and lock-in.[30] The whole CE framework designed for product reuse, remanufacturing, and refurbishment must compete with the existing product line manufactured using the LE principle and low-cost recycled products using fossil fuels.

Governance and Management — Before they end up as waste in the environment, the physical flows of resources and energy derived from nature move through several different interdependent sections within the economic production-consumption mechanism. Often, these movements do not respect institutional or regional boundaries, sectoral domains, and corporate jurisdictions.[31] The CE business model embraces resource sharing, multiple lifecycles, leasing, and renting; all these require sustainable management and co-operation between suppliers and customers. CE protocols are yet to be devised for governance and management; for instance, who is the decision-maker, who bears the greatest responsibility, who gains the most from the operation of the network, who loses the most, etc.[26]

Social and Cultural limits — Human society is continually evolving, and the definition of waste differs from country to country. It depends on culture, society, group knowledge, background, and how much society has grown. Waste and resources have an intricate relationship; it is hard to define the specific moment when a resource's worth shifts from being profitable to being garbage. Waste is generally viewed as a valuable resource when it has some monetary value; otherwise, it is redundant. However, the difference between waste and by-product is not as straightforward as one would expect.[26] It is challenging to promote waste utilization when adopting the CE theory without proper descriptions of some forms or phases of physical resource flows in economic systems.

2.5. The Broken Link: Social Sustainability

The idea of a CE is based on various schools of thought aimed at sustainable development. However, CE priorities, which resonate with company growth, are intended to drive *economic* and *environmental* improvements, and struggles to adequately resolve the *social component of sustainability*, including human needs and geographical consequences.[27] CE businesses embrace materials savings and limited resource consumption to improve profit. On the other hand, governments are concerned about the existence of critical resources in the future. It seems CE formulations have trivial importance towards social interactions and well-being.

Repair, refurbish, and remanufacture are core activities of CE implementation that require an intensive workforce. Indeed, without a doubt, these sectors would create immense job opportunities than conventional industrial practices.[32] However, where will the employment opportunities be, locally or internationally?[13] Besides, misuse of power, unfair employment practices, and disregard for human rights would further threaten the fundamental needs of people. There is also no clear explanation on how a CE will lead to socio-economic inclusion, intra-generational justice, as well as gender, ethnic, and religious equality. Thus, the CE principles do not fulfill all aspects of sustainability.[13] Hence, as seen in Figure 2.6, the social part of the CE is still being developed and is regarded as a missing link to fully embrace sustainability.

The conceptual connection between the CE definition, tools, and social dimension is not evident, but there are distinct advantages that CE may presumably offer to society. For instance, CE social dimensional investigation and systematic review have been performed by Alejandro *et al.*, who outlined various social impacts that can be associated with

Environment   Social   Economy

Figure 2.6.   Social sustainability — Broken link.

the CE.[33] Besides, the *social CE* is still a relatively new concept, which is emerging to create values and advantages for people, the planet, and the economy. This evolving concept will hopefully integrate environmental principles and visions of social enterprise to support the economic prosperity.[34]

Concluding Remarks

Moving towards the CE model requires all the economic players to recognize the importance of circular thought. Governments need to implement the CE policy framework; businesses need to incorporate CE principles in their product design; financial institutions should invest in CE business ideas; and individuals need to recognize the consequences of the LE system and foster CE practice.

The ideas introduced by the CE, amid all these obstacles, make several opportunities. It rivals the conventional LE production method, identifies business opportunities, supports environmental preservation, and utilizes innovative concepts to develop values. The CE framework has multiple limitations, but it is continually improving by incorporating resilience in all dimensions, accepting different schools of thought, implementing innovative business models, and fostering sustainable development.

Conceptually, a CE is more sustainable, and appears to be more supportive for sustainable development. However, some hypotheses are unsound since there are significant trade-offs in current structures. Across numerous researches on the CE, it is found that several organizations and communities struggle to understand its social implications. We shall investigate the intricate relationship between sustainability and the CE paradigm in the next chapter.

References

1. Circular economy: A definition and most important aspects. https:// kenniskaarten.hetgroenebrein.nl/en/knowledge-map-circular-economy/what-is-the-definition-a-circular-economy/.
2. Towards a circular economy: business rationale for an accelerated transition. https://www.ellenmacarthurfoundation.org/assets/downloads/TCE_Ellen-MacArthur-Foundation_9-Dec-2015.pdf.

3. Torres, A. S. & Parini, F. P. Circular Economy: Perspective of Changes in Entrepreneurial Dynamics. In: L. C. Carvalho, C. Rego, M. R. Lucas, M. I. Sánchez-Hernández & A. Noronha (eds.), *New Paths of Entrepreneurship Development*, pp. 315–349, Springer (2019).

4. Hebel, D. E., Wisniewska, M. H. & Heisel, F. Constructing waste — investigating an alternative resource for future cities. doi:10.3929/ethz-a-010636987 (2016).

5. Antikainen, R., Lazarevic, D. & Seppälä, J. Circular Economy: Origins and Future Orientations. In: H. Lehmann (ed.), *Factor X*, pp. 115–129, Springer (2018).

6. Lopes, J. & Farinha, L. Industrial symbiosis in a circular economy: Towards firms' sustainable competitive advantage. *Int. J. Mechatronics Appl. Mech.* **2019**, 206–220 (2019).

7. Stahel, W. R. *The Performance Economy* (2nd edition). Palgrave Macmillian (2010).

8. Ghisellini, P., Cialani, C. & Ulgiati, S. A review on circular economy: The expected transition to a balanced interplay of environmental and economic systems. *J. Clean. Prod.* **114**, 11–32 (2016).

9. Ankrah, N. A., Manu, E. & Booth, C. Cradle to cradle implementation in business sites and the perspectives of tenant stakeholders. *Energy Procedia* **83**, 31–40 (2015).

10. Pauli, G. *The Blue Economy*. Paradigm Publications (2011).

11. Leube, M. & Walcher, D. Designing for the next (Circular) economy. An appeal to renew the curricula of design schools. *Des. J.* **20**, S492–S501 (2017).

12. Blomsma, F. & Brennan, G. The emergence of circular economy: A new framing around prolonging resource productivity. *J. Ind. Ecol.* **21**, 603–614 (2017).

13. Mouazan, E. Understanding circular business models: Drivers, obstacles and conditions towards a successful transition (Master's Thesis). http://epub.lib.aalto.fi/fi/ethesis/pdf/14782/hse_ethesis_14782.pdf.

14. Wautelet, T. The concept of circular economy: Its origins and its evolution. doi:10.13140/RG.2.2.17021.87523 (2018).

15. Understanding the challenge of finite resources. http://cdn.worldslargestlesson.globalgoals.org/2016/07/3_Ellen-MacA_Understanding-the-Challenge-of-Finite-Resources.pdf.

16. Deselnicu, D. C., Militaru, G., Deselnicu, V., Zăinescu, G. & Albu, L. Towards a circular economy — a zero waste programme for Europe. doi:10.24264/icams-2018.xi.4 (2018).

17. Ramakrishna, S. & Lerwen, L. *An Introduction to Circular Economy*. Springer (2021).
18. What is a Circular Economy? | Ellen MacArthur Foundation. https://www.ellenmacarthurfoundation.org/circular-economy/concept.
19. Cecchin, A., Salomone, R., Deutz, P., Raggi, A. & Cutaia, L. Relating Industrial Symbiosis and Circular Economy to the Sustainable Development Debate. In: R. Salomone, A. Cecchin, P. Deutz, A. Raggi & L. Cutaia (eds.), *Industrial Symbiosis for the Circular Economy*, pp. 1–25, Springer (2020).
20. Bassi, A. M., Bianchi, M., Guzzetti, M., Pallaske, G. & Tapia, C. Improving the understanding of circular economy potential at territorial level using systems thinking. *Sustain. Prod. Consum.* **27**, 128–140 (2021).
21. McGuinness, M. The circular economy could unlock $4.5 Trillion of economic growth, finds new book by Accenture | Accenture Newsroom. https://newsroom.accenture.com/news/the-circular-economy-could-unlock-4-5-trillion-of-economic-growth-finds-new-book-by-accenture.htm.
22. Circular economy — definition, principles, benefits and barriers. https://youmatter.world/en/definition/definitions-circular-economy-meaning-definition-benefits-barriers/.
23. Ali, K. A., Ahmad, M. I. & Yusup, Y. Issues, impacts, and mitigations of carbon dioxide emissions in the building sector. *Sustain.* **12**, 7427 (2020).
24. de Wit, M., Verstraeten-Jochemsen, J., Hoogzaad, J. & Kubbinga, B. The Circularity gap report 2019: Closing the circularity gap in a 9% world. https://circulareconomy.europa.eu/platform/sites/default/files/circularity_gap_report_2019.pdf.
25. Montt, G., Fraga, F. & Harsdorff, M. The future of work in a changing natural environment: Climate change, degradation and sustainability. https://www.ilo.org/wcmsp5/groups/public/---dgreports/---cabinet/documents/publication/wcms_644145.pdf.
26. Korhonen, J., Honkasalo, A. & Seppälä, J. Circular economy: The concept and its limitations. *Ecol. Econ.* **143**, 37–46 (2018).
27. Mentink, B. Circular Business Model Innovation (Master's Thesis). https://repository.tudelft.nl/islandora/object/uuid%3Ac2554c91-8aaf-4fdd-91b7-4ca08e8ea621.
28. Sariatli, F. Linear economy versus circular economy: A comparative and analyzer study for optimization of economy for sustainability. *Visegr. J. Bioeconomy Sustain. Dev.* **6**, 31–34 (2017).
29. Mayer, A. L., Kauppi, P. E., Angelstam, P. K., Zhang, Y. & Tikka, P. M. Importing timber, exporting ecological impact. *Science* **308**, 359–360 (2005).

30. Norton, B. G. The evolution of preferences: Why 'sovereign' preferences may not lead to sustainable policies and what to do about it, with Robert Constanza and Richard C. Bishop. *Search. Sustain.* **24**, 249–276 (2010).
31. Seuring, S. & Gold, S. Sustainability management beyond corporate boundaries: From stakeholders to performance. *J. Clean. Prod.* **56**, 1–6 (2013).
32. Stahel, W. R. Policy for material efficiency — Sustainable taxation as a departure from the throwaway society. *Philos. Trans. R. Soc. A Math. Phys. Eng. Sci.* **371**, 20110567 (2013).
33. Padilla-Rivera, A., Russo-Garrido, S. & Merveille, N. Addressing the social aspects of a circular economy: A systematic literature review. *Sustain.* **12**, 1–17 (2020).
34. Robinson, S. *Social Circular Economy: Opportunities for People, Planet and Profit.* Winston Churchill Memorial Trust & The Frank Jackson Foundation (2019).

Exercises

1) The term "Circular Economy" refers to the following:
   (A) Closed loop
   (B) Open loop
   (C) Interconnected
   (D) Perplexed
2) What are the key foundational rules of the CE concept?
   (A) Repair, Recycle, Reuse
   (B) Repair, Reinstate, Recycle
   (C) Recycle, Reuse, Reconcile
   (D) Reduce, Repair, Reuse
3) European Commission defines CE as an economic growth approach that incorporates the following elements:
   (A) Less resource consumption and highly efficient product design
   (B) Redesign industrial systems and highly competent delivery
   (C) Less resource consumption and redesign industrial systems at the system level
   (D) Highly efficient product and low operating cost
4) When describing the CE system, what are the two clusters suggested by the Ellen MacArthur Foundation?
   (A) Technical and Non-technical materials
   (B) Technical and Organic materials
   (C) Biological and Technical materials
   (D) Biological and Organic materials

5) The CE paradigm ensures continuous flow of materials/products is within the system and as a result
   (A) Waste generation is limited
   (B) Waste generated is avoided
   (C) Waste generation is multiplied
   (D) Waste generation is balanced
6) Which parts of the social aspect of sustainability are the CE's greatest challenges?
   (A) Wealth distribution and gender equality
   (B) Poverty and basic human needs
   (C) Human needs and geographical consequences
   (D) Work-life balance and racial tension
7) In CE, the material loop is theoretically impracticable because of
   (A) System boundary limit
   (B) Spatial limit
   (C) Temporal limit
   (D) Thermodynamic limit
8) What does the term "broken link" mean in the context of CE?
   (A) Social sustainability
   (B) Economic sustainability
   (C) Environmental sustainability
   (D) Artificial sustainability
9) What are the social factors that threaten the implementation of the CE?
   (A) Misuse of power, fair employment practice, disregard for human rights
   (B) Misuse of power, unfair employment practice, disregard for human health
   (C) Misuse of power, unfair employment practice, disregard for human rights
   (D) Misuse of money, fair employment practice, disregard for human rights
10) What facets are needed to achieve sustainability?
   (A) Environment, Economy, and Society
   (B) Environment, Economy, and Energy
   (C) Environment, Energy, and Society
   (D) Environment, Politics, and Society

CHAPTER THREE
SUSTAINABILITY AND SUSTAINABLE DEVELOPMENT

Introduction

This chapter aims to provide a fundamental outline of sustainable development (SD) and sustainability. In the last chapter, we explored the basic implementation of the Circular Economy (CE) alongside its benefits and drawbacks, and mentioned the absence of a social viewpoint in line with sustainability articulation. While CE is advocated as a viable economic outlook to resolve environmental impacts, we require a deeper understanding and clarification between *sustainability* and the *definition of CE*.

This chapter aims to examine the roots of sustainability, evolution, and the modern need for SD. We will explore some of the popular sustainability notions and discuss the context of the CE foundation and connectivity of sustainability developed by CE pioneers, as well as how CE has culminated in sustainability benefits, and the three foundations of sustainable growth (social, economic, and environmental sustainability).

3.1. Sustainability Evolution and Timeline

In 1713, Hans Carlowitz suggested "Nachhaltigkeit", which can be interpreted in English as "sustainability". Concerned about a shortage of wood for mining and metallurgy activities, he set the goal for sustainability: the amount of wood extracted should not surpass the amount that grows again.[1] He was one of the early pioneers in setting sustainability objectives.

Subsequently, over the course of the 20th century, continuous attempts were made to quantify the environmental impacts such as climate change, resource depletion, biodiversity loss due to the Industrial Revolution, and growing population. For example, Hardin's *Tragedy of the Commons* was published in 1968,[2] and underlined the issues connected with the overconsumption of natural resources. This essay highlighted a concern for the environment and the necessity, from a moralistic view, to protect it.

In the early 1970s, scholars came together to define the effect of human activity on the atmosphere owing to increasing environmental awareness. Ehrlich & Commoner, for example, created a mathematical equation ($I = P \times A \times T$) in 1970.[3] The expression equates human impact on the environment (I) to the product of three factors: population (P), affluence (A), and technology (T).

Following that, environmental tension has accumulated across the world, sustainability has risen to the forefront, and policymakers have begun to look at it. The UN Conference on the Human Environment was held in 1972 in Stockholm.[4] As a result of this conference, the United National Environment Program (UNEP) was formed. Subsequently, the UNEP, in 1980, set up the World Conservation Strategy, outlined long-term solutions, and merged environmental and sustainability goals.

In the 1970s, sustainability policies centered mostly on environment conservation and did not consider the holistic facets of sustainability, such as the economy and people. A concept of SD that considered other aspects of sustainability originated in 1987 with the Brundtland Report.[3] It defined sustainability as *"development that meets the needs of the present without compromising the ability of future generations to meet their own needs"*.[5,6]

After the publishing of the Brundtland Report, the basic concept of sustainability combining *people*, *economy*, and *the planet* received greater attention, transformed our perception, and was infused in policies. In this direction, nations recognized the importance of a newly formed sustainability framework and defined environmental policies associating economy and people.

The 1992 Rio Earth Summit on Environment and Prosperity was the next important step in the development of sustainability awareness.[7] This was followed by the UN World Summit on Sustainable Development (2002) which recognized the need for integrated incorporation of economic, environmental, and social sustainability (shown in Figure 3.1). The 2012 UN conference in Rio de Janeiro culminated in a report that outlined a concrete set of steps that would implement sustainable growth principles.

In 2015, the UN Summit on Sustainable Development outlined the 2030 plan. The 2030 Agenda for Sustainable Development will aim to find new ways to improve the lives of people, eradicate poverty, promote prosperity and well-being for all, protect the environment, and fight against climate change.[8] Graphical representation of the sustainability concept, formulation, and evolution is presented in Figure 3.1 for quick reference.

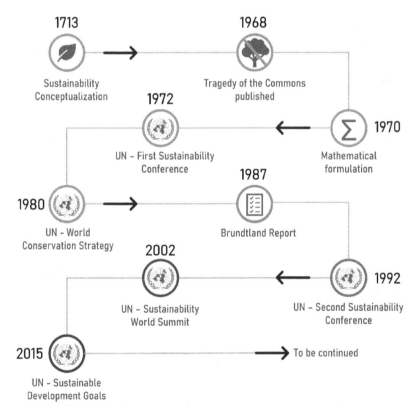

Figure 3.1.   Timeline of sustainability concept, formulation, and evolution.

3.2. Definitions and Components

P. Johnston stated that there are around three hundred distinct notions of sustainability and sustainable growth within the environmental management and related fields, either directly or indirectly.[9] In the earlier section, we discussed the conceptualization and formulation of sustainability; the definition of sustainability and SD was first broadly expressed in the **Brundtland Report** of 1987. The 'Brundtland definition' of SD was framed as *"development that meets the needs of the present without compromising the ability of future generations to meet their own needs"*. It aims to balance economic development with social and environmental equilibrium security.[10] Recently, **Prof. Seeram Ramakrishna FREng**, Chair of Circular Economy Taskforce, National University of Singapore, defined sustainability as follows:

> *Sustainability is about the implications of every human 'action' on the Earth's systems and beings, objectively assessed by the methods namely carbon foot-printing, circularity gap, ESG ratings, life cycle impact assessment, resource efficiency, biodiversity loss, etc., and taking actions to stimulate economic growth, mitigate undesirable effects on the health and well-being of humans, support social security, protect planet Earth's all other beings, and the planet itself, and to conserve it for the well-being of future generations.*

These definitions aim to articulate the nature of sustainability goals by integrating the three dimensions — economic development, social progress, and environmental conservation; in other words, they act as interdependent and mutually reinforcing pillars. A conceptual representation of how these three facets ought to connect to achieve this sustainability goal is depicted in Figure 3.2.

The three components (economic, social, environmental) of sustainability depiction have been primarily used to describe a broad spectrum of sustainability philosophy; this model of three interlinked circles is widely accepted and referred to by scholars (Figure 3.2). The model acknowledges that there are strong ties between the pair of circles. For example, a strong *community economy* emerges from the combination

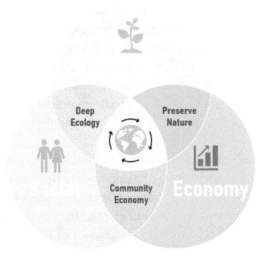

Figure 3.2. Three facets of sustainability.

of Social and Economy circles; similarly, *preserving nature* emerges from the unification of Economy and Environment circles.

By incorporating intergenerational economic, social, and environmental efficiency, sustainability is recognized to be comprehensive, equitable, resilient, and well balanced. Instead of establishing naive targets, sustainability paves the way to shared agendas; sustainability demands that several standards be formed for what can be built, what is to be maintained, for how long, and for the benefit of whom. It has facilitated discussion on how intragenerational prosperity can be improved while establishing the life support required to fulfill intergenerational needs at the same time.

3.3. Is the Circular Economy Wholly Sustainable?

The idea of SD can be viewed in various contexts, but at its center is a development strategy that aims at achieving long-term economic and environmental prosperity, which can only be accomplished by the incorporation and consideration of economic, environmental, and social issues in the decision-making phase. We addressed the relevance and drawbacks of the CE in Chapter 2, and outlined the problems raised by the academic community and practitioners: *"Is the CE wholly sustainable?"*

Debate continues regarding the ongoing challenges of a *sustainable society* and *CE* and the suitable methods/tools to accomplish these objectives. Hence, this debate demands new interpretations, explanations, science/technology, and epistemological perspectives.[11] While the ambition of the CE is to reform the present linear industrial model and work towards sustainability, due to the absence of social/community establishment, CE alone is not adequate for the economy to be sustainable; we discussed this point earlier.

Today's issues call for a holistic commitment to SD that allows for all the implications — planned and unplanned — to be considered. In CE, as the ecosystem is a dynamic and complex structure, rather than considering just particular sections of the framework, the whole system and its interconnections must be studied. An absence of such systems thinking during the decision-making process may contribute to misallocation or negative outcomes in other parts of the system.[13] Specifically, tools and methods for CE SD that have found their way to parts of businesses often fail to address another side of the problem. For example, recycling is the prime mover of CE businesses, and intentionally recycling would stimulate the circular materials economy; on the other hand, it inhibits the usage of advanced materials.[12] Furthermore, as shown in Figure 3.3, a significant portion of greenhouse gas emissions comes from electricity production via fossil fuels. To mitigate this adverse environmental effect, we must switch to renewable or clean energies. However, this trade-off results in reliance on scarce metals for clean energy production. Indeed, this situation is constrained by the current technical limitations.

Hence, these constraints imply that although the CE model may enable businesses to step closer to SD and foster new business concepts, it does

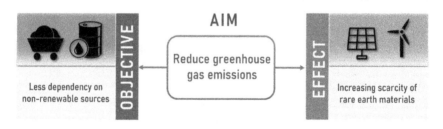

Figure 3.3.   Example of an unsustainable CE practice with the aim of promoting SD.

not contribute to maximum sustainability.[14] A technological connection between the facets of sustainability with quantified outcomes is needed. We need to establish the CE as a critical strategy reinforced with engineering and social philosophies to achieve SD to get the insights we need.[11]

Walter Stahel, a pioneer CE researcher, has suggested a synergistic relationship between CE and Sustainability. Indeed, the CE promotes businesses and focuses on maintaining and sustaining natural resources, while the sustainability definition emphasizes social, economic, and environmental protection. Stahel proposes sustainability and CE as two sides of the same coin (shown in Figure 3.4). Global resources may be interpreted as the sum of three components: *the net manufactured capital, the net human capital, and the net natural capital.*[1]

The sum of its three components equates to the nation's wealth. In this frame of reference, *strong sustainability* is the stage where growth is realized in all three realms. On the other hand, *weak sustainability* is the stage that generates positive holistic wealth and guarantees that this capital goes on to future generations;[12] however, weak sustainability relies highly on technology and believes that technological strategies will alleviate environmental issues exacerbated by increased output of products and services.[15] An example of weak and strong sustainability realms, representing environmental sustainability, is given in Figure 3.5.

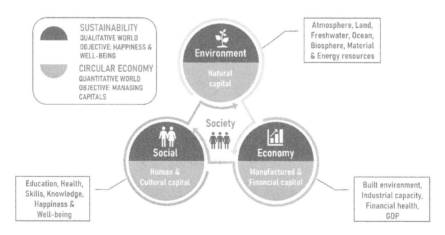

Figure 3.4.   Integrated CE and sustainability representation. (Source: Walter Stahel, Michael F. Ashby.)

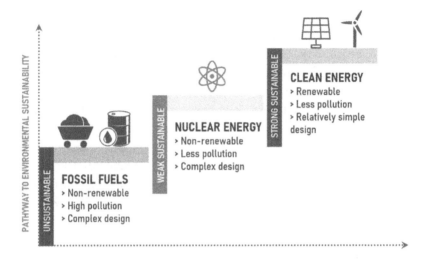

Figure 3.5. Transition from unstainable to strong sustainable realm.

In short, a CE is seen as a condition for realizing the principle of sustainability. It has the essential components of sustainability – encouraging environmental protection, stimulating economic development, though often missing the social aspect (still debatable), etc. With the aid of sustainable engineering practices, software tools, and regulations, the CE will one day become a large-scale sustainable activity. The challenge is to examine the interconnections, experiences, interactions, and synergies with CE between these three aspects of sustainability and how these reciprocal links may behave in the modern world without compromising one another.

3.4. Sustainable Development

SD has been the catchword for many years among governments, scholars, practitioners, and industries with different concepts, interpretations, and explanations. SD implies development that can be sustained over infinite time or for a specified period. More precisely, SD is the way society should be structured to survive in the long term.[16] It ensures that all current and potential precepts, such as ecosystem preservation, social and economic justice, etc., are considered while making decisions. The idea of SD, in the shape of an expression composed of two terms, *"sustainable"* and *"development"*, has been considered from various viewpoints, contributing to a multitude of meanings of the term. While SD definitions vary, the description most frequently quoted is the one suggested by the Brundtland Commission Study: a *development that meets the needs of the current generation without compromising the ability of future generations to meet their own needs.*

Often, *Sustainability* and *Sustainable Development* are confused. Sustainability is the aim or endpoint of SD. Sustainability refers to a condition; SD refers to the mechanism for reaching this condition.[16] The need for SD intensifies much further nowadays because the population continues to expand while the critical resources (discussed in Chapter 1) required to meet human needs are gradually diminishing. As a result, it is becoming challenging to embrace SD in this aspect; for instance, how will we have enough food and water for the increasing population without depleting natural resources or destroying biodiversity? What if the price of non-polluting electricity products rises? What target should be prioritized?[17] Indeed, SD would have a challenging implementation process; holistically, we can maximize one objective at a time and leverage other facets simultaneously.

The three sustainability facets (Figure 3.2) illustrated have relevance at the same level. While economists assign more importance to the economic goals, ecologists consider biodiversity concerns, and social scientists the social issues. We need to analyze the sustainability goals and their internal reasoning before we can begin to reconcile these diverse viewpoints. Hence, as indicated by the Balaton research on sustainability indicators, we must start by considering and assessing each component independently.[18]

3.4.1. *Components of Sustainable Development*

SD fosters an optimistic direction of change focused fundamentally on social sustainability, economic sustainability, and environmental sustainability; let us explore how each discipline offers its points of view on this subject.

A) Economic sustainability

"The general definition of economic sustainability is the ability of an economy to support a defined level of economic production indefinitely."[19]

Before we begin, let us unpack the integrated components of economic sustainability. In general, an economy, either linear or sustainable, is measured by A) *growth*, B) *high employment*, and C) *price stability*. Economists use figures called economic indicators to get a feel of where the economy is going in the future and understand the country's overall economic performance by analyzing gross domestic product (GDP) — the market price of all products and services generated by the economy in a single year. The above three indices should always be positive to realize a stable and strong economy.[20]

Traditionally, strong economy implies continuously growing GDP; an ideal GDP growth rate for a nation is between 2% and 3%.[21] Despite rising GDP, we cannot assume that a country is pursuing economic sustainability. National GDP, while significant, is not representative of the average person's income in a country. It does not reflect the percentage of individuals who are in the lowest of the income tier either. Hence measuring economic sustainability via the conventional GDP method is obsolete.[19]

There is an intricate relationship between GDP and the biocapacity of the Earth. Biocapacity refers to the biologically active area's capacity to produce a continuous supply of renewable resources and consume its spillover pollution.[22] Our economy (global GDP) has been growing since post-World War II with numerous technological advancements since the 1960s.[23] On the other hand, as seen in Figure 3.6, we have seen a significant shrinkage in our biocapacity owing to the influx of new technology developments and the rising population.[24] If we relate GDP growth with biocapacity, it becomes apparent that the global GDP is unsustainable and neglects the social and environmental facets of SD.

Daly & Cobb, in 1989, proposed a statistic tool, Genuine Progress Index (GPI), to substitute or complement GDP to calculate real *economic sustainability*.[25] GPI brings fruitful insights to people and politicians by understanding economic development that weakens environmental and human wealth. To do this, we need to develop economic indicators complying with three fundamental concepts as follows[26]:

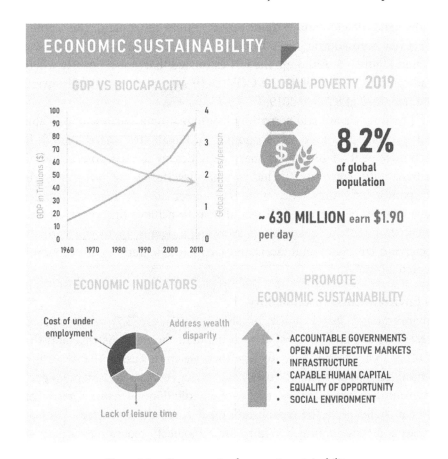

Figure 3.6.   Components of economic sustainability.

- *Define and deduct impacts on the environment, well-being, and lack of leisure time*
- *Cost of underemployment*
- *Address wealth disparity*

In this direction, Ida Kubiszewski, in 2013, reported that the global GDP and GPI of 17 countries followed the same trend between 1945 and 1965. However, GDP tends to rise while GPI depletes post-1960s due to rapid industrialization. A significant change in our economy has started since then; natural resources, human rights, and wealth inequality have been deteriorating.[24] This trend sets up a massive accumulation of wealth in the hands of a few and extreme poverty on the other hand. This rippling effect has been continuing until now, and extreme poverty still exists, as seen in Figure 3.6. Although the UN estimated that global poverty will be eradicated in 2030 (before the COVID-19 situation), the global poverty rate remained at 8.2% in 2019.[27]

In short, we are still some way from creating a reliable, impeccable, and prosperous mode of economic sustainability. There should be encouragement of interdisciplinary activities to discuss core economic sustainability concerns, including the description of priorities, the acceptance of limitations, and the agreement of related disputes. Leveraging tools such as GPI would help to achieve this vision as well. Scientists ought to make use of knowledge details associated with the social and environmental facets and facilitate integration with economic sustainability.[28]

B) Environmental sustainability

Environmental sustainability, as shown in Figure 3.7, is the idea of preserving the natural ecosystem to maintain human existence and that of other living beings.[16] To achieve that, we must ensure that we utilize natural resources such as fuels, soil, water, etc., at a sustained pace. Environmentalists perceive the over-exploitation of natural resources to be a challenge to the equilibrium on Earth and the welfare of human beings and the economy.[29] Within the ecological accounting scheme, we should treat wastes produced by human activities and maintenance of natural resources as sources of economic input. In addition, fostering economic growth using virgin natural resources needs to be minimized, resource depletion and ecosystem disruption due to mining should be acknowledged, and CE practices have to be implemented suitably.

In 1990, Herman Daly, one of the first theorists of sustainable environmental growth, studied the issue from the viewpoint of preserving natural resources and formulated three ecological principles[30]:

1. *Sustainable yield* — The harvest rate does not surpass the recovery rate.
2. *Sustainable disposal* — The waste generation rates from projects should not exceed the environmental assimilation capability.
3. *Sustainable substitute* — The loss of non-renewable resources should entail equal production of renewable alternatives.

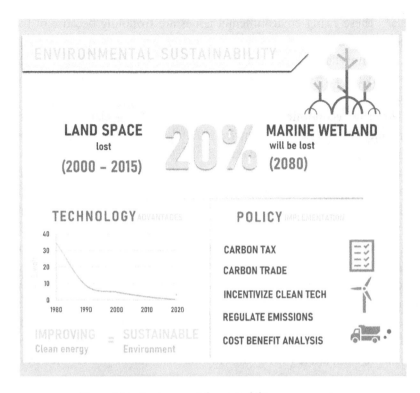

Figure 3.7.   Environmental sustainability — an overview.

The UN Food and Agriculture Organization (FAO) reported that forests cover nearly 31% of the planet's land area in 2020, and around 1.6 billion people depend on forests for their livelihood. Forests are also the ideal environment for more than 80% of all animals, plants, and insects. Owing to human activity, the biodiversity is disappearing faster more than ever before. In the 21st century, between 2000 and 2015, nearly 20% of the planet's land surface area has been degraded.[31] Worldwide environmental concerns have grown owing to harmful activities and emphasis on social and economic aspects; for instance, the effects of global warming due to shrinking forests give a convincing argument for the need for a sustainable environment.

Climate change has already exhibited signs of affecting beings and the ecosystem, for example, biodiversity loss, changes in animal reproduction behavior, acid rain, etc. According to the FAO, by the year 2080, some 20% of marine wetlands will be destroyed due to climate change and rising sea levels.[32] These rising environmental issues are troubling because of their direct effects on the ecosystem's stability, the efficacy of its preservation, and human welfare. Unfortunately, as we have been centered on economic prosperity for the past few decades, we did not recognize the environmental impacts.

From an economic perspective, Selden & Song claimed that both economic development and environmental sustainability are consistent with one another. They said economic growth allows environmental sustainability to grow naturally in line with the progressing economy.[33] The team identified an inverted U-relationship between GDP growth and a few environmental efficiency indicators. The term 'Environmental Kuznets Curve' (EKC) was coined for this phenomenon.[34]

To boost overall economic development, developments in technology and/or efficiency are crucial. In this context, we can appreciate how advances in solar energy have minimized the potential for environmental harm via better technology. The prices of solar energy have declined substantially in recent years, fulfilling the promise of renewable technology. Therefore, it can be viewed that economic growth using technological advancements can still be compatible with environmental sustainability, as claimed by the EKC principle.[35]

Tools like Environmental Sustainability Index (ESI) and Environmental Performance Index (EPI) measure overall environmental sustainability.[34,36] Lee & Chung used it to identify the effect of income on environmental sustainability, controlling for population density and civil-political liberty. The analysis showed that wealth has a positive impact on many pollution controls but harms many ecological measures.[36] Indeed, there are negative criticisms linked to the tools and EKC systems, such as elevated production of greenhouse gases, no assurance that SD reduces pollutants, and a weak relationship between social and environmental aspects. Economic development can be consistent with a sustainable environment, but it needs a very careful collection of policies and a commitment to generate the most environmentally responsible energy resources and materials.[35]

C) Social sustainability

Historically, for a couple of centuries, we progressed immensely by focusing only on the economic aspect. Subsequently, with increasing concerns over climate change and biodiversity loss, we centered on environmental issues.

In this journey, we humans often ignored the fundamental aspects of our social welfare. The significant yet practical facets of economic development and natural co-existence have been recognized and accepted in recent years as social sustainability. The increasing knowledge of the challenges of fragility, persistent injustice, and ethnic discrimination has prompted social sustainability to work alongside economic and environmental sustainability.[37]

Achieving societal goals and favorable working conditions is the primary goal of pursuing social sustainability. This objective can be related to two aspects of social sustainability: A) Macro-preservation and reproduction of the core system of society and B) the living standards of individuals.[38] Numerous topics that all contribute to social sustainability can be seen in the literature. These involve (but are not limited to) social equity, distributive justice, cultural inclusion, social harmony, social stability, social capital, recognition, social compatibility, involvement, jobs, schooling, equitable opportunity, the standard of living, decent quality of life, health security, and the fulfillment of basic needs.[16]

The five dimensions of social sustainability are:

- Quality of Life
- Equality
- Diversity
- Social Cohesion
- Democracy and Governance

Social sustainability and equal economic opportunities will accelerate change, generate enough employment for everyone, and raise living standards. However, getting a job does not always ensure a decent quality of life. In reality, over 8.2% of the global workforce lived in severe poverty in 2019 and were unable to maintain a reliable source of income.[27] Productivity and fair jobs are core components of globalization and poverty eradication. Fair jobs imply providing opportunities for everyone to showcase productivity and achieving reasonable wages, social stability, and inclusion.

Given the prevalence of injustice, inequality, racial discrimination, and exploitation, the expense is significant to both person and society. Globally, the loss of human capital resources owing to gender disparity is estimated

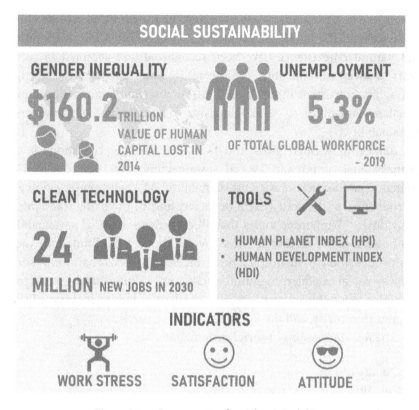

Figure 3.8.   Components of social sustainability.

at $160.2 trillion in 2014, as seen in Figure 3.8 (about twice the value of global GDP).[39] Besides, the World Bank estimates that in 2019, global unemployment was 5.3% of the total global workforce.[40]

If the planet progresses to a greener future, it would result in 6 million workers losing jobs owing to the decline in the usage of fossil fuels. However, a green economy might generate 24 million new jobs by 2030 once SD policies are aligned, as suggested by the International Labor Organization (ILO).[41] The main challenge for the future is that most countries would find it unsustainable unless they concentrate on improving workforce job conditions. Prevailing simulations indicate that as citizens migrate out of poverty it results in growth of the global ecological footprint, but this could contribute to environmental destruction. On the other hand, the current situation would kill employment and wages, creating rippling effects among poor, indigenous, tribal people.[42] Therefore, the goal of sustainable prosperity and decent work growth would require an environmentally friendly course of action. Social sustainability, similar to environmental sustainability, upholds the principle that future generations shall be able to access social services as the present generation without compromising the quality. By leveraging tools such as the Human Planet Index (HPI) and Human Development Index (HDI), as shown in Figure 3.8, we could achieve such a goal.

Concluding Remarks

Sustainability in the context of academia, policy, and economic growth has received considerable interest. Practitioners and policymakers tirelessly promote SD issues such as global warming, ozone layer depletion, water shortage, lack of biodiversity, injustice, unemployment, malnutrition, hunger, and poverty to garner people's attention and invoke action.

SD can best be accomplished by coordinated societal, economic, and environmental activities at different levels. Most notably, multinational bodies and institutions, such as the UN, non-governmental organizations, democratic institutions, and charity organizations should get involved in resolving conflicts of sustainability development and economic growth.

Sustainability and Sustainable Development involve new concepts, revolutionary modeling methods, and engineering/corporate tools to assess productivity and sustainable growth. Companies, governments, scholars, and legal professionals have begun to incorporate the tools into their existing expertise. The next chapter will introduce a list of available engineering tools and their basic introduction to measuring sustainability in all aspects.

References

1. Stahel, W. R. *The Circular Economy: A User's Guide.* Taylor & Francis (2019).
2. Hardin, G. Tragedy of the commons. *Science* **162**, 1243–1248 (1968).
3. Geissdoerfer, M., Savaget, P., Bocken, N. M. P. & Hultink, E. J. The circular economy — A new sustainability paradigm? *J. Clean. Prod.* **143**, 757–768 (2017).

4. United Nations Conference on the Environment, 5–16 June 1972, Stockholm | United Nations. https://www.un.org/en/conferences/environment/stockholm1972.

5. 1987: Brundtland Report. https://www.are.admin.ch/are/en/home/sustainable-development/international-cooperation/2030agenda/un-_-milestones-in-sustainable-development/1987--brundtland-report.html.

6. Chatterjee, D. K. World Commission on Environment and Development. In: D. K. Chatterjee (ed.), *Encyclopedia of Global Justice*, pp. 1163–1163, Springer (2011).

7. United Nations Conference on Environment and Development, Rio de Janeiro, Brazil, 3–14 June 1992 | United Nations. https://www.un.org/en/conferences/environment/rio1992.

8. United Nations Summit on Sustainable Development, 26 August-4 September 2002, Johannesburg | United Nations. https://www.un.org/en/conferences/environment/johannesburg2002.

9. Johnston, P., Everard, M., Santillo, D. & Robèrt, K. H. Reclaiming the definition of sustainability. *Environ. Sci. Pollut. Res.* **14**, 60–66 (2007).

10. Keeble, B. R. The Brundtland Report: 'Our Common Future'. *Med. War* **4**, 17–25 (1988).

11. Stefanakis, A. I. How to achieve sustainability? Through Circular Economy! | Springer Nature Sustainability Community. https://sustainabilitycommunity.springernature.com/posts/how-to-achieve-sustainability-through-circular-economy.

12. Ashby, M. F. What is a "Sustainable Development"? In: M. F. Ashby (ed.), *Materials and Sustainable Development*, pp. 27–38, Butterworth-Heinemann (2016).

13. Robèrt, K. H. Tools and concepts for sustainable development, how do they relate to a general framework for sustainable development, and to each other? *J. Clean. Prod.* **8**, 243–254 (2000).

14. Bechtel, N., Bojko, R. & Völkel, R. Be in the Loop: Circular Economy & Strategic Sustainable Development (Master Thesis). https://www.diva-portal.org/smash/get/diva2:829199/FULLTEXT01.pdf (2013).

15. Pelenc, J. & Ballet, J. Weak sustainability versus strong sustainability. https://sustainabledevelopment.un.org/content/documents/6569122-Pelenc-Weak%20Sustainability%20versus%20Strong%20Sustainability.pdf (2015).

16. Mensah, J. Sustainable development: Meaning, history, principles, pillars, and implications for human action: Literature review. *Cogent Soc. Sci.* **5**, 1653531 (2019).

17. Muschett, F. D. *Principles of Sustainable Development*. CRC Press (1997).

18. Meadows, D. Indicators and information systems for sustainable development. https://donellameadows.org/wp-content/userfiles/Indicators Information.pdf (1998).

19. Definition of economic sustainability | Thwink. https://www.thwink.org/sustain/glossary/EconomicSustainability.htm.

20. Reading: measuring the health of the economy | Introduction to Business. https://courses.lumenlearning.com/baycollege-introbusiness/chapter/reading-measuring-the-health-of-the-economy/.

21. What is the ideal GDP growth rate? https://www.thebalance.com/what-is-the-ideal-gdp-growth-rate-3306017.

22. Glossary: Biocapacity. https://www.greenfacts.org/glossary/abc/biocapacity.htm.

23. World GDP over the last two millennia. https://ourworldindata.org/grapher/world-gdp-over-the-last-two-millennia?time=1950..2015.

24. Kubiszewski, I. *et al.* Beyond GDP: Measuring and achieving global genuine progress. *Ecol. Econ.* **93**, 57–68 (2013).

25. Daly, H. E. & Cobb Jr., J. B. *For the Common Good: Redirecting the Economy toward Community, the Environment, and a Sustainable Future.* Beacon Press (1989).

26. What is the genuine progress indicator. https://dnr.maryland.gov/mdgpi/Pages/what-is-the-GPI.aspx.

27. End poverty in all its forms everywhere. https://unstats.un.org/sdgs/report/2020/goal-01/.

28. SLX. https://hub.slxlearning.com/.

29. Sustainability and sustainable development — Circular Ecology. https://circularecology.com/sustainability-and-sustainable-development.html.

30. Daly, H. E. Toward some operational principles of sustainable development. *Ecol. Econ.* **2**, 1–6 (1990).

31. FAO & UNEP. The state of the world's forests 2020. doi:10.4060/ca8642en (2020).

32. Cheung, W., Bruggeman, J. & Butenschon, M. Projected Changes in Global and National Potential Marine Fisheries Catch Under Climate Change Scenarios in the Twenty-First Century. In: Barange, M. *et al.* (eds.), *Impacts of Climate Change on Fisheries and Aquaculture*, pp. 63–86, FAO (2018).

33. Selden, T. M. & Song, D. Environmental quality and development: Is there a kuznets curve for air pollution emissions? *J. Environ. Econ. Manage.* **27**, 147–162 (1994).

34. Alam, M. S. & Kabir, M. N. Economic growth and environmental sustainability: Empirical evidence from east and south-east asia. *Int. J. Econ. Financ.* **5**, 86–97 (2013).

35. Environmental Kuznets curve — Economics Help. https://www.economicshelp.org/blog/14337/environment/environmental-kuznets-curve/.

36. Lee, H., Chung, R. K. & Koo, C. M. On the relationship between economic growth and environmental sustainability. https://citeseerx.ist.psu.edu/viewdoc/download?doi=10.1.1.586.3088&rep=rep1&type=pdf (2005).

37. Five things you need to know about social sustainability and inclusion | World Bank. https://www.worldbank.org/en/news/feature/2020/09/02/five-things-about-social-sustainability-and-inclusion.
38. Setton, D. Social Sustainability: Making Energy Transitions Fair to the People. In: O. Renn, F. Ulmer & A. Deckert (eds.), *The Role of Public Participation in Energy Transitions*, pp. 201–221, Academic Press (2020).
39. Wodon, Q. *et al.* How large is the gender dividend? Measuring selected impacts and costs of gender inequality. doi:10.1596/33396 (2020).
40. Unemployment, total (% of total labor force) (modeled ILO estimate) | Data | World Bank. https://data.worldbank.org/indicator/SL.UEM.TOTL.ZS.
41. Green economy could create 24 million new jobs — United Nations Sustainable Development. https://www.un.org/sustainabledevelopment/blog/2019/04/green-economy-could-create-24-million-new-jobs/.
42. Magis, K. Community resilience: An indicator of social sustainability. *Soc. Nat. Resour.* **23**, 401–416 (2010).

Exercises

1) Ehrlich & Commoner define human influence on the environment (I) as the sum of three factors:
   (A) Population (P), Affluence (A), and Technology (T)
   (B) Population (P), Affirmation (A), and Technology (T)
   (C) Pollution (P), Affluence (A), and Technology (T)
   (D) Population (P), Affluence (A), and Training (T)
2) According to the Brundtland report, SD is defined as
   (A) development that meets the needs of the future without compromising the ability of future generations to meet their own needs
   (B) development that meets the needs of the future without compromising the ability of present generations to meet their own needs
   (C) development that meets the needs of the present by slightly compromising the ability of future generations to meet their own needs
   (D) development that meets the needs of the present without compromising the ability of future generations to meet their own needs
3) Who is regarded as a pioneer in the field of CE research?
   (A) Walter Stahel
   (B) Walter Murray
   (C) Murray Walter
   (D) Walter Stanley

4) Which technology has shown to be effective in achieving strong sustainability?
   (A) Fossil fuels
   (B) Nuclear energy
   (C) Clean energy
   (D) Biomass energy
5) What are the components of SD?
   (A) Economic sustainability, Environmental sustainability, Social sustainability
   (B) Economic sustainability, Artificial sustainability, Social sustainability
   (C) Commercial sustainability, Environmental sustainability, Social sustainability
   (D) Economic sustainability, Environmental sustainability, Cultural sustainability
6) What are the three indicators used to assess the country's overall economic performance to realize a stable and strong economy?
   (A) growth, low employment, and price stability
   (B) growth, high employment, and price stability
   (C) growth, high employment, and price instability
   (D) growth, high poverty, and price stability
7) According to the UNFAO, by the year 2080, some 20% of marine wetlands will be destroyed due to
   (A) Climate change and pollution
   (B) Climate change and lower sea levels
   (C) Climate change and rising sea levels
   (D) Climate change and deforestation
8) What are the policies needed for environmental sustainability?
   (A) Carbon tax and incentivizing clean tech
   (B) Carbon tax and avoiding clean tech
   (C) Income tax and incentivizing clean tech
   (D) No tax and incentivizing clean tech
9) Which of the following indicators is not regarded as a measure of social sustainability?
   (A) Work stress
   (B) Job satisfaction
   (C) Attitude
   (D) Corruption
10) Which technology may create 24 million new jobs in 2030?
   (A) Clean technology
   (B) Communication technology
   (C) Manufacturing technology
   (D) Information technology

CHAPTER FOUR
SUSTAINABILITY FRAMEWORK, INDICATORS AND ASSESSMENT

Introduction

In the previous chapter, we discussed the factors, components, and conditions for Sustainable Development (SD). We have also stated that growing GDP does not guarantee sustainable growth in the future. The UN in 2008 reported that SD cannot be evaluated by rising standards of living or growing GDP; this situation will obscure conditions where vulnerable people are slipping backwards amid the increase in average living standards.[1] The SD process needs to include critical features such as clean air, water, and an endangered environment. Besides, we also need to consider the importance of capital assets to well-being and social growth beyond the economy.[2]

This chapter will take you through a common framework established for SD. Subsets of the sustainability framework, i.e., indicators and assessment, are discussed. Indicators are an integral part of SD, and this chapter outlines these parts in detail with examples, such as the Human Development Indicator. Assessments are of utmost importance as well; hence, you will gain insights into the sustainable assessment framework and its components such as tools, principles, etc.

4.1. Framework for Sustainability

There have been various and varied strategies for measuring SD. Many of the initiatives focus on identifying sustainability metrics and determining how to aggregate specific attributes. The consensus of all approaches is that the three facets of our existence (social, environmental, economic) must be incorporated in order to be called sustainable. Alfsen & Greaker state, from a broader viewpoint, that a balanced SD measure should have[3]:

1) *A specific strategy to use natural wealth, social indicators, and sustainable accounting.*
2) *A shared framework centered upon resources or capital for the international community.*

When it comes to practical implementation, SD must be regarded as a decision-making technique since decision-making is at the core of all action plans. *A policy or strategy is a path ahead to bring about a desirable outcome without compromising goals and objectives of current development and future generation needs.* Decision-makers/governments/institutions depend on evidence/knowledge and subjective considerations such as philosophy, principles, standards, desires, relationships of influence, and systemic background throughout the decision-making phase.[4] Scientific context, on the other hand, is likely to have less influence despite strong foundations. For instance, as we speak about empirical dimensions of SD, several scientific papers have suggested hypotheses, postulates, and studies about sustainability assessment and indicators. As a result, we may conclude that sustainability and decision-making are inextricably linked. But to put it in a tangible perspective, we need to resolve the following three topics[5]:

1. *Interpretation* — Institutional decision with socio-environmental settings.
2. *Information-structuring* — Underlying multidisciplinary ambiguity may be compiled into intelligent units (Assessment and Indicators).
3. *Influence* — Knowledge outcomes can be used to guide policies to help create sustainable activities.

As shown in Figure 4.1, sustainability assessment (SA) and sustainability indicators (SI) are resources that can be used to support

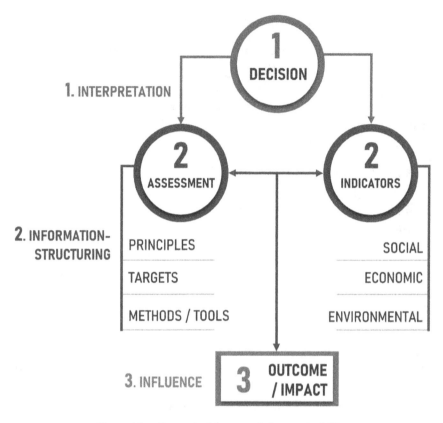

Figure 4.1.   Conceptual framework for sustainability.

decision-making, make recommendations, and bring policies in motion to fix sustainability concerns.[6] Due to the increasing volume of information and multidimensional nature of SD with uncertain outcomes and risks, SI and SA appear to be considerably complicated to comprehend, evaluate and assess. Nevertheless, they have widely been used, encouraging decision-making and presenting opportunities to understand the growing dynamics of SD.

4.2. Sustainability Indicators

The SI is an integral part of SD that captures the relative information, defines relationships, clarifies the current situation, rate and direction of change, and assists policy formulation. Over a couple of decades, there have been numerous attempts to develop, build, and articulate the SIs by governments, academics, NGOs, businesses, and practitioners.[7] In layman terms, indicators are an integral part of the day-to-day life. We intuitively rely on many indicators to understand and interpret situations and outcomes. For example, we choose different outfits in line with changing weather conditions. In the economic aspect, the commodity price hike is an indicator of inflation, and in an environmental context, the rising sea level is an indicator of global warming. So, instinctively, we know what an indicator is and how to relate it to a scenario and predict the expected result.

From a sustainable perspective, SIs are used to define the "system".[8] They help to analyze vital ties, patterns, and action points with influence. System properties shift over time, and we use indicators to inform us about the situation; for instance, is the population or economy rising more quickly or slowly than before? Hence, complex operations and behaviors of the system are dissected and studied using indicators.[9]

Figure 4.2(a) and 4.2(b) are examples of systems with indicators. Generally, the **stock** is the component of the system that tends to vary from time to time, e.g., the nation's population, forest biomass, money in the

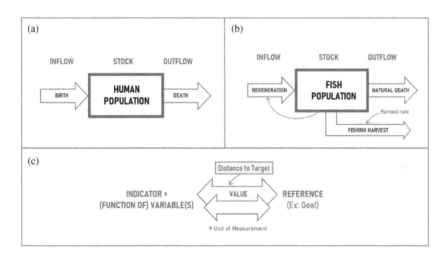

Figure 4.2.   Representation of sustainability indicators. (a) "System" and its components with indicators. (b) "System" with dynamic indicators. (c) Technical perspective of an indicator. (Source: The Balaton Group report, Waas *et al.*)

bank, etc. Inflow and outflow are **indicators** (measured per time unit) of the system which define the features, characteristics, quality, and property of the stock. Stocks are time-dependent. For instance, accumulated stock such as population in a country is declining due to a contagious disease, and most of the working population are deceased. Thus it would take a longer time to replenish the workforce (stocks) needed to revive the economy. Similarly, if we apply the same analogy to the fish population and introduce one more variable (fish harvesting), we end up with a *dynamic indicator* (human activity). These valuable *dynamic indicators*, such as turnaround time, regeneration ability, harvest rate, etc., help us understand the system/ stock and make modifications to preserve it in a sustainable manner.[7]

An *indicator* is, from a technical point of view, a *variable* or an aggregation/function of many variables, connected to a reference value (goal/target) that gives significance to the values taken by the variables.[10] Waas *et al.*, as shown in Figure 4.2(c), articulated the relationship between the variables, values, and references in their publication.[6] *Indicators* are linked to *reference values* to establish a shared understanding of the system that affects the result. If the indicator is not related to the reference value (goal/target/norm/standard), it has no significance, and the system state cannot be identified clearly. These indicators determine the difference between the variable's actual or expected values and the reference value and illustrate success as a distance-to-target calculation. The reference value (goal/target/norm/standard) here indicates the successful accomplishment of SD utilizing indicators.

The graphical presentation (Figure 4.2) is of practical benefit, as it enhances comprehension of the subject, and it is specific to establish the SI framework. These indicators and systems could serve as the fundamental components for any SI implementation, and any SI framework could conveniently be related to current and potential operations. For example, Pressure-State-Response (PSR),[11] the three-dimensional sustainability triangle,[7] or nested sustainability representations[12] are all applicable. Many publications propose new ideas and methods representing the SI framework; however, we shall focus on the widely adopted PSR framework (shown in Figure 4.3).[13]

The International Institute for Sustainable Development (IISD) used the PSR model to calculate aspects of societal, economic, and biophysical

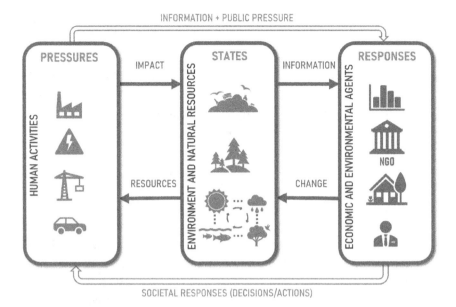

Figure 4.3. General framework of a Pressure-State-Response model — sustainable indicator.

environments within states and broad municipalities. It advocates that two components need to be considered to understand the maximum potential of indicators: a) indicator selection and b) issue-based indicator selection. In their report, the IISD presented a detailed study of how to select indicators surrounding problems.[13] For now, we shall understand the connection between each component and study the framework as follows:

(a) the **pressure** that people exert on the environment (in the form of pollution and resource exhaustion)
(b) the resulting **state** of the environment (especially the incurred changes) compared to desirable (sustainable) states
(c) the **response** by human activity, specifically in the context of political and social actions, interventions, and policies

The model categorizes environmental, economic, and social variables according to their roles in the causal chain, as seen in Figure 4.3. The first set of indicators in the PSR model refers to human activity and the impacting nature. It offers details on the triggers of environmental problems (for example, resource depletion, accumulation of wastes, toxic gas release, etc.) and the magnitude of the activities that impose strain on our ecosystem. The second group of indicators offers relevant statistics on the quality of the environment and the adjustments in the quality induced by human actions (for example, greenhouse gas emission, seawater level rise, ozone layer depletion, etc.). The third group of indicators provides information about the action items taken by political, social, and other organizations to return the ecosystem to its former condition. These indicators enable the policymakers to impose sanctions such as carbon tax for high-polluting vehicles and introduce new regulations to retain the environmental equilibrium.

SI initiatives are continuously evolving, and scholars, NGOs, and governments are continually developing the concept in line with the dynamic nature of technological advancements, waste generation, and environmental impacts. As we discussed earlier, SIs are the components of the decision-making process to promote SD. Therefore, to resolve growing environmental implications, new laws should be formulated and drafted continually along the road.

The SI framework will include a shared outlook for sustainable growth, independent of political dynamics, which will continue to occupy an influential role on every nation's agenda. To reinforce this statement, the US interagency working group has developed a list of 41 SIs to foster sustainability. Table 4.1 provides a handful of SIs pertaining to three aspects of sustainability for comparison.

As seen in Table 4.1, the indicators are focused on the three components of sustainability: environmental, economic, and social. While there are about 41 metrics in the original table, it is understood that not all of them are suitable for all companies/organizations/governments to implement SD. *An indicator should be selected based on the availability of data and the ease of study.* For that reason, the methodology is designed to be resilient to enable the simultaneous incorporation of other modules. For example, from a nation's viewpoint, the government will concentrate on environmental improvement due to growing concerns; therefore, environmental indicators would be promoted, and priorities will be given. Subsequently, other indicators such as economic and social will be introduced and integrated accordingly.[14]

Table 4.1. Sustainable indicators. (Source: US Interagency.)

ECONOMY	ENVIRONMENT	SOCIAL
› Capital assets	› Water quality	› Population
› Labour productivity	› Ozone layer status	› Crime rate
› Energy and Material consumption/capita/ $ of GDP	› Greenhouse emissions	› Life expectancy
› Inflation	› Soil erosion rates	› Educational achievement rates
› Income distribution	› Conversion of cropland to other usages	› Home ownership rates
› Unemployment	› Extreme weather events	› Teacher training level

4.3. Application of Sustainability Indicators

4.3.1. *Ecological/Environmental Footprint*

The environmental footprint estimates the need and effect of human activities on the planet. it assesses the availability of land area and water needed to sustain human existence at their level of use and resource quality and comparing this footprint value to the available biocapacity. **Biocapacity** refers to the biological efficiency of land area providing a sufficient supply of renewable resources and consuming its discharged waste. Research by the Global Footprint Network suggests that we are using up 1.52 Earths. By 2025, we would need to use up to 2.8 times of Earth services per human.[15] The team has developed a software tool to demonstrate the footprint value by collecting individual parameters such as food, housing, etc., to forecast personal impact on the global footprint. In this accounting method, consumable resources such as energy, biomass, construction materials, land occupancy, water, and other resources are converted into normalized land units called global hectares (gha).

Bastianoni *et al.* (2012)[16] proposed an ecological footprint (EF) estimation approach:

$$EF_{TOT} = EF_{DIR} + EF_{INDIR} \qquad (1)$$

where EF_{TOT} is the total ecological footprint and EF_{DIR} is related to direct occupation of land for crop cultivation, and it is expressed as

$$EF_{DIR} = \frac{Q}{Y_W} \times EQF_{cropland} \qquad (2)$$

where Q is the amount of generic crop harvested (in tonnes) and Y_W is the average yield of generic crop production globally. EQF (equivalence factor) is a scaling factor needed to convert a specific land-use type into a universal unit of biologically productive area (global hectare).

The term EF_{INDIR} takes all indirect land uses into account and is the contribution of the n inventoried inputs required for crop production (such as fuels, fertilizers, chemicals). It is evaluated as

$$EF_{INDIR} = \sum_{i=1}^{n} EF_i \qquad (3)$$

$$EF_i = \sum_{j=1}^{6} A_i \times YF_j \times EQF_j = \sum_{j=1}^{6} \frac{Q_i}{Y_i} \times YF_j \times EQF_j \qquad (4)$$

where A is the total area required (in physical hectares, ha) given by the ratio of the quantity (Q_i) of a generic input (i) to the yield (Y_i).

— The subscript i (= 1, …, n) refers to the inputs inventoried.
— The subscript j (= 1, …, 6) indicates the six land-use types of National Footprint Accounts (i.e., cropland, grazing, fishing grounds, forest, built-up and carbon footprint).
— YF_j is the Yield Factor specific for country and j-land type.
— EQF_j is the Equivalence Factor specific for each j-land type.

Crop production is essential for human existence. We use the massive land area to grow food resulting in overexploitation of the fertility of soils, overuse of water, deforestation, etc. When the demand for other natural resources (fishing grounds, forest, built-up) continues to grow, the greenhouse gas emission becomes significant simultaneously. The ecological footprint tests the minimum needs for living within the regenerative potential of the Earth and prepares human society for sustainable growth. Therefore, tracking the ecological footprint is crucial in maintaining the indicators within the threshold that our world can withstand the harmfulness and retain its regenerative capacity. Readers are advised to visit the website (https:// data.footprintnetwork.org/?_ga=2.248110660.2119166138.1619285535- 1570826653.1619285535#/) to get more insights about the ecological footprint, where values can be visually seen and downloaded.

4.3.2. *Economic Indicators*

4.3.2.1. *Genuine Saving Indicator*

In 2000, the World Bank created the Genuine Saving Index to measure the sustainability of the economy.[17] Perhaps this was the first step that aimed to implement social and environmental aspects in the economy, drawing inspiration from Hartwick's rule. Hartwick's law (although debatable) states the country is on a sustainable path if the savings exceed the depreciation caused by loss of natural or human wealth.[18]

The formula used by the World Bank to measure genuine savings, now referred to as 'adjusted net saving', is[2,17]:

GS = investment in produced capital – net foreign borrowing + net official transfers – depreciation of produced capital – net depreciation of natural capital + current education expenditures

where net depreciation of natural capital is the sum of resource depletion and environmental degradation (as we know, resource depletion is the loss of natural resources such as coal, crude oil, natural gas, and environmental degradation refers to greenhouse gas emissions). The Genuine Saving Indicator is a measure of weak sustainability, in other words, failure of reversibility. This indicator states that developing countries primarily depend on non-renewable (unsustainable) resources to fuel their economy, but fails to elaborate for developed nations. This imperfection is criticized by scholars and competing models such as

Non-Declining Natural Capital Stocks and *Daly's Operational Principles* have been proposed. Despite the debate, the Genuine Saving Indicator concept is a valuable and realistic model that is grounded in economic principles.[18]

For more details about 'adjusted net saving', readers are advised to visit (https://data.worldbank.org/indicator/NY.ADJ.NNTY.PC.KD?end=2018 &start=1970&view=map) to get more insights.

4.3.2.2. *Economic Performance Indicator*

Financial indicators (such as return on equity, profitability, solvency, and risk factors) indicate the economic benefit that a business or a country brings to the economy,[19] for example, Value Added (VA) or contribution to GDP. The primary function of these indicators is pointed at increasing the value and assets of a company. Therefore, the VA approach is typically employed to realize this objective. VA is a value that analysts refer to as surplus profits, which means that a business retains a certain sum of revenue after covering all its expenses. VA from a company's perspective is calculated as Net income = Value of sales − (Expense on raw materials + Other purchases).[20]

The VA method of evaluation has been popular to determine the performance of a company. Nevertheless, it is only recently that corporations have found and begun to incorporate this economic success indicator into the management accounting framework. Lately, this indicator has transformed into EVA (Economic Value Added), which represents net operating profit minus a charge for the capital invested.[21]

The EVA index can be mathematically expressed as

$$EC_{eva} = \sum_{l=1}^{L} \sum_{c=1}^{LC} \left[NOPAT_{c,l} - (C_{c,l} \times CA_{c,l}) \right] \qquad (5)$$

Equation (5) is expressed in currency, where *NOPAT* is net operating profit before interest but after tax, *C* is the cost of capital in the organization and *CA* is capital employed in the organization. Further detailed mathematical expressions can be seen in Azapagic *et al.*'s paper.[14] Refer to the link (https://www.wallstreetmojo.com/economic-value-added-eva/) for a detailed understanding of EVA.

The EVA indicators are useful for quantifying the economic effects of improvements. The measure, though, has certain drawbacks and is sometimes criticized because of its sluggish nature when handling other factors.[22] Nonetheless, it may be useful as a metric of sustainable growth when used in combination with other indicators such as GDP and VA. The GDP, an indicator of the manufacturing sector, would reflect its growth potential and expansion ability in both national and global markets. When it is paired with the VA indicator, it performs a dual function. The hybrid indicator will be able to calculate sustainable industrial development and capture the essence of sustainability by regulating resource depletion.[14]

In this direction, to calculate the macroeconomics, a few other indicators were proposed, such as the Index of Sustainable Economic Welfare (ISEW), Net Economic Welfare (NEW), and ISEW-based Genuine Progress Indicator (GPI).[23] These indicators are more inclusive considering the social factors in the economic domain acknowledging sustainable values, such as community, economic advancement, environmental services, natural resources, etc.

4.3.3. *Social Indicators — Human Development Indicator*

The UNDP proposed the Human Development Index (HDI). It described the HDI as a combination of long and healthy life, knowledge, and a decent standard of living. *Income distribution* is a prime factor for all citizens to enjoy a decent standard of living.[24] Income distribution can be defined as the ratio of the top 10% (CEO, managers) and the bottom 10% of people (technicians, operators) of a company. The Income Distribution of Social Indicator (SI_{id}) is expressed as[14]

$$SI_{id} = \frac{\sum_{c=1}^{c} \frac{IT_c}{IB_c}}{C} \tag{6}$$

where *IT* and *IB* represent income of the top and bottom 10%, respectively. In company-oriented analysis, $C = 1$; for process- and product-analysis, C includes all major suppliers in the life cycle. As it indicates the distribution of wealth between individuals, this indicator is often linked to social equity

Table 4.2.   An example for income distribution of social indicator.

	Employees	Cumulative income/year
IT_c	CEO	$ 250,000 / Year
	CFO	
	Director	
IT_b	Security	$ 85,000 / Year
	Clerk	
	Driver	

$$\frac{IT_c}{IB_c} = \frac{250{,}000}{85{,}000} = 2.94$$

and harmony. To ensure strong social sustainability there should be a closer balance between the two components (*IT* and *IB*).

The SI_{id} value (2.94) represents modest sustainability, as seen in Table 4.2, but the indicator value should be as low as possible in the future to reach high social sustainability within organizations.

From Equation (6), the social aspect is studied in an economic context by leveraging the income distribution. However, an environmental facet is still needed to fulfill the criteria of sustainability. The scholars applied a green aspect to the HDI by factoring in CO_2 pollution per capita, also known as the Green HDI.[25] In this way, Green HDI or Sustainable HDI, holistically considering the environmental components such as air, water, and soil, has been developed.

4.4. Sustainability Assessment

We discussed the common framework and the indicators used for SD in previous sections. In this direction, let us evaluate how the sustainability implementation (e.g., sustainable projects) process is being assessed in detail. Sustainable assessment is gaining momentum among financial institutions, governments, academics, and NGOs. SA delivers unique insights by evaluating the impacts/outcome directed towards sustainable growth strategy and decision-making. A few SA definitions are as follows:

> "Sustainability assessment is...a tool that can help decision-makers and policy-makers decide what actions they should take and should not take in an attempt to make society more sustainable."[26]

or

> *"The goal of sustainability assessment is to pursue plans and activities that make an optimal contribution to sustainable development."*[27]

4.4.1. SA Background

As currently articulated in the literature, the modern SA has primarily emerged from work conducted by environmental impact assessment (EIA) professionals and strategic environmental assessment (SEA). Both EIA and SEA are often labeled as *impact assessment* methods fostering environmental sustainability. The EIA and SEA experts have significantly established lots of SA thinking that were feasible and practicable.[28] Therefore, these proposals were viewed as the new environmental assessment trend in the 20th century.

Impact assessment can be characterized as forecasting the effects of actual or planned action. The EIA was first established in the US as part of the National Environmental Policy Act (NEPA) introduced in 1970. The EIA determines the environmental impacts of planned actions and identifies ways to reduce the consequences.[29] The EIA reflects the feasibility of alternative strategies and mitigation steps to avoid environmental harm by leveraging interagency collaboration. Also, the EIA was upgraded to the SEA by including policies and higher-level impact studies of planning. Therivel[30] defines SEA as *the formalized, systematic and comprehensive process of evaluating the environmental effects of a policy, plan, or program and its alternatives, including the preparation of a written report on the findings of that evaluation, and using the findings in publicly accountable decision-making.*

In a nutshell, the EIA relates to projects, and the SEA is related to policies, plans, and programs. It seems these two (EIA and SEA) techniques emphasize the environmental aspect at their core. To encourage complete sustainable assessment, the EIA and the SEA must incorporate other elements of sustainability. Thus, *EIA-driven integrated assessment* emerged; it integrates social and economic outcomes, including environmental impacts, into a project.[29]

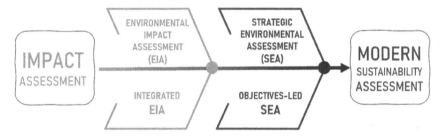

Figure 4.4.   Sustainable assessment evolution.

Similarly, an *objectives-led integrated assessment* has been proposed based on SEA.[31] The *EIA-driven integrated assessment* is a powerful technique, but the outcome is inhibited. Naturally, SEA is an upgraded version of EIA and driven by objectives, outcomes, targets, etc. Hence, objectives-led SEA is likely to achieve wholly sustainable assessment by integrating policy framework, project plans, and targeted objectives. Figure 4.4 provides an overview of evolution of SA starting from impact assessment to modern SA.

The modern SA refers to recent progress and advancements (i.e., 21st century). For example, Bond *et al.*[32] regard SA as a *recent paradigm for an impact assessment* often referred to as the "**third generation**" alongside EIA and SEA methods. In this way, other scholars contributed to the modern SA practice, such as indicator development, product-related assessment, and innovative integrated assessment techniques.[6]

4.4.2. *SA Framework*

We need to grasp the framework and the integral components of SA, accompanied by the evolution of SA. In general, a framework includes a conceptual nexus, models, methodology, and components with the intent of functionalities that outline the implementation of an action. While considering SA, there appears to be a broad spectrum of SA practices and definitions from the literature, and the framework will be hard to pinpoint. Regardless, lets us aim to spot widely accepted SA principles and frameworks from the scholarly articles.

Table 4.3. Aspects of Sustainable Assessment (SA) and corresponding Bellagio STAMP principles. (Source: IISD.)

ASPECTS OF SA	BELLAGIO STAMP PRINCIPLES
ESTABLISH A VISION	› Guiding vision and Goals 01
CONTENT	› Essential consideration › Framework and indicators › Adequate scope 02–04
KEY ISSUES AND PROCESS	› Broad participation › Effective communications › Transparency 05–07
ESTABLISH CAPACITY OF ASSESSMENT	› Continuity and capacity 08

In 1996, global SA professionals drafted the "Bellagio Principles — Guidelines for Practical Assessment of Progress Toward Sustainable Development". The principles have acted as general guidance for SA since then. Given the evolving definitions, the standards were re-evaluated and re-named as "Sustainability Assessment and Measurement Principles" ("Bellagio STAMP") in subsequent decades.[33]

The concepts of the Bellagio STAMP, as seen in Table 4.3, address four aspects of the SA process for SD. The first aspect of assessment deals with principle 1, establishing a clear vision and goals. Likewise, other aspects of assessment deal with different principles establishing distinct strategies for SA accomplishment.

Now let us establish the linkage between Bellagio STAMP principles and the sustainable assessment concept. As shown in Figure 4.5, Sala *et al.* suggested that the SA is a convergence of Bellagio STAMP principles

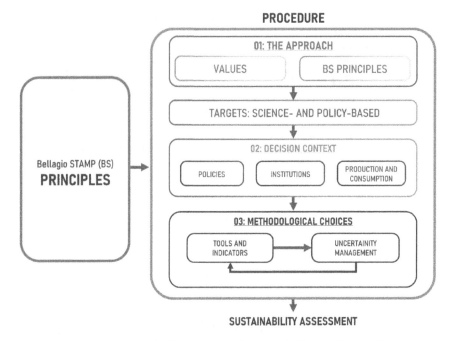

Figure 4.5.   Sustainable assessment framework. (Source: Sala *et al.*)

and the evaluation methods (approach, decision, and methods).[34] To start the SA, it is essential to thoroughly understand the definitions of Bellagio STAMP sustainability principles (shown in Table 4.3). Pintér *et al.*[33] specifically offered a comprehensive elaboration of these principles, so let us not get into discussing these principles in depth. The bottom line is, as stated by Sala *et al.*, that these sustainability principles are crucial, because they reinforce the values of assessment and assisting practitioners with quantifying outcomes.

4.4.2.1. *The Approach*

The approach to sustainable practice is often described as a perspective of assessment (for example, weak or strong sustainability). It is further classified and directed towards values and principles to determine the characteristics of the outcome. Values, for instance, are often handled by experts and assessed objectively due to their vagueness. However, it is expected that a consistent expression of values is necessary for the integrity and robustness of the SA (e.g., strong versus weak sustainability, and a clear definition of the guiding vision and perspective).[34]

As shown in Table 4.3, different sustainability principles (01–08) related to SA provide the essence of relationships. Values and principles are interrelated, and at the same time, they may operate individually. Values define the attribute of sustainability (weak/strong). On the other hand, principles reflect core ideas regardless of conflicting values. For example, cultural and social values are important while building a sustainable ecosystem. But the ecosystem should comply with the planetary boundary principles; therefore, any proposed values should not hinder principles and inhibit growth.[35]

The next stage refers to sustainable targets. Ideation of targets should reflect the values and principles and be backed by empirical evidence. Holistically, to obtain a concrete result, targets should resonate with scientific contexts following the decision-making process.

4.4.2.2. *Decision Context*

Decision context is influenced by external factors rather than following a guided path as the approach stage. External factors are highly uncertain and change from time to time, so a cohesive effort is required to analyze the fuzzy messages and translate them into a quantitative decision context. Some of the influential factors are (a) the actor — assessment driver; (b) the scale of assessment; (c) complexity of decision; (d) the uncertainty of the decision; (e) time horizon — unpredictable events; and (f) the activity affected by the decision (e.g., investment, decommissioning).[34]

Besides, two more strategies should been considered during the decision-making process: 1) Threshold and 2) Scenario planning. As we know, the threshold may be defined as a critical limit for any given conditions; if crossed or violated, adverse consequences become inevitable. Polasky *et al.*[36] have elaborated a scenario considering the threshold factor which influences the decision-making process and identifies its limitations related to an uncertain outcome. Assume CO_2 in the atmosphere is beyond the threshold level; it does not mean that just below the threshold level is good for health. Ideally, placing the threshold value in an evaluation is difficult, and relying on these fixed values may lead to misinterpretation. Hence probability distribution is highly suited for this kind of assessment.

The second is scenario planning; scenarios are a set of possible futures that are evaluated based on different criteria. Hence, individual criteria and scenarios must be studied following the three pillars of SA (i.e., multicriteria assessment).[34]

4.4.2.3. *Methodological Choices*

The methodological choices stage is considered at the forefront of SA due to its significant integrated components. Tools and Indicators play a vital role in SA, and we have seen the importance of indicators with some examples in the previous section. We have also studied the evolution, framework, and conceptualization of these indicators suggesting sustainable assessment. Likewise, Tools are the software, application, and database that facilitate the research analysis following a specific method and similar models. There are many commercial and open-source software tools that help to conduct various levels of assessment. Figure 4.6 shows the classification and collection tools for SA.

These tools assist professionals in creating sustainability projects by anticipating the results of multiple scenarios and conditions. For instance, Life Cycle Assessment (**LCA**) helps to evaluate and quantify the environmental impact of product/process/service through evaluation of its entire life cycle or lifespan by a defined systematic procedure from extraction, processing, and process development to use and disposal.[37] Similarly, Social LCA (**SCLA**) is used for the social and socio-economic impacts of the product

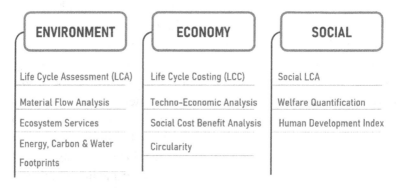

Figure 4.6.   Tools for sustainable assessment. (Source: Institute for European Environmental Policy, Seeram *et al.*)

system throughout its life cycle, which directly/indirectly and positively/negatively influence participants/stakeholders.[38] Life Cycle Costing (**LCC**) applies to both costs and benefits linked to the product system during the life cycle, considering external relevant cost and advantages.[38] To put it in a sustainable perspective, Kloepffer (2008) proposed life cycle sustainability assessment (**LCSA**), and it can be defined as[39]

$$LCSA + LCA + LCC + SLCA \qquad (7)$$

Equation (7) discusses the environmental, economic, and social factors correlated with the sustainable product life cycle. We will discuss this equation in detail with case studies in the next chapter.

In Figure 4.5, under methodological choices, uncertainty management applies to how we plan for unseen incidents and situations and how we will effectively reduce them in the process of SA. There would be so many uncertainties that the project or any development activities would meet unknowingly. For example, global warming is a direct negative consequence of CO_2 emissions from burning fossil fuels. We were not sure about the harmful impacts of burning fossil fuels in the early days because we have not witnessed immediate adverse effects. But now we are observing acid rain, sea-level rise, etc. In the future, to avoid such negative impacts and ambiguities, we need to apply uncertainty management in SA, for example, using the LCA to analyze the CO_2 emission and estimate the environmental degradation.

Concluding Remarks

SD must be regarded as a decision-making tool for all parties from the local to the global level. The framework and its constituent elements should be studied and understood to achieve the full competitiveness of sustainability. We began by studying the framework for SD and associated components (indicators and assessment). We have analyzed the ways sustainable indicators assist practitioners and experts in making decisions that predict the future based on empirical data.

Following that, we have been acquainted with the fundamentals of sustainable assessment with the framework and integral components, and collection and classification of tools with functionalities. The central idea of this chapter is that profound understanding is needed concerning sustainable indicators and sustainable assessment rules. The knowledge gained from this chapter can be applied for policy formulation, the assessment of goods and services, or measuring public sector efficiencies. Sustainability principles with indicators and tools can efficiently facilitate SD and we have seen the importance of integration within the framework.

Finally, we concluded the chapter with the importance of tools and how to access sustainability with the help of analytical tools such as LCSA. We shall study the components, implementation, and case studies in the next chapter.

References

1. Creative economy report 2008 — the challenge of assessing the creative economy: towards informed policy-making. https://unctad.org/system/files/official-document/ditc20082cer_en.pdf.
2. Evans, A., Strezov, V. & Evans, T. Measuring tools for quantifying sustainable development. *Eur. J. Sustain. Dev.* **4**, 291–300 (2015).
3. Alfsen, K. H. & Greaker, M. From natural resources and environmental accounting to construction of indicators for sustainable development. *Ecol. Econ.* **61**, 600–610 (2007).
4. Dahl, A. L. Achievements and gaps in indicators for sustainability. *Ecol. Indic.* **17**, 14–19 (2012).
5. Hugé, J., Waas, T., Eggermont, G. & Verbruggen, A. Impact assessment for a sustainable energy future-reflections and practical experiences. *Energy Policy* **39**, 6243–6253 (2011).
6. Waas, T. *et al.* Sustainability assessment and indicators: Tools in a decision-making strategy for sustainable development. *Sustain.* **6**, 5512–5534 (2014).
7. Meadows, D. Indicators and information systems for sustainable. https://donellameadows.org/wp-content/userfiles/IndicatorsInformation.pdf.
8. Indicators of sustainable development: guidelines and methodologies. https://www.un.org/esa/sustdev/natlinfo/indicators/guidelines.pdf.
9. Martinet, V. Defining sustainability objectives. https://are.berkeley.edu/fields/erep/seminar/s2009/MMR.pdf.
10. Searcy, C. The role of sustainable development indicators in corporate decision. https://www.iisd.org/system/files/publications/role_of_sustainability_indicators.pdf.

11. Linster, M. & Fletcher, J. Using the pressure-state-response model to develop indicators of sustainability. http://documentacion.ideam.gov.co/openbiblio/bvirtual/017931/DocumentosIndicadores/Temasvarios/Docum26.pdf.
12. Smeets, E. & Weterings, R. Environmental indicators: Typology and overview Prepared. https://www.eea.europa.eu/publications/TEC25.
13. Hardi, P. & Pinter, L. Models and methods of measuring sustainable development performance. https://www.iisd.org/system/files?file=publications/measure_models_methods_sd.pdf.
14. Azapagic, A. & Perdan, S. Indicators of sustainable development for industry: A general framework. *Trans. I. Chem. E. Vol 78, Part B* **41**, 629–637 (2000).
15. Gray, N. F. *Facing Up to Global Warming: What is Going on and How You Can Make a Difference?* Springer (2015).
16. Bastianoni, S., Niccolucci, V., Pulselli, R. M. & Marchettini, N. Indicator and indicandum: 'Sustainable way' vs 'prevailing conditions' in the Ecological Footprint. *Ecol. Indic.* **16**, 47–50 (2012).
17. Hamilton, K. Genuine saving as a sustainability indicator. https://documents.worldbank.org/en/publication/documents-reports/documentdetail/908161468740713285/genuine-saving-as-a-sustainability-indicator.
18. Chang, Y. A path towards strong sustainability. https://eneken.ieej.or.jp/3rd_IAEE_Asia/pdf/paper/103p.pdf.
19. Financial indicators. https://www.unescap.org/ttdw/ppp/ppp_primer/46_financial_indicators.html.
20. Gilchrist, R. R. *Managing for Profit: The Added Value Concept.* Allen & Unwin (1971).
21. Ehrbar, A. *EVA: The Real Key to Creating Wealth.* Wiley (1998).
22. Shil, N. C. Performance measures: An application of economic value added. *Int. J. Bus. Manag.* **4**, 169–177 (2009).
23. Schiller, B. & Gebhardt, K. *The Macro Economy Today* (14th edition). McGraw-Hill Education (2015).
24. Human Development Index (HDI) | Human Development Reports. http://hdr.undp.org/en/content/human-development-index-hdi.
25. Dietz, S. & Neumayer, E. Weak and strong sustainability in the SEEA: Concepts and measurement. *Ecol. Econ.* **61**, 617–626 (2007).
26. Devuyst, D. Sustainability assessment: The application of a methodological framework. *J. Environ. Assess. Policy Manag.* **1**, 459–487 (1999).
27. Verheem, R. A. A. Recommendations for Sustainability Assessment in the Netherlands. In: *Environmental Impact Assessment in the Netherlands — Views from the Commission for EIA in 2002*, pp. 9–14, Commission for EIA (2002).

28. Gibson, R. B. *et al.* Specification of sustainability based environmental assessment decision criteria and implications for determining significance in environment. https://static.twoday.net/NE1BOKU0607/files/Gibson_ Sustainability-EA.pdf.

29. Pope, J., Annandale, D. & Morrison-Saunders, A. Conceptualising sustainability assessment. *Environ. Impact Assess. Rev.* **24**, 595–616 (2004).

30. Therivel, R. *Strategic Environmental Assessment in Action.* Taylor & Francis (1992).

31. Sheate, W. R. *et al.* Integrating the environment into strategic decision-making: Conceptualizing policy sea. *Eur. Environ.* **13**, 1–18 (2003).

32. Bond, A., Morrison-Saunders, A. & Pope, J. Sustainability assessment: The state of the art. *Impact Assess. Proj. Apprais.* **30**, 53–62 (2012).

33. Pintér, L., Hardi, P., Martinuzzi, A. & Hall, J. Bellagio STAMP: Principles for sustainability assessment and measurement. *Ecol. Indic.* **17**, 20–28 (2012).

34. Sala, S., Ciuffo, B. & Nijkamp, P. A systemic framework for sustainability assessment. *Ecol. Econ.* **119**, 314–325 (2015).

35. Rockström, J. *et al.* Planetary boundaries: Exploring the safe operating space for humanity. *Ecol. Soc.* **14**, 32 (2009).

36. Polasky, S., Carpenter, S. R., Folke, C. & Keeler, B. Decision-making under great uncertainty: Environmental management in an era of global change. *Trends Ecol. Evol.* **26**, 398–404 (2011).

37. Dahiya, S., Katakojwala, R., Ramakrishna, S. & Mohan, S. V. Biobased products and life cycle assessment in the context of circular economy and sustainability. *Mater. Circ. Econ.* **2**, 7 (2020).

38. Luu, L. Q. & Halog, A. Life Cycle Sustainability Assessment: A Holistic Evaluation of Social, Economic, and Environmental Impacts. In: G. Ruiz-Mercado & H. Cabezas (eds.), *Sustainability in the Design, Synthesis and Analysis of Chemical Engineering Processes*, pp. 327–352, Butterworth-Heinemann (2016).

39. Hauschild, M. Z., Rosenbaum, R. K. & Olsen, S. I. *Life Cycle Assessment: Theory and Practice.* Springer (2017).

Exercises

1) What are the three stages that describe the sustainability framework?
   (A) Decision, Assessment & Indicators, Outcome/Impact
   (B) Arrangement, Assessment & Indicators, Outcome/Impact
   (C) Arrangement, Assessment & Indicators, Methods
   (D) Decision, Assessment & Indicators, Measurement

2) Which component in the 'System' of SIs varies from time to time?
   (A) Commission
   (B) Price
   (C) Stock
   (D) Percentage
3) SIs are measured using
   (A) Time
   (B) Speed
   (C) Power
   (D) Force
4) PSR stands for:
   (A) Pressure, State, React
   (B) Point, State, Response
   (C) Pressure, Sell, Response
   (D) Pressure, State, Response
5) What are the sustainable indicators used for measuring environmental performance?
   (A) Water quality, Greenhouse, Extreme weather events
   (B) Water quality, Unemployment, Extreme weather events
   (C) Quality life, Greenhouse, Extreme weather events
   (D) Water quality, Greenhouse, Education
6) EF stands for:
   (A) Ecological Force
   (B) Ecological Footprint
   (C) Element Force
   (D) Ecological Finance
7) Who founded the Genuine Saving Index?
   (A) American bank
   (B) Reserve bank
   (C) World bank
   (D) Citi bank
8) Which of the following tools are considered to measure environmental assessment?
   (A) Life Cycle Assessment (LCA)
   (B) Material Flow Analysis (MFA)
   (C) Ecosystem services
   (D) All the above

9) What is the eighth principle of Bellagio Stamp Principles?
   (A) Transparency
   (B) Broad Participation
   (C) Consultancy and capacity
   (D) Adequate scope
10) LCSA stands for
   (A) Life Cycle Sustainability Assessment
   (B) Long-term Cycle Sustainability Assessment
   (C) Life Cycle Standard Assessment
   (D) Life Cycle Sustainability Appraisal

CHAPTER FIVE

SUSTAINABILITY ASSESSMENT-CASE STUDIES

Introduction

As we discussed in the last chapter, we were aiming to conduct Life Cycle Sustainability Assessment (**LCSA**). **LCSA** = Life Cycle Assessment (**LCA**) + Life Cycle Costing (**LCC**) + Social Life Cycle Assessment (**SLCA**). But conducting **LCSA** is not cost-effective and requires a licensed software tool. We wish to gain only a basic understanding of SA as well as some practical knowledge. Thus we choose *openLCA*, an open-source software tool, in this chapter to perform the SA. When it comes to performing an environmental analysis (**LCA**) on any product development or process, openLCA is user-friendly, and the databases are accessible for free on the openLCA website.

We begin this chapter by presenting a brief introduction to the LCA and discussing the framework developed by the International Organization for Standardization (ISO). We elaborate on each component of the LCA framework by giving examples so that readers can grasp the definition quickly. Following that, the chapter compares the environmental effects of coal-fired power plants and solar panel production scenarios, focusing on airborne pollution, using a 100 MW electricity production example. This comparison would use the LCA method to understand our current situation and the benefits of clean energy in light of environmental emissions.

5.1. Life Cycle Assessment

Life Cycle Assessment (LCA) is a method that aims to evaluate and quantify the environmental effects of a product/process/service via a given systemic protocol from extraction, manufacturing, and process creation to usage and disposal, through assessing its entire life cycle or lifetime (shown in Figure 5.1).[1] In other words, LCA evaluates the environmental value of goods and their impacts on the ecosystem. Thus, the LCA is deemed an appropriate method for rendering environmental choices for the businesses who make the products, and helps to convey environmental concerns constructively. Businesses and governments have started incorporating the tool in their product developments and policymaking. Following the ISO's guidance of 1997, increasing attention has arisen for LCA.[2]

Among several LCA techniques, a familiar and widely agreed approach to carry out LCA is the ISO LCA Norm. The ISO 14040 series is a compilation of guidelines stipulating how an LCA should be applied while developing products or services. LCA is defined in these criteria as a "product environmental assessment method" and consists of four different phases,[3] as seen in Figure 5.2. The LCA framework complying with ISO Standard 14040 consists of (a) goal and scope definition, (b) inventory analysis, (c) impact assessment, and (d) interpretation as detailed in Table 5.1. The LCA is very

Figure 5.1.   Life Cycle Assessment.

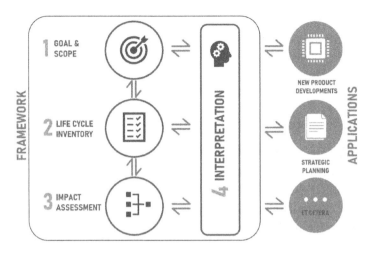

Figure 5.2.   Overview of ISO LCA framework.

Table 5.1.   Methodology for performing LCA. (Source: S. Dahiya *et al.*)

S.No	Phases	Factors
1	Goal and scope	› Definition of the system boundaries › Variation of life cycle (cradle-cradle, cradle-gate, cradle-wheel, gate-gate, etc.) › Fixing the functional unit for the study
2	Inventory analysis	› Selecting and separating primary and secondary sources of data › Data and data quality's requirements › Kind of assumptions employed or to be employed › Value choices and optional elements › Cut-off criteria to be employed
3	Impact assessment	› Selection of impact categories and classification › Characterization and the optional steps › Normalization (optional) › Weighing (optional)
4	Interpretation	› LCA methodology to be implemented › Critical review of results and interpretation › Uncertainty analysis › Preparation of final report

versatile and precise concerning the goal of the research. LCA application and outcome are custom-designed depending upon the study. For example, LCA can be implemented at any stage starting from product development, improvement, to end-of-life.[1]

5.2. The Essence of Environmental LCA and How It Is Applied

In short, LCA is a method that helps to analyze the different environmental factors connected with a product/service throughout its lifespan. Environmental LCA is carried out in four steps, as set out in the ISO 14040 and 14044 specifications, and these phases are typically interlinked, as shown in Figure 5.2. A detailed elaboration of these different stages is outlined in Table 5.1.

5.2.1. *Goal and Scope*

5.2.1.1. *Goal*

The purpose of an LCA must be evident. The target statement must contain the following aspects as defined by ISO:

› *Why are you doing the LCA analysis? Concretely, what are the objectives of conducting the LCA study?*
› *What are the application areas of the LCA results?*
› *Who are the potential audiences?*
› *Can the findings be revealed and used in comparative statements that are made public?*

Example:
Evaluate potential environmental impacts of a 100 MW coal-fired power station.

5.2.1.2. *Scope*

The scope is not a single document, but perhaps a set of qualitative and quantitative details that denotes what is involved in the research and key criteria that explain how it is performed. Once the goal of the study is defined, the scope is formulated which essentially includes A) Functional unit and product system, B) System boundaries and inventory inputs and outputs, and C) LCIA methods used.

A. Functional Unit and Product System

There is a relationship between (2) product system and (1) functional unit. A **product system** is a set of processes that serves a **function**. In layman's words, "what would it do?" For instance, a power plant is a **product system** that has the **function** of generating electricity. As seen in Table 5.2, the functional unit must be explicitly and quantitatively (e.g., 100 MWh) described by a calculation comparing the function to the inputs and outputs to be analyzed.[2]

B. System Boundary and Input and Output Flow

The system boundary is a subset of the overall collection of *processes* (mining, transport, recycling) and *flows* (energy, materials) of the **product system** that are part of the study within stated study goals. The system boundary helps the audience to ascertain the overall project scope and limits and evaluate the functions of flow, process, and product system. A simple system boundary depiction is given in Figure 5.3.[4] Input and output flows do not have any standards based on ISO recommendations. These flows are customizable depending on the project specifications. As an example, Figure 5.3 depicts the input and output flows for coal-driven power plants.

C. LCIA Methods

LCIA stands for Life Cycle Impact Assessment. As mentioned in the goal definition, there are different impact assessment methods available for assessing the performance/output of the project. We will review this definition in depth in section 5.2.3.

Table 5.2.   Linkages between function, functional unit and product system for hypothetical LCA studies. (Source: Matthews *et al.*)

Product System	Function	Functional Unit
Power plant	Generating electricity	100 MWh of electricity
Light bulb	Providing light	100 lumens of light for 1 hour (100 lumens/hr)

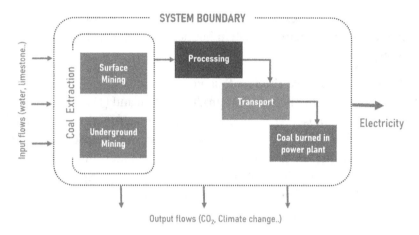

Figure 5.3.   Conceptual system boundary of coal-driven power station.

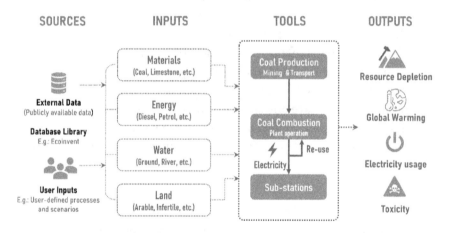

Figure 5.4.   Conceptual life cycle inventory of coal-driven power station.

5.2.2. *Life Cycle Inventory*

If the goal and scope have been established, the next phase is to gather data from the *life cycle inventory* that contains inputs and outputs from each process at each point of the life cycle. In other words, all emissions discharged into the atmosphere (e.g., CO_2, CFC), impacts (e.g., resource depletion), and resources derived from the environment (e.g., water, limestone, coal) along with the life cycle of products are summed in an inventory.[5] The inventory is a list of elementary flows as shown in Figure 5.4.

Inputs are typically obtained from external data (public information) or software database/occasionally user-specific data (as seen in Figure 5.4). Once the inventory is listed, it is important to create consistent output flows (intended to assess) such as resource depletion, toxicity level, etc.[6] (Note: The output here refers to end-point impact assessment, the next section would elaborate this concept clearly.)

5.2.3. *Impact Assessment*

This phase is referred to as life cycle impact assessment (LCIA). This phase includes sorting all emissions and resources according to different types of impacts and translating them into comparable impact units. In other words, we are translating Life Cycle Inventory output into environmental-related measures or impact on resources/ecosystem/well-being. Impact Assessment can be carried out by two methods: (i) midpoint and (ii) endpoint.

The midpoint method (as shown in Figure 5.5) refers to elementary flow (input and output) assigned to midpoint impact categories such as

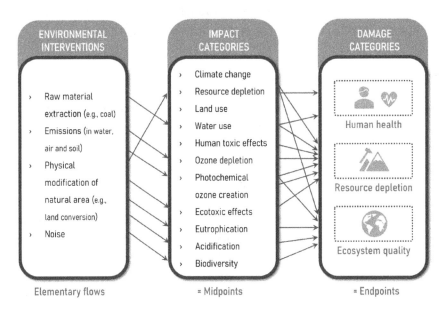

Figure 5.5. Overall UNEP/SETAC scheme of the environmental LCIA framework, linking LCI results via the midpoint categories to damage categories. (Source: Jolliet *et al.*)

ozone depletion, climate change, etc. Some LCIA tool such as CML and TRACI follow the midpoint method, whereas ReCiPe and IMPACT follow endpoint method. The LCIA is carried out in four steps: (i) Characterization, (ii) Normalization, (iii) Aggregation, and (iv) Weighting. Among them, the ISO has advised *Characterization* as most significant when compared to the other three steps. *Characterization* translates one parameter (raw material extraction, e.g., coal) into corresponding impact categories, as shown in Figure 5.5, for further processing and interpretation.[7]

5.2.4. *Interpretation*

The interpretation stage converts all the empirical information carried out in previous phases into relevant data for the target group, consistent with the goal and scope. This stage is necessary for defining, quantifying, reviewing, and assessing information from the outcomes of the Life Cycle Inventory and Life Cycle Impact Assessment. This stage draws concluding remarks by identifying the environmental hotspots and analyzing the environmental impact of products or services.[8] Subsequently, based on the findings obtained from the analysis, product improvement, development, policymaking, etc., can be implemented as seen in Figure 5.2.

5.3. Power Plants Comparison

We will compare a coal-fired power plant with a solar power panels fabrication facility in this segment, with both power plants providing a 100 MW power generation capability. Two power plants and their energy generation scenario are depicted in Figures 5.6 and 5.7 using Sankey diagrams. As shown in Figure 5.6, the coal-fired power production life cycle starts with the extraction and refining of raw materials such as coal, limestone, and crude oil. These raw materials are then transported to the power plant to prepare for the electricity generation process. In the power plant, coal is crushed into pulverized coal and fed into the combustion boiler. Simultaneously, limestone is pumped into the boiler to reduce SO_2 emissions. At the bottom of the furnace, a series of air nozzles are used to pump a combination of hot air and gas into the combustion chamber, thus increasing the combustion efficiency. The studied coal-fired power plant

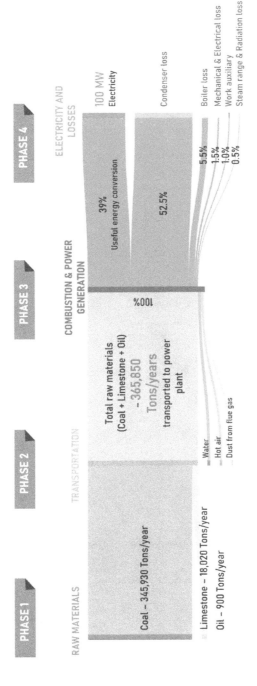

Figure 5.6.   Sankey diagram of 100 MWh coal-fired power station.

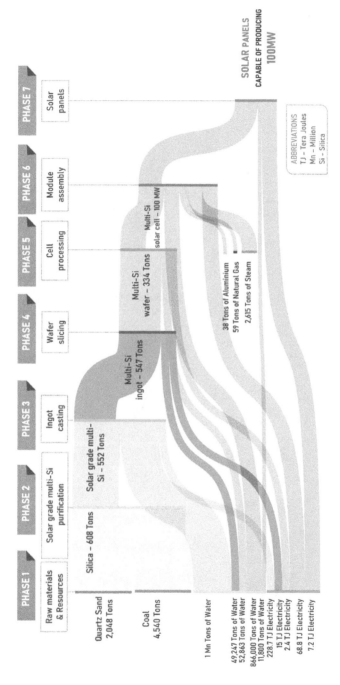

Figure 5.7.   Sankey diagram of 100 MWh solar panels production.

utilizes a circulating fluidized bed combustion technology with the added benefit of two cyclones that collect dust particles from flue gas and return them to the boiler bed to mix with coal and limestone. The combustion phase heats the feed water, resulting in the production of high-pressure steam. After that, the steam vapor is routed to the steam turbine, which generates electricity. After driving the turbine, the steam is stored, filtered, and returned to the boiler for reuse. The typical coal-fired plant has a maximum energy conversion efficiency of 39%,[9] and the remaining 61% of energy is lost in the process of energy generation, as shown in Figure 5.6.

Similarly, Figure 5.7 illustrates the manufacturing life cycle scenario for solar panels. The seven-phase manufacturing method begins with raw materials such as quartz sand and coal mining and services such as water and electricity.[10] Although additional resources such as chemicals, glass, and plastics are needed for the operation, we have considered only water and electricity in addition to raw materials for simplicity. Assuming that all raw materials and services are accessible in the factory, solar panel manufacturing must follow a seven-stage method, as shown in Figure 5.7. A typical industry standard solar panel would be 1.6 m × 1 m (length × breadth) that generates an average of 320 W at its peak efficiency.[11] In a similar setup, building 100 MW capacity would require ~380,000–400,000 solar panels with an area covering ~2 km². A typical industry standard solar panel has a conversion efficiency of 24.1%,[12] which means that 100% of incident light energy is converted to 24.1% electrical energy. The remaining 75.9% of energy is lost through DC to AC conversion, dirt loss, ohmic loss, temperature loss, transformer loss, and module mismatch loss.[13]

5.3.1. *Coal-Fired Power Plant*

Figure 5.8 shows the boundary conditions for a coal-fired power plant with a capacity of 100 MWh. This exercise aims to gain a reasonable understanding of LCA analysis of coal-fired power plants, so the boundary conditions presented might not be relevant in a realistic situation. The LCA analysis is performed via the OpenLCA, an open-source software program using the ecoinvent database, and the Life Cycle Impact Assessment (LCIA) performed in this study is ReCiPe midpoint.

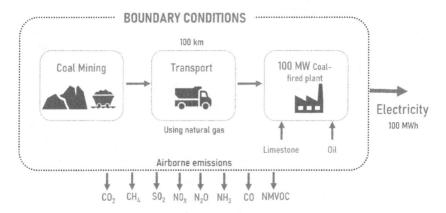

Figure 5.8.   Boundary conditions for 100 MWh coal-fired powered plant used in this study.

Table 5.3.   Technical characteristics for coal-fired plant and solar power plant considered in this study. (Source: Luu *et al.*[14])

Technical Characteristics	Coal-Fired Power Plant 100 MW	Solar-Based Power Plant 100 MW
Operating lifetime	30 years	25 years
Raw material consumption	Coal, Limestone, Oil, Water	
Total Area	NA	~ 2 km²
Operating hours	8760 h/year	2900/year
Installed capacity	100 MW	100 MW
Efficiency	39%	25%
Input material consumption	40 tonne/hour	-
Heavy fuel oil for start-up	102 kg/hour	NA
Limestone for neutralizing SO_2	2057 kg/hour	NA

The technical characteristics and input parameters of the coal-fired station are shown in Tables 5.3 and 5.4, respectively. The coal-fired station runs 24 hours a day, consuming 40 tonnes of coal/hour and other materials (oil, limestone) to generate 100 MWh electricity. In this example, only airborne emissions such as CO_2, CH_4, SO_2, NO_x, N_2O, NH_3, CO, and NMVOCs in low population areas are considered. The cumulative results from the ReCiPe midpoint are shown in Table 5.5.

Since we are interested in airborne pollutants (boldface in Table 5.5), the LCIA observation for producing 100 MWh electricity is a significant

Table 5.4.   Input parameters (airborne emissions) for coal-fired plant considered in this study. (Source: Wang *et al.*)

Constituents	Mining	Transport	Combustion
CO_2 (g/KWh)	50.328	11.981	910.22
CH_4 (g/KWh)	3.58E+00	1.93E–04	3.73E+00
SO_2 (g/KWh)	4.01E–01	7.98E–02	9.54E–01
NO_x (g/KWh)	3.67E–01	2.64E–03	8.20E–01
N_2O (g/KWh)	0	0	0.04
NH_3 (g/KWh)	2.50E–04	0.00E+00	6.31E–03
CO (g/KWh)	1.11E–01	1.90E–02	1.68E–01
NMVOC (g/KWh)	3.24E–02	3.21E–03	2.35E–02

Table 5.5.   Life Cycle Impact Assessment using Midpoint ReCiPe of coal-fired plant.

Impact Category	Result	Reference Unit
agricultural land occupation (ALOP)	0	m_2a
climate change (GWP20)	0	kg CO_2-Eq
fossil depletion (FDP)	**19202.08**	**kg oil-Eq**
freshwater ecotoxicity (FETP100)	0	kg 1,4-DCB-Eq
freshwater eutrophication (FEP)	0	kg P-Eq
human toxicity (HTP100)	0	kg 1,4-DCB-Eq
ionising radiation (IRP_I)	0	kg U235-Eq
marine ectotoxicity (METP100)	0	kg 1,4-DCB-Eq
marine eutrophication (MEP)	**0.577590961**	**kg N-Eq**
metal depletion (MDP)	0	kg Fe-Eq
natural land transformation (NLTP)	0	m_2
ozone depletion (ODPinf)	0	kg CFC-11-Eq
Particulate matter formation (PMFP)	**7.102805219**	**kg PM10-Eq**
Photochemical oxidant formation (POFP)	**17.77063607**	**kg NMVOC-Eq**
terrestrial acidification (TAP20)	**26.49821236**	**kg SO_2-Eq**
terrestrial ecotoxicity (TETP100)	0	kg 1,4-DCB-Eq
urban land occupation (ULOP)	0	m_2a
water depletion (WDP)	0	m_3 water-Eq

effect on our environment due to pumping of hazardous substances. These toxic airborne pollutants, such as particulate matter formation (PMFP), photochemical oxidant formation, and terrestrial acidification could affect human internal organs over time, as seen in Table 5.5.

5.3.2. *Solar Power Plant — Panel Production*

Coal-fired power plants continually release toxic pollutants into the environment in normal working circumstances, while solar energy is less polluting or nearly emit zero pollutants. Hence, to make a fair comparison, the solar panel production scenario is considered for the LCA study, and the airborne emissions are calculated. Figure 5.9 shows the boundary conditions, Table 5.6 shows input parameters (airborne emissions) for the study considering the fabrication of 1 KWh solar panels, and Table 5.7 shows Life Cycle Impact Assessment using Midpoint ReCiPe of 1 KWh solar panels production illustrating the airborne emissions (e.g., fossil depletion, marine eutrophication, particulate matter formation, photochemical oxidant formation, terrestrial acidification, etc.)

5.3.3. *Comparing Airborne Emission of the Coal-Fired Power Plant and Solar Panels Production*

As compared to a coal-fired facility, the energy produced by solar panels is renewable and less polluting, as shown by the literature and real-time applications. However, we continue to use coal for electricity generation for

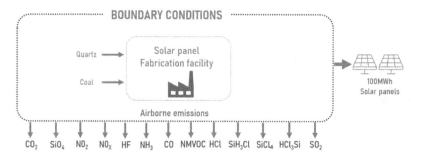

Figure 5.9.   Boundary conditions for 100 MWh solar panel fabrication facility used in this study.

Table 5.6. Input parameters (airborne emissions) for solar panel fabrication considered in this study. (Source: Wang *et al.*)

Raw materials used for manufacturing 1 KWh solar panel		
Quartz sand	35.85	kg
Coal	45.4	kg
Emissions into air from 1 KWh solar panel fabrication			
Carbon dioxide	CO_2	132.91	kg
Carbon monoxide	CO	1.7	kg
Nitrogen oxides	NO_x	340.5	g
Silicon dioxide	SiO_2	1.7	kg
Sulfur dioxide	SO_2	0.79	kg
Nitrogen dioxide	NO_2	3.15	g
Hydrogen fluoride	HF	4.75	g
Ammonia	NH_3	7.68	g
Hydrogen chloride	HCl	41.16	g
	NMVOC	34.64	g
Chlorosilane	SiH_3Cl	28.56	g
Silicon tetrachloride	$SiCl_4$	9.23	g
Trichlorosilane	HCl_3Si	31.3	g

many reasons, including its low cost of extraction, better energy conversion performance, and so on. In practice, as we strive to be more sustainable, our environment is an essential factor to recognize, and emissions should be reduced immediately.

This comparison aims to use an LCA to better grasp our current situation and the advantages of renewable energy. But in a real-time examination, several other considerations such as water, electricity, recycling, and so on, must be taken into account for accurate calculations. We may quickly infer from this basic comparative analysis that solar energy is much superior to coal-fired power plants. PMFP is compared between two power plants in Figure 5.10 to confirm this justification.

As previously said, solar panels produce very little to no emissions when in use. Thus, solar panel manufacturing is compared to the operation of a coal-fired power plant. Particulate matter, a very toxic substance, is emitted in both cases, as seen in Figure 5.10. However, when looking at the

Table 5.7.   Life Cycle Impact Assessment using Midpoint ReCiPe of 1 KWh solar panels production.

Impact Category	Result	Reference Unit
agricultural and occupation (ALOP)	0	m_2a
climate change (GWP20)	0	kg CO_2-Eq
fossil depletion (FDP)	**1970360**	**kg oil-Eq**
freshwater ecotoxicity (FETP100)	0	kg 1,4-DCB-Eq
freshwater eutrophication (FEP)	0	kg P-Eq
human toxicity (HTP100)	3876	kg1,4-DCB-Eq
ionising radiation (IRP_I)	0	kg U235-Eq
marine ecotoxicity (METP100)	0	kg 1,4-DCB-Eq
marine eutrophication (MEP)	**1398.606**	**kg N-Eq**
metal depletion (MDP)	0	kg Fe-Eq
natural land transformation (NLTP)	0	m_2
ozone depletion (ODPinf)	0	kg CFC-11-Eq
particulate matter formation (PMFP)	**21736.76**	**kg PM10-Eq**
photochemical oxidant formation (POFP)	**43191**	**kg NMVOC-Eq**
terrestrial acidification (TAP20)	**88212.82**	**kg SO_2-Eq**
terrestrial ecotoxicity (TETPl00)	0	kg l,4-DCB-Eq
urban land occupation (ULOP)	0	m_2a
water depletion (WDP)	0	m_3 water-Eq

100 MW Coal-fired power plant	7.1 kg / hour
100 MW Solar panels production	21,736.76 kg / entire production

In just over **128 DAYS** of service, a 100 MWh coal-fired power plant will achieve the total PMFP pollution amount of 100 MW solar panel production.

Figure 5.10.   Comparison of particulate matter formation emission from 100 MW solar panel fabrication facility and 100 MWh coal-fired power station.

amount of pollution, 100 MW solar panels appear to produce 21,736.76 kg during the production process, while 100 MW coal production facility emits 7.1 kg in one hour of service.

A 100 MWh coal-fired power station could surpass the PMFP emission from the entire 100 MW solar panels production in just over 128 days. The coal-fired plant is planned to run for 30 years; imagine the volume of PMFP that will be released into the environment, causing harm to humans and other living things. This comparison analysis will educate newcomers interested in fostering sustainability, academics, lawmakers, non-governmental organizations, and businesses advocating sustainable practices and recognizing adverse effects. As a response, we should trust sustainable energy to boost our environment and well-being by switching from non-renewable to renewable sources.

Concluding Remarks

Globalization accelerates the use of energy. Global electrical energy demand has been satisfied by coal-fired power plants, resulting in extreme environmental pollution. On the other hand, less polluting or green energy is picking up widely to combat pollution. This chapter has performed an LCA on a coal-fired plant and solar panel production to measure the airborne emissions.

To conduct the LCA, an open-source software tool called OpenLCA was used and an LCIA was performed using the ReCiPe midpoint method. Approximately 40 tonnes of coal are needed to produce 100 MWh of electricity from the coal-fired plant, which results in the emission of 7.1 kg of particulate matter (a hazardous gas). On the other end, attempting to manufacture solar panels with a capacity of 100 MW results in the emission of 21,736.76 kg of particulate matter into the atmosphere. This straightforward life cycle assessment shows that a 100 MWh coal-fired power plant will emit more particulate matter than the total amount from 100 MW solar panel generation in just over 128 days.

References

1. Dahiya, S., Katakojwala, R., Ramakrishna, S. & Mohan, S. V. Biobased products and life cycle assessment in the context of circular economy and sustainability. *Mater. Circ. Econ.* **2**, 7 (2020).

2. Matthews, H. S., Hendrickson, C. T. & Matthews, D. H. *Life Cycle Assessment: Quantitative Approaches for Decisions that Matter* (Open-access textbook). https//www.lcatextbook.com/.

3. Lee, K.-M. & Inaba, A. Life cycle assessment: best practices of international organization for standardization (ISO) 14040 series. https://www.apec.org/Publications/2004/02/Life-Cycle-Assessment-Best-Practices-of-International-Organization-for-Standardization-ISO-14040-Ser#:~:text=The%20ISO%2014040%20series%20standards,all%20four%20phases%20of%20LCA.

4. Hyder, Z., Ripepi, N. S. & Karmis, M. E. A life cycle comparison of greenhouse emissions for power generation from coal mining and underground coal gasification. *Mitig. Adapt. Strateg. Glob. Change* **21**, 515–546 (2016).

5. Ciroth, A. *et al. Towards A Life Cycle Sustainability Assessment: Making Informed Choice on Products.* https://www.lifecycleinitiative.org/wp-content/uploads/2012/12/2011%20-%20Towards%20LCSA.pdf.

6. Shi, J., Mu, D. & Wang, C. An LCI study on waste gas emission of electricity coal supply chain. In: R. Zhang, Z. Zhang, K. Liu & J. Zhang (eds.), *LISS 2013*, pp. 209–213, Springer (2015).

7. Jolliet, O. *et al.* IMPACT 2002+: A new life cycle impact assessment methodology olivier. *Int. J. Life Cycle Assess.* **8**, 411–424 (2003).

8. Liu, L. & Ramakrishna, S. *An Introduction to Circular Economy.* Springer (2020).

9. Room document: baseline efficiency analysis of fossil fuel power plants. https://unece.org/fileadmin/DAM/energy/se/pdfs/CES/pub/RoomDoc_Baseline_EE__PowerPlants_DRAFT.pdf.

10. Fu, Y., Liu, X. & Yuan, Z. Life-cycle assessment of multi-crystalline photovoltaic (PV) systems in China. *J. Clean. Prod.* **86**, 180–190 (2015).

11. How much power do 5kW solar systems produce per day? https://gosolarquotes.com.au/how-much-power-does-a-5kw-solar-system-produce-per-day/.

12. Polman, A., Knight, M., Garnett, E. C., Ehrler, B. & Sinke, W. C. Photovoltaic materials: Present efficiencies and future challenges. *Science* **352**, aad4424 (2016).

13. Estimation of solar PV system output. https://firstgreenconsulting.wordpress.com/2012/12/26/estimation-of-solar-pv-system-output/.

14. Luu, L. Q. & Halog, A. Life cycle sustainability assessment: A holistic evaluation of social, economic, and environmental impacts. In: G. Ruiz-Mercado & H. Cabezas (eds.), *Sustainability in the Design, Synthesis and Analysis of Chemical Engineering Processes*, pp. 327–352, Butterworth-Heinemann (2016).

Exercises

1) Which aspect of a product's impact is LCA used to evaluate and quantify?
   (A) Social
   (B) Environmental
   (C) Economic
   (D) Performance

2) ISO stands for
   (A) International Organization for Substitution
   (B) International Organization for Sustainability
   (C) International Organization for Standardization
   (D) International Organization for Solicitation

3) A product system is a set of processes that serves a:
   (A) Function
   (B) Unit
   (C) Time
   (D) Value

4) What are the examples of input flows for the coal-fired power plant?
   (A) Water and Climate change
   (B) Electricity and Emissions
   (C) Water and CO_2
   (D) Water and Limestone

5) What does LCIA stand for?
   (A) Life Cycle Inverse Assessment
   (B) Life Cycle Impact Assessment
   (C) Life Cycle Impact Advice
   (D) Life Cycle Impact Appraisal

6) Assume a power plant is a product system in the context of a life cycle assessment. What is the power plant's function?
   (A) Generate pollution
   (B) Generate electricity
   (C) Distribute electricity
   (D) Distribute resources

7) SO_2 is an example of
   (A) Waterborne emission
   (B) Landborne emission
   (C) Airborne emission
   (D) Soilborne emission

8) Which of the following resources are raw materials that are not considered for solar panel production?
   (A) Quartz, water, and electricity
   (B) Quartz, coal, and limestone
   (C) Quartz, coal, electricity
   (D) Quartz, coal, water, and electricity
9) What does PMFP stand for?
   (A) Particulate Matter Formulation
   (B) Particulate Matter Formation
   (C) Particulate Material Formulation
   (D) Particulate Material Formation
10) In comparison to solar, coal is regarded to be a preferred source of energy because of its
   (A) Low extraction costs and high energy conversion efficiency
   (B) Low extraction costs and low amounts of waste heat by-product
   (C) Abundance and low extraction cost
   (D) None of the above

CHAPTER SIX
ENVIRONMENTAL, SOCIAL AND GOVERNANCE — INTRODUCTION

Introduction

This chapter provides a broad description of Environmental, Social, and Governance (ESG) metrics. We first highlight the sustainability concerns in companies and how individual (E, S, G) components evolved in the 20th century. Following that, the chapter discusses the basis of sustainable or responsible investment strategies. Sustainable investments traditionally fall into three buckets: impact, socially responsible, and ESG investment. As a result, as a newcomer to the investing world, we introduce the latest ESG investment pattern in this segment.

The chapter further examines the ESG success of businesses and how ESG matters from both company and investor perspectives. As a reader, you will get to understand how businesses and investors interact with each other via ESG considerations and how they promote sustainability. The section further describes the significance of rating agencies and how they support investors making investment choices.

Three ESG rating agents (MCSI, Sustainalytics, Refinitv) and their model system/framework, rating methodology, scoring scheme, input sources, insights, and key ESG considerations are discussed. A quantitative comparison of the three rating agencies addressing different factors, describing commonalities and divergence is presented via a table. Rating agencies depend upon multiple sources to collect data to produce ESG ratings. The chapter considers data quality and examines how the scientific community comments on discrepancies and inconsistencies among rating agencies.

6.1. ESG — Introduction and Evolution

Businesses need employees, a constant supply of material resources, stakeholders, and good leadership to run efficiently. For the sake of efficient business operations, companies usually adopt standard operating procedures. The companies understand their real values when they follow government guidelines and regulations and organic business principles. Hence, if we look at companies in this direction and the essence of integration towards the environment and society, we arrive at ESG. The entities we interact with every day are inevitably connected to numerous ESG matters to a certain degree. Figure 6.1 shows the parameters and components of the ESG nexus that promote business sustainability.[1]

Figure 6.1.   Illustration of ESG nexus from a sustainable business perspective.

The **Environmental (E)** component indicates consumption of energy/materials/resources and discharged waste and impacts on the ecosystem by a company. Carbon emissions and their contributions to climate change are the two most significant and recurrent parameters that reflect the company's ecological footprint.

The **Social (S)** dimension denotes the company's integrity and connections the company has earned with workers, customers, and institutions in the society where the business is based. It primarily demonstrates the egalitarian community and diversity of a company's human resources to meet social needs.

The **Governance (G)** aspect defines the in-house processes and procedures of a company for making choices, obeying the laws, and addressing the demands of stakeholders. In the long term, this setup guarantees the survival of the business.

The formal idea of ESG integration with traditional business was initiated by the UN Secretary-General, Kofi Annan, in 2004. The 50 top CEOs of global financial firms around the world met to build ideas for identifying sustainable business and develop guidelines and suggestions.[2] The overarching aim of this effort was to outline ways to combine ESG concerns in asset management, securities brokerage services, and relevant analysis functions. A collaborative effort by the International Finance Corporation (IFC) and the Swiss government was initiated to encourage the early implementation of ESG principles. Subsequently, in a seminal study undertaken by the IFC titled "Who Cares Wins", the word ESG was formulated in 2005 to explore the function of environmental, social, and governance value factors in asset management and financial research.[3]

While ESG has been coined in the 21st century, even before the ESG concept was adopted, there have been traces of ESG in the previous century. World wars significantly affected the global economy, and an intense labor force was needed to restore the damage caused to the economy. Between the 1950s and 1970s, global labor shortage escalated.[4] To reduce labor exploitation and acknowledge welfare and employee rights, labor unions were formed. Mutual arrangements between the employees and businesses defining a common framework arose. Subsequently, these new policies were included in the business scopes and governance that established the founding values of the ESG concept. Social concerns (civil rights and consumer rights) also gained prominence in the 1960s and 1970s owing to the formation of many public campaigns.[5]

Developed countries and companies have widely embraced human rights in their policies and operations. Overall, we seem to have effectively incorporated social justice into our economy. Since encompassing social justice, our emphasis has increasingly turned to environmental disruption. Disasters stemming from industrial activities have had a noticeable effect on the environment and its well-being. For example, in the late 1980s, our environmental perception was sparked by the nuclear catastrophe in Chernobyl in Ukraine, the Bhopal gas tragedy in India, and the Exxon Valdez oil spill in Alaska, USA. Following these tragedies, businesses inducted environmental ethics along with social justice in their operations. This persistent deterioration of the ecosystem has contributed to a radically new collection of systematic company rankings focusing on the environment. The EIRIS (Ethical Investment Consulting Services) Base, for example, was an early ranking institution that provided investors with a benchmark for investments in sustainable firms.[5]

Governance is the final element of ESG. Transparent corporate governance practice is essential for good employee-investor partnerships. In the 1990s, a few publicly listed companies had CEOs, CFOs, and other higher-level executives embroiled in financial controversies. This situation elevated concerns between stakeholders and the company's management.[6] New rules and laws were introduced because of these scandals to improve the accuracy of financial statements for public corporations. A detailed timeline and evolution of the ESG concept is given in Figure 6.2.

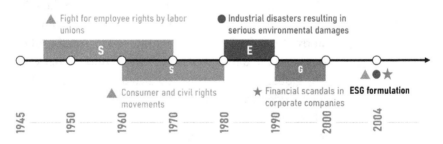

Figure 6.2.   Timeline and evolution of ESG.

6.2. Understanding Sustainable or Responsible Investment

We have studied the basics of sustainability and sustainable developments (SDs) in the third chapter. A simple but meaningful definition for sustainability given by the Bruntland Commission is *"development that meets the needs of the current generation without compromising the ability of future generations to meet their own needs"*.

Holistically, the idea behind SD is to foster economic, environmental, and social (people). So far, we have seen SD from the policymakers' and academic viewpoints. Henceforth, we shall understand SD from an institutional and business perspective. In general, any developments (not limited to SD) require investments to construct infrastructures, pay wages, procure components, etc. A strong value proposition, combined with consumers, is a principal ingredient to attract funds. Thereafter, the business will increase in scale, the economy will improve, and the GDP will grow.

Social and environmental causes have started to draw investors since the 19th century. The influential industrialist, renowned business magnate, and philanthropist Andrew Carnegie encouraged the affluent to contribute to social causes. Subsequently, Rockefeller followed Carnegie's footsteps. These activities sparked corporate philanthropy and catalyzed companies to integrate the Corporate Social Responsibility (CSR) scheme.[7]

6.2.1. *Corporate Social Responsibility*

The CSR strategy was generally adopted in the US after Howard Bowen, an American economist and father of CSR, published a book titled *Social Responsibilities of the Businessman* in 1953. After the Committee for Economic Development developed the Social Contract in 1971, CSR started to gain momentum in the US in the 1970s. The Social Contract advocates that *the business has an obligation to constructively serve the needs of society.*[8]

After the publication by Howard Bowen, CSR has become an exciting subject, and various research studies have been carried out.[9] CSR is a self-regulatory business framework that allows a business to be socially responsible to itself, its customers, and the public. By fostering the CSR methodology, the company will be able to quantify the societal, financial, and environmental effects of its goods and services.

6.2.1.1. *CSR of Starbucks*

Starbucks is a globally recognized company that commits to CSR. As indicated by the company, Starbucks' CSR and sustainability are about being accountable and doing things that are good for the planet and each other.

Starbucks' CSR actions involve[10]:

- Starbucks Youth Action Grants: Culminate and inspire young minds by grant schemes.
- Ethos Water Fund: Promote access to clean water and ensure clean water for children.
- Ethical Sourcing: Dedication to sourcing and serving coffee that is ethically traded.
- Green Buildings: Use energy-efficient green buildings for shops.

In a nutshell, CSR outlines how an organization tackles social and environmental concerns. To encourage investors and the public to participate in them, most corporations display their CSR operations openly. While sustainability investment has become extremely relevant, it is challenging for investors to assess businesses that embrace sustainable values. Regardless, investors leverage CSR principles of companies in their decision-making process to invest wisely and sustainably. In this direction, the following sections will discuss the classification and consideration of sustainable investing. Figure 6.3 outlines the group of Sustainable investments.

6.2.2. *Impact Investment*

In 2007, a consortium of investors and business leaders met to explore the idea of "impact investing". Impact investment focuses on the premise that investors should seek capital gains while intentionally tackling social and environmental concerns. According to the Gates Foundation, impact investing and philanthropy are two sides of a coin because impact

Figure 6.3.   Classification of sustainable investments.

investments yield profits that are channeled back into the foundation.[11] For instance, a Hong Kong citizen chooses to use her money to help fund micro-entrepreneurs in rural Mexico, with the aim to lift people from poverty. As a result, the impact investing firm raised over $300 million in its initial public offering on the Mexican stock exchange.[12]

Additionally, philanthropic activities have a small difference in terms of outcome. For example, the Gates Foundation announced its plan to spend $40 million in agricultural science and innovation. The dairy sector plays a significant function in agricultural production, and dairy farming contributes significantly to greenhouse gas emissions (GHG).[11] The Foundation believes that cutting-edge technology and scientific findings can help to address global GHG. Because of philanthropic activities, the research output and technology know-how will be produced as returns rather than financial returns. Eventually, inventions may be commercialized, but that is not the main goal here. Financial organizations, rich individuals, and policymakers collaborating to solve social and environmental problems, providing the requisite financial stimulus and positively transforming society is the ideal of impact investment.[13]

6.2.3. *Socially Responsible Investment*

Socially Responsible Investment (SRI) is a distinct, but equal, path to sustainable investment. The literature describes SRI as both "a consequence of increasing social consciousness brought on by institutions" as well as "primarily related to the public (beneficiary) involvement in social accountability".[14] The investment method of SRI, also known as value-added investing, aims to incorporate non-financial considerations into investment decision-making or portfolio creation. Investing in this way has two goals: to optimize financial reward, while simultaneously recognizing the effect that the investment would have on the environment and local society.[15]

In SRI, equities are compared to the social problems they impact. Thus, investors focus on businesses with a positive societal stigma. For example, businesses engaged in the manufacturing of arms, cigarettes, or online gaming are avoided in the portfolio. Companies with histories of dealings with minorities, women, and their respective groups often feature on this list in contrast.[16]

Traditional investors and socially responsible investors follow stakeholder theory and the ethical finance model.[17] In this way, a socially responsible investor is more inclined to pursue investment options that provide the best financial gains while still being aware of social and environmental problems. SRI utilizes CSR as a benchmark to assess an organization before investing in it, as demonstrated by the literature. According to empirical evidence, SRI coupled with sustainability values has catalyzed the importance of ESG and offered investors a fresh viewpoint.[18,19]

6.2.4. *ESG Investment*

ESG investment has European origins and has developed based on the sustainability principles we discussed in Chapter 4. ESG investments have been fueled by growing Environmental (climate change), Social (children welfare), and Governance (transparent operations) concerns. These pragmatic considerations have tweaked global investors' thinking towards the real issues rather than just focusing on financial returns.

ESG investments have surged globally. The Global Sustainable Investment Alliance reported that the ESG sector attracted over US$30 trillion in 2018.[20] As of 2020, the ESG assets have increased to US$40.5 trillion, as stated by Pensions & Investments.[21] The investments are doubling owing to transparent policymaking at the management level and the visible socio-environmental benefits.

On the academic line, ESG seems to be an evolution of SRI integrated with sustainable values. Based on the available literature, we can deduce that SRI is very agile when making investment decisions. While SRI performs well in screenings (excluding tobacco, firearms, etc.), the literature suggests that it prioritizes performance/returns and sometimes excludes ethical guidance.[22] Perhaps to address these concerns, the UN has established six modern responsible or sustainable investing principles to support investors in their assessment before making a decision.[23]

Investors make logical judgments based on ESG ratings issued by private institutions (we will go over ratings in more depth in the next section). The ESG metrics we addressed in section 6.1 are, in general, the main success measures used to assess firms. Unlike SRI, the ESG investment approach prioritizes valuable ideas to the community/environment, rather than merely beneficial ones, by leveraging positive screening methods[13] or norm-based screening[24] (excluding investments that violate ESG norms). From an investment perspective, a higher weighting is assigned to firms with better ESG scores, while low or zero weight is allocated to firms with lower or no ESG scores. Figure 6.4 shows detailed strategies and a map of ESG,[25] and Table 6.1 shows the comparison of Sustainable or Responsible Investments.

6.3. ESG Performance Assessment

ESG performance is becoming popular among investors to evaluate the financial performance and socio-economic concerns of companies. Nearly 96% of G250 companies[26] (G250 applies to the world's top 250 corporations in terms of revenue) offered sustainability reports by 2020, according to the

Figure 6.4.   Detailed strategies and map of ESG.

Table 6.1.   Classification of sustainable or responsible investments.

S.No	Investment scheme	Outcome	Origin	Theory	Screening	References
1	IMPACT investment	› Socio-environmental benefits with minor equity ‹br› › Research output	USA	—	—	11,12
2	SRI investment	› Financial returns	USA	› Stakeholder theory ‹br› › Ethical finance	Positive	9,17,19
3	ESG investment	› Financial returns	Europe	› Sustainable principles ‹br› › Our common future	› Positive and best in ESG ratings ‹br› › Norm-based (excludes firms that violate ESG norms)	17,19,24

KPMG Study of Corporate Responsibility Reporting, and these numbers are rising. It indicates that big companies are coming forward to report their ESG performances, and their level of commitment towards sustainability is growing every year.

ESG performance of the company at a conceptual level represents combining non-financial elements (environmental stewardship, social contribution) in their annual reports. Bringing these non-financial considerations together will enable businesses to leverage ESG ratings and prove their ability to make strategic commitments. For this purpose, companies can use ESG ratings to explain their values and governance ethics to investors and the public to make decision investments.

Top organizations adhere to globally accepted standards such as the Global Reporting Initiative (GRI) and the ISO 14000, ISO 50001, etc., for reporting ESG performances. These criteria will assist businesses to self-evaluate their ESG performance and improve the integrity of their knowledge disclosures.[5] The self-reported ESG evaluation documents are studied and checked by ESG ranking agencies, which we will address in the next segment, to retrieve ESG ratings.

Unquestionably, ESG transparency plays a crucial role. Ernst & Young (EY) commissioned a study that showed that approximately 97% of investors focus their judgments on non-financial disclosures (ESG) of the company to make a decision.[27] According to the report, ESG performance is crucial in investment decision-making, and it is backed up by effective governance processes, assessments, and controls.

So far, we have learned that businesses present their ESG scores publicly, and studies (KMPG and EY) indicate that investors choose these companies based on their ESG performances. Through introducing this creative approach, ambiguities between businesses and stakeholders are eliminated. Hence, efficient control of investment choices that obey existing legislation is preserved in the corporate communities.

As a commoner, while studying the ESG performance of any company, two aspects are explicitly used: (i) companies foster sustainability by leveraging ESG metrics, and (ii) investors use ESG metrics to evaluate companies to make investment decisions. From a systemic viewpoint, we can infer that sustainability is at the forefront of companies and stakeholders to make a meaningful change to society.

6.4. ESG Rating Companies

Investors, executives, and legislators spend trillions of dollars on companies based on the specific distribution of ESG-related knowledge. There are several private firms in the marketplace that deliver up-to-date ESG data. These private firms act as intermediaries for investors and companies, and they provide detailed clarity about companies by harnessing ESG data. In this section, we will analyze these ranking institutions and their rating methodology.

Nearly 150 rating agencies are in the market to provide ESG ratings, rankings, and indices.[28] Market leaders in ESG ratings include MCSI, Refinitiv (formerly Thomson Reuters), Sustainalytics Inc., RobecoSAM, Bloomberg, etc. These ESG rating agencies gather and compile information regarding an organization and generate an ESG ranking focused on various publications (e.g., NGOs, CSR), data collection by interactions/interviews with company officials, and unbiased judgments. These companies provide cumulative ESG data (e.g., MCSI) or individual E, S, G data (e.g., Refinitiv) to publicly traded equities listed in large global stock indices.[29]

Since each rating organization uses a different computational formula and marketing strategy, there could be process discrepancies. What each rating agency must do, therefore, is to start with the details presented, determine which metrics to evaluate, measure variables that are not usually quantifiable, analyze the results, and produce a final rating. Let us look at various ranking processes, criteria, and their significance in generating an ESG score in this chapter. To keep it easy, we will include only three major industry participants: MCSI, Refinitiv, and Sustainalytics.

6.4.1. *MCSI*

MSCI methodology used to analyze ESG risks of an organization is analogous to a top-down funnel: they compile various data points (1,000+) on company management, processes, and practices to produce a comprehensive data set for review and drawing a conclusion.[30] The MCSI rating model in Figure 6.5(a) shows how data is collected, processed, and insights perceived.

The MSCI ESG Rating Model aims to address four main questions[30]:

1) What are the most significant ESG risks and opportunities facing a company and its industry?

2) How exposed is the company to those key risks and/or opportunities?
3) How well is the company managing key risks and opportunities?
4) What is the overall picture for the company and how does it compare to its global industry peers?

6.4.1.1. *MCSI Rating Model*

A) *Data Collection* — 1,000+ data points on ESG policies, programs, and performance; data on 100,000 individual directors; up to 20 years of shareholder meeting results.
B) *Exposure and Management metrics* — Collected data (point A) are analyzed against points (2) and (3) above.
C) *Key issue scores and weights* — 35 key issues are selected annually for each industry and weighted based on MSCI's mapping framework.
D) *ESG rating (AAA-CCC)* — Issue scores and weights combine to give an overall ESG rating relative to industry peers.

6.4.1.2. *MCSI Outcome*

MCSI implements a 35-key issues strategy. An entity is analyzed against these key issues, examined for how it behaves, and studied for risk and exposure. For each issue, the outcome is weighed based on the defined mapping framework. The findings are translated into letter ratings (AAA — best ESG; CCC — worst ESG) and compared with industry peers, and a ranking is generated. For detailed information, please refer to the MCSI ESG rating methodology.[30]

6.4.2. **Sustainalytics**

Sustainalytics analyze the ESG risk of a firm based on a *quantitative score* and a *risk category*. A quantitative score is an arbitrary unit of unmanaged ESG risk. That is, a lower level of unmanaged ESG risk equals a lower quantitative score, and vice versa. Companies are grouped into one of five risk categories depending on their quantitative scores (negligible, low, medium, high, severe). In their evaluation system, the rating agency offers direct and explanatory details on their methodology and operation.[31] Rating statistics are available for nearly 12,000 companies (as of 05 March 2021).

6.4.2.1. *Sustainalytics Rating Model*

The Sustainalytics rating method (as shown in Figure 6.5(b)) is based on three pillars. A) Corporate Governance, B) Material ESG Issues, and C) Idiosyncratic Issues.[31]

A) *Corporate Governance* is a significant component of ESG Risk Ratings and accounts for nearly 20% of the company's overall unmanaged risk ranking.
B) *Material ESG Issues* is the building block of the ESG Risk Ratings. This segment focuses on human resources, employee-related concerns, growth, diversity, safety, relationship with the company, etc.
C) *Idiosyncratic Issues* refer to unexpected or unpredictable risks for a business and its industry. If an idiosyncratic problem occurred, it impacts the company involved, keeping the rest of the industry untouched.

6.4.2.2. *Sustainalytics Outcome*

Sustainalytics models are designed to rank business risk in the entire rating process. The rating agency produces an absolute risk score, which means one firm (such as a bank) is comparable to another firm (e.g., oil industry). The rating is arrived at by measuring a number from 0 to 100.[31]

6.4.3. *Refinitiv*

Refinitiv produces the ESG scores by assessing the relative ESG performance, engagement, and effectiveness of an organization, based on the company-reported data (CSR). Rating statistics were available on nearly 10,000 organizations (as of 05 March 2021), with time-series data beginning in 2002 covering over 70% of the global market cap.[32] Refinitv reflects the ESG performance of the internationally listed companies and is calculated using ten key metrics. This covers emissions, innovation, resource use, community, human rights, shareholders, product responsibility, workforce, management, and CSR strategy.

Scholars often quoted that the Refinitiv ESG scores are believed to be less biased because of several controls, such as company scale, number of workers, etc.[33]

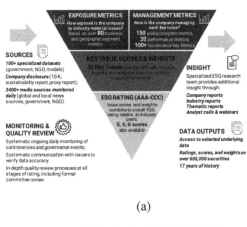

(a)

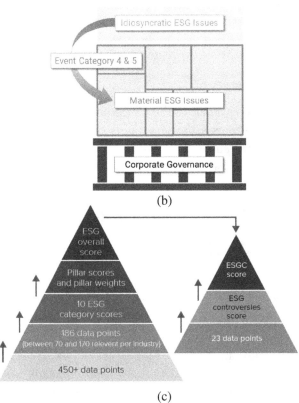

(b)

(c)

Figure 6.5. ESG rating model (framework): (a) MCSI, (b) Sustainalytics, (c) Refinitiv. (Source: MCSI, Sustainalytics, Refinitiv.)

6.4.3.1. *Refinitiv Rating Model*

Refinitiv employs (as shown in Figure 6.5(c)) a bottom-up funnel technique (inverse of MCSI) to measure an *ESG Combined (ESGC) score.* The overall ESGC is generated based on A) an ESG score and B) an ESG controversies score, according to the Refinitiv ranking model.[32]

A) *ESG score* — a measure of ESG performance, based on publicly available data, is assessed/funneled using four components: (i) collection of 450+ data points, (ii) 180 data points (industry-specific), (iii) 10 ESG metrics (mentioned earlier), and (iv) pillar score and weights.
B) *ESG controversies score* — The ESG controversies score is calculated based on 23 ESG controversy topics collected from media and news reports. If a company is involved in scandals, legal disputes, etc., this may affect the ESGC score.

6.4.3.2. *Refinitiv Outcome*

The ESGC value is an average of the ESG score and the ESG controversies score. If the controversies scores are higher than the ESG score, the ESG and ESGC scores are equal. The results are presented in scores varying from 0–100, reflecting the 10 key metrics we discussed.[32]

6.5. Data Collection and Quality of Data

A quantitative comparison of the three rating agencies is included in Table 6.2. We have seen three different rating companies and their unique methodology to come up with ESG ratings. For these companies to interpret and generate results from data, they first need to gather data. While most rating companies use the same data collection methodologies, there might be certain discrepancies in collection methods depending on their market scope, relations, and rating model. MSCI, for example, collects knowledge from governments, NGOs, stock exchanges, company websites, and business disclosures such as financial/annual statements and sustainability (CSR) reports. Similarly, Refinitiv, for instance, employs data analysts and follows the same methodology as MCSI. Another fascinating point about Refinitiv is that it contains the ESG controversies ranking, which is

Table 6.2. Overview of findings by rating firms. (Source: Rydholm *et al.*, Douglas *et al.*, MCSI, Sustainalytics, Refinitiv.)

Questions / Method	MCSI	Sustainalytics	Refinitiv
Number of data points/ Indicators	1,000+	70	450+
Quantitative or qualitative process	N/A	Quantitative	Quantitative
Types of data input sources	Government sources, company disclosers, annual reports, sustainability reports, and media channels	Three pillars: annual reports, official sources, and interviews	Stock filings, CSR reports, news sources, company websites, NGOs, and annual reports
Usage of standards	N/A	Yes, Global Reporting Initiative	N/A
Approach to rating	Funnel/top-down	N/A	Bottom-up
Industry comparison	Relative, suitable for intra-industry comparison	Absolute, ranks comparable to other industries	Relative, suitable for intra-industry comparison
Key issues measured	35	N/A	178
How are risks perceived?	Cost to the business and possible opportunity	Exposure to firm and management conduct	Controversy score, 23 measures
Weight of risks?	2-dimensional matrix: time frame and contribution	Emphasis on governance pillar and material ESG risks	Emphasis on management and governance pillar
Rating scale and method	Letter	Numbers	Numbers
Rating Resolution	7 categories, AAA to CCC	1–100	1–100
Target market	Investors	Investors	Investors
Model methodology	Hybrid	Analyst-based	Hybrid
Market coverage*	2800 firms	12,000 firms	10,000 firms

(*Number of publicly listed firms on rating agencies website as of 05-March-2021) competitive and needs frequent media and press coverage on businesses. In conclusion, these companies have deployed enormous capital in data collection to remain competitive, and as a result, fantastic job prospects are accessible in this domain.

As previously stated, ranking firms produce ESG ratings based on company sustainability reports. Hence there is a correlation between sustainability reports, ratings, and investment decisions. Investors should be mindful that ESG results (CSR reports) would not follow financial consistency requirements, because organizations do not disclose their output using a single metric. As a result, there is no consistent criterion for investors to use when evaluating businesses solely based on ESG results. Businesses may communicate on either measurable or non-measurable ESG considerations on specific goals or the entire supply chain. Either they will use global ESG guidelines like GRI, or their own reporting requirements. Also, an independent audit is at the absolute discretion of the company.[28]

ESG ranking agencies, on the other hand, measure ESG scores using a variety of methodologies and input sources, resulting in large differences in ESG scores across ESG databases. For these reasons, ESG scores may deviate and are often inconsistent among rating agencies. Many research scholars have identified this gap, and observed significant ESG discrepancies and varied ESG performances across rating agents.[34,35]

The authors have acknowledged that ESG ratings provided by various rating agencies are sometimes incompatible since rating providers rely on different topics, metrics, and details.[36] That is, of course, something crucial to be aware of when choosing a ranking company for investment decision-making. These ESG data providers are most interested in attracting investors as clients. Investors prefer to depend on rating agents to select the best firms for portfolios, regardless of divergent rating systems. Investors ought to assess the amount and consistency of data that rating agencies produce, as well as the approach they employ to synthesize their data.

Concluding Remarks

In a nutshell, ESG has to do with how an organization treats the environment, personnel, and management activities. The CSR movement is speeding up, which indicates that businesses are gravitating toward establishing long-term sustainability targets and moving away from conventional settings. ESG, from a company perspective, is a self-regulatory tool/method to measure the performance of businesses and stakeholders towards sustainability. Fostering and nurturing ESG values in companies can result in greater productivity, overall fairness, inclusiveness, accessibility, and respect for the community.

In recent years, because of the increased emphasis on social and environmental sustainability, financial markets have entered the sustainability arena. Traditionally investors focus on company financial reports to evaluate the effectiveness, growth, return on investments, etc. Increasing social and environmental consciousness along with transparent management have catalyzed investors to rethink their investment strategies. In this way, investors believe ESG ratings of a company may reduce financial risks and improve accountability while simultaneously addressing global social and environmental challenges.

Rating agencies such as MCSI, Refinitv, etc., act as a bridge between investors and companies. Rating agencies collect data from many sources, derive insights, and present them to investors. The development of responsible investing and the integration of ESG considerations into investment decision-making has been fueled by the emergence of ESG data analysis and ranking providers. However, the scientific community speculates and questions the rating agents about data quality, rating methodologies, and consistency across rating industries. Investors are the primary customers of ESG rating agencies, and they rely on ESG rating agencies to pick the best firms to invest based on ESG metrics regardless of rating methodology, data accuracy, etc. More context and information from these divergent ESG rating agencies should be provided to investors so that they can come to an accurate conclusion about an investment opportunity.

References

1. The time is now | DBS Group. https://www.dbs.com/sustainability/responsible-banking/sustainable-financing/sustainable-investing/the-time-is-now.
2. The rise of responsible investment — KPMG Singapore. https://home.kpmg/sg/en/home/insights/2019/03/the-rise-of-responsible-investment-fs.html.

3. Who cares wins: connecting financial markets to a changing world. https://www.unepfi.org/fileadmin/events/2004/stocks/who_cares_wins_global_compact_2004.pdf.

4. Young, S. Environmental, Social, and Governance Risk. In: S. O. Idowu, N. Capaldi, L. Zu & A. D. Gupta (eds.), *Encyclopedia of Corporate Social Responsibility*, pp. 1025–1032, Springer (2013).

5. Patil, R. A., Ghisellini, P. & Ramakrishna, S. Towards Sustainable Business Strategies for a Circular Economy: Environmental, Social and Governance (ESG) Performance and Evaluation. In: L. Liu & S. Ramakrishna (eds.), *An Introduction to Circular Economy*, pp. 527–554, Springer (2021).

6. Financial scandals of enron, worldcom, and tyco occurred... | Bartleby. https://www.bartleby.com/essay/Financial-Scandals-Of-Enron-Worldcom-And-Tyco-P3RHPHQ5G385.

7. Corporate social responsibility: a brief history. https://www.accprof.org/ACCP/ACCP/About_the_Field/Blogs/Blog_Pages/Corporate-Social-Responsibility-Brief-History.aspx.

8. Bowen, H. R. *Social Responsibilities of the Businessman.* University of Iowa Press (2013).

9. Matos, P. ESG and responsible institutional investing around the world: a critical review. doi:10.2139/ssrn.3668998 (2020).

10. Corporate social responsibility (CSR) — types and business benefits. https://corporatefinanceinstitute.com/resources/knowledge/other/corporate-social-responsibility-csr/.

11. Bill Gates — upping the stakes with impact investing | Candriam Academy. https://academy.candriam.com/us/microsoft-founder-and-philanthropist-bill-gates-is-a-pioneer-in-whats-known-as-impact-investing-private-investment-that-not-only-has-a-measurable-bottom-line-but-also-a-real-environm/.

12. Bugg-Levine, A. & Emerson, J. Impact investing. *Innov. Technol. Gov. Glob.* **6**, 9–18 (2011).

13. Cardoso, F. S. The Growing Role of ESG in Investment Decisions — Investors' Preference: Low Sustainability High Returns? (Master's Thesis). https://research-api.cbs.dk/ws/portalfiles/portal/59750983/688418_The_Growing_Role_of_ESG_in_Investment_Decisions_Investors_Preference.final.pdf.

14. Sciarelli, M., Cosimato, S., Landi, G. & Iandolo, F. Socially responsible investment strategies for the transition towards sustainable development: the importance of integrating and communicating ESG. *TQM J.* **33**, 39–56 (2021).

15. Galema, R., Plantinga, A. & Scholtens, B. The stocks at stake: Return and risk in socially responsible investment. *J. Bank. Financ.* **32**, 2646–2654 (2008).

16. Hill, R. P., Ainscough, T., Shank, T. & Manullang, D. Corporate social responsibility and socially responsible investing: A global perspective. *J. Bus. Ethics* **70**, 165–174 (2007).

17. Standard Ethics — Solicited Sustainability Rating — ESG Model. https://www.standardethics.eu/company/esg-model.

18. Dorfleitner, G., Halbritter, G. & Nguyen, M. Measuring the level and risk of corporate responsibility — An empirical comparison of different ESG rating approaches. *J. Asset Manag.* **16**, 450–466 (2015).

19. Townsend, B. From SRI to ESG. *J. Impact ESG Invest.* **39**, 72–77 (2009).

20. Global sustainable investment review. http://www.gsi-alliance.org/wp-content/uploads/2019/03/GSIR_Review2018.3.28.pdf.

21. Global ESG-data driven assets hit $40.5 trillion. https://www.pionline.com/esg/global-esg-data-driven-assets-hit-405-trillion.

22. Amir, A. Z. & Serafeim, G. Why and how investors use ESG information: Evidence from a global survey. doi:10.2469/faj.v74.n3.2 (2017).

23. Principles for responsible investment | United Nations. https://www.unpri.org/download?ac=10948.

24. ESG investing: the rise of a new standard | BankingHub. https://www.bankinghub.eu/banking/research-markets/esg-investments-current-trends.

25. Eurosif: European SRI study. https://www.eurosif.org/wp-content/uploads/2018/11/European-SRI-2018-Study.pdf.

26. Tempero, M. The time has come! *J. Nat. Compr. Canc. Netw.* **17**, 295 (2019).

27. Does your nonfinancial reporting tell your value creation story? | EY Singapore. https://www.ey.com/en_sg/assurance/does-nonfinancial-reporting-tell-value-creation-story.

28. Douglas, E., Van Holt, T. & Whelan, T. Responsible investing: guide to ESG data providers and relevant trends. *J. Environ. Invest.* **8**, 1–23 (2017).

29. Hinze, A.-K. & Sump, F. Corporate social responsibility and financial analysts: a review of the literature. *Sustain. Account. Manag. Policy J.* **10**, 183–207 (2019).

30. MCSI ESG ratings methodology. https://www.msci.com/documents/1296102/21901542/MSCI+ESG+Ratings+Methodology+-+Exec+Summary+Nov+2020.pdf.

31. ESG risk ratings — methodology abstract. https://connect.sustainalytics.com/hubfs/INV/Methodology/Sustainalytics_ESG%20Ratings_Methodology%20Abstract.pdf.

32. Environmental, Social and Governance (ESG) scores from Refinitiv. https://www.refinitiv.com/content/dam/marketing/en_us/documents/methodology/esg-scores-methodology.pdf.

33. Rajesh, R. Exploring the sustainability performances of firms using environmental, social, and governance scores. *J. Clean. Prod.* **247**, 119600 (2020).
34. Berg, F., Kölbel, J. & Rigobon, R. Aggregate confusion: the divergence of ESG ratings. doi:10.2139/ssrn.3438533 (2019).
35. Chatterji, A., Durand, R., Levine, D. & Touboul, S. Do ratings of forms converge? Implications for Managers and Strategy reseachers. *Strateg. Manag. J.* **37**, 1597–1614 (2015).
36. Kotsantonis, S. & Serafeim, G. Four things no one will tell you about ESG data. *J. Appl. Corp. Financ.* **31**, 50–58 (2019).

Exercises

1) Which of the following components is more significant when evaluating a company's ecological footprint?
   (A) Plastic reduction and marine pollution
   (B) Plastic reduction and carbon emission
   (C) Carbon emissions and climate change
   (D) Carbon emission and deforestation

2) Who is considered the founder of CSR?
   (A) Howard Bowen
   (B) Kenneth Boulding
   (C) Andrew Carnegie
   (D) Kofi Annan

3) Which investment theory is followed by traditional investors and socially responsible investors?
   (A) Number theory
   (B) Social theory
   (C) Stakeholder theory
   (D) Systems theory

4) Which investment strategy emphasizes the 'socio-environmental with minor equity' component?
   (A) Impact investment
   (B) ESG investment
   (C) Socially responsible investment
   (D) All the above

5) The ESG investment concept originated in
   (A) America
   (B) Europe
   (C) Australia
   (D) India

6) Why do investors rely on ESG data from the rating agencies?
   (A) To leverage the company's performance
   (B) To maintain the integrity with workers
   (C) To make investment decisions
   (D) To support the company's long-term goal
7) Who are the customers of companies such as Refinitiv and Sustainalytics that have ESG ratings?
   (A) People
   (B) Entrepreneurs
   (C) Scholars
   (D) Investors
8) Why are ESG scores often inconsistent among rating agencies?
   (A) Due to different frameworks used by agencies
   (B) Due to various sources of information
   (C) Due to different rating models and methodologies
   (D) All the above
9) What parameters have catalyzed investors to rethink their investment strategies?
   (A) Environmental concern, Social involvement, and transparent Governance
   (B) Political concern, Social involvement, and transparent Governance
   (C) Environmental concern, Social involvement, and logical Governance
   (D) Environmental concern, Political involvement, and logical Governance
10) Rating agencies such as MCSI and Refinitv act as a bridge between
   (A) Investors and People
   (B) Investors and Companies
   (C) Investors and Governments
   (D) Investors and Universities

CHAPTER SEVEN

ESG PRACTICES WITH CASE STUDIES

Introduction

This chapter presents an introduction to ESG reporting with examples of good practices. The chapter utilizes a range of terms to express the same concept, such as Sustainability reporting (SR), Corporate Social Responsibility (CSR) reporting, and Environmental, Social, Governance (ESG) reporting. We begin by outlining the UN Sustainable Development Goals (SDGs) and then discuss how companies utilize the UN SDGs as a guideline for CSR preparation.

This chapter further focuses on the academic perspective of SR and presents the process and implementation methods. SR reflects the ESG performance of an organization, but it is challenging to comprehend due to a lack of reporting standards. Nevertheless, SR companies do follow some standards such as Global Reporting Initiative, etc. Hence, in this aspect, this chapter will provide insights on how SR may be prepared and explains the process steps based on empirical studies.

Following that, top-performing ESG reporting firms such as Singapore Airlines, Microsoft Corporation, and Samsung Electronics are considered for case studies based on Refinitiv ESG scores. Each company considered for case studies and its respective ESG components is neatly illustrated with detailed insights provided on their ESG performances. In the final segment, the importance of ESG from an investor's perspective is discussed.

The role of ESG incorporation in the investment decision-making phase is explicitly mentioned, along with an example of how investment risks are measured.

7.1. Sustainability Reporting and Sustainable Development Goals

In the business world, SR is interchangeable with other non-financial reporting terms, such as triple bottom line reporting, CSR reporting, etc.[1] The sustainability report represents financial, environmental, and social costs associated with the day-to-day operations of organizations. A sustainability report also describes an organization's values and governance, and how they relate to global sustainability key concepts such as environmental preservation, social concerns, and transparent operations.

Many corporations have incorporated SR to present their ESG activities and sustainable initiatives and enable investors to study them.[2] ESG rating agencies will then process this knowledge and provide their ESG metrics of the companies, as we mentioned in Chapter 6. Companies publish their CSR or sustainability report every year by aligning their business interests/outcomes towards SDGs envisioned by the UN in 2015.[3] In this way, business communities report their efforts to address global challenges by reducing social and environmental impacts via transparent operations.

We shall go through the SDGs in detail before considering the SR implementation process and a correlation between SDGs and SR. The SDGs are a collection of 17 promising goals combating global challenges by enabling a sustainable/prosperous future for everyone.[4] Despite the growing population, constant political shifts, environmental destruction, and other factors, the optimistic plans seek to achieve these targets by 2030. Figure 7.1 shows 17 individual goals developed by the UN advocating SD.

The UN SDGs gave businesses the chance to restructure their current unsustainable business practices by removing adverse environmental practices and incorporating social consensus. Consequently, investors and the public became more concerned about corporate governance, thereby pushing management to have greater transparency. Companies believed

Figure 7.1.   The UN Sustainable Development Goals: Agenda 2030.

that it was necessary to address global challenges while at the same time exploiting operational transparency to lift the firm's appeal. Hence, a holistic nexus between E, S, G has been established by fostering UN SGDs. Companies developed new sustainable policies, formed new teams, and adopted an updated code of ethics, enabling them to make a positive contribution to the community and the world.

As we addressed in Chapter 6, SR is a voluntary self-reporting framework for measuring, monitoring, and managing sustainability issues in an organization. In this way, increasing environmental issues (climate change), new sustainable legislation (carbon tax), government programs (grants), and other facets of sustainability have driven businesses to integrate green practices through the supply chain. Thus, we must examine how SR has been developed as a comprehensive model from a business viewpoint, and we shall have a look at its implementation process in the next segment.

7.2. Process and Implementation of Sustainability Reporting

In Chapter 6, we have discussed that CSR received much attention after the publication made by Howard Bowen, an American economist, in 1953. Since then, several researchers have attempted to estimate the performance of social and economic factors using structured CSR models. For example, Carroll (1979) introduced a conceptual model that defines the corporate social performance of an organization.[5] Subsequently, he introduced Carroll's pyramid of CSR in 1991. The pyramid model proposes economic, legal, ethical, and philanthropic responsibilities.[6] Similarly, other CSR models such as the Friedman model,[7] Ackerman model,[8] corporate citizen model,[9] and New CSR model[10] have been proposed to advance theoretical, moral, and ethical groundings for CSR initiatives. Naturally, these initiatives were criticized for lack of rationale, complexity, and advice to business executives to perform CSR strategic implementation.[11]

(The phrases "CSR" and "Sustainable Reporting (SR)" represent the same meaning; CSR evolved from the United States, while SR evolved from Europe. Owing to the implementation of the UN SDGs, the term SR has become widespread.)

It is challenging to comprehend the process and implementation of SR at the business level. Since SR is optional, as previously stated, it helps to represent the company's sustainability status. As there is no global regulation enforcing documentation obligations for sustainability reports, it is solely up to the organization to provide relevant details and facts. Also, existing local legislation concerning how an organization responds to sustainability is regionally specific; thus, SR outcomes may differ based on the geographical location and ongoing regional challenges. Furthermore, there is no international process flow for SR deployment. But regardless of whether it would be subject to legislation, all components in the process implementation must be considered by a decision-maker. Based on these points, it is suggested that international SR guidelines should be updated, and a standard form of implementation is needed.

*(Note: European Union Regulation, **directive 2014/95**, advises businesses to disclose their non-financial details regarding social and environmental issues.)*

Empirical studies continue to analyze and propose aspects of sustainability implementation at the business level. For example, Francesca *et al.*[12] reported how top businesses in the EU have applied 2014/95 recommendations to deliver SR. Subsequently, Francesca *et al.*[13] again accounted on SR implementation formats in public sector organizations. Similarly, Kurniawan[14] presented the SR model in village-owned enterprises and small and medium enterprises. Karaman *et al.*[15] proposed the SR process for aviation industries, and Loh *et al.* investigated the SR implementation process of publicly listed companies in Singapore.

Bergman *et al.*[16] have proposed a systematic and detailed SR framework after discussing it with industrial experts. The team recommended that the SR framework involve four dimensions (like Carroll's pyramid concept), as seen in Figure 7.2, which illustrates the SR implementation model from the company's viewpoint.

7.2.1. *Identify and Develop the Aspects of the Report*

The first step is to identify the overall impacts of its operations across its value chain. For starters, consider how the disclosing organization addresses environmental concerns such as energy usage and emissions.

Figure 7.2.   Process of SR with expected outcomes.

The next step is to outline the five aspects of reporting representing the organization's point of interest, attributes to include or exclude, current and future position, etc. The five aspects are: 1) Subject (total impact), 2) Audience (e.g., shareholders, peers), 3) Content (e.g., finance spent on social causes), 4) Motivation (e.g., to maintain the position of power), and 5) Reliability (e.g., external audit).[17]

The proposed SR document draft should reflect facts and evidence, stakeholder involvement and analysis, and help develop a code of conduct. This stage is time-consuming, knowledge-demanding, and expensive. Thus, the company may opt for sourcing in-house or out-house expertise, inviting stakeholders for discussion, and engaging sustainability experts to expedite the process.

7.2.2. Choose Reporting Framework

Since there are no global guidelines for choosing reporting frameworks, companies may select based on specific market interests or legal criteria. However, there are a few standard SR frameworks on the market (shown in Table 7.1), which the companies may gain some insights from while preparing reports.

Table 7.1.   SR frameworks. (Source: measurabl, GRI, BlackRock SASB report, SASB, Frasers ESG report, Singapore Airlines ESG report.)

Standard	Focus	Who Reports	Example
Global Reporting Initiative (GRI)	Corporate social responsibility with an equal weight on ESG factors. Heavy on stakeholder engagement to determine materiality.	Public and private companies, government agencies, universitites, hospitals, etc.	Singapore Airlines — commercial and cargo freight services
Sustainability Acconting Standards Board (SASB)	US public companies only. Industry-specific issues deemed material to investors.	Public and private companies	BlackRock, Inc. — investment management corporation
GRESB	ESG performance in global commercial real estate only.	Commercial real estate owners, asset mangers, developers	Frasers Property Australia

7.2.3. *Conduct an Independent Assurance*

Adding accountability and transparency to the report is a primary goal of this phase. An external assurer performs independent assurance by vetting the company's financial and non-financial results. External assurers may be financial auditing firms or authorized sustainability advisory boards. Companies may also use reporting framework vendors (e.g., GRI, SASB) to obtain further assurance and transparency for their reports.

7.2.4. *Level of Assurance*

The level of assurance has two parts: (A) restrict, and (B) reasonable.

A) Restrict contents for specific parts of the report (intend not to disclose)
B) Apply reasonable methods for other sections of the reporting document

The outcome from SR represents quantified individual E, S, G components presenting factors, impacting scenarios, countermeasures, and other aspects related to sustainability.

7.3. ESG Reporting: Case Studies

So far, we have looked at how corporations prepare their CSR and investigated the various components and procedure measures that go through CSR documentation. Due to ongoing environmental demands, ethical commitments, and the need for transparent operations, several businesses have improved their environmental and social performances and changed their internal governance to improve their ESG ratings.

The number of businesses reporting their CSR has risen and become popular since the turn of the 21st century. Let us look at the CSR efforts of three corporations, namely Singapore Airlines, Microsoft Corporation, and Samsung Electronics, as case studies in the following sections. The case studies will illustrate an overview of how the leading industries have improved their ESG practices.

Although the above mentioned three companies reported their CSR comprising all E, S, G factors, for simplicity, we decided to focus on individual factors for specific industries. For example, the Environmental (E) performance (as shown in Figure 7.3) is studied for Singapore Airlines because of its excellent environmental performance relative to its peers, according to Refinitiv ESG scores. Microsoft is well known for its social contributions and initiatives based on Refinitiv ESG ratings. Hence, the Social (S) performance, as shown in Figure 7.4, is considered for Microsoft Corporation. Also, Refinitiv ranked Samsung Electronics at 1st place for its ESG ratings among 100 other companies. Hence its Governance (G) performance, as shown in Figure 7.5, is featured. (Standards such as GRI, SASB, and their details are not discussed. Readers may read more about them by visiting their webpage.)

7.3.1. *Singapore Airlines*

Singapore Airlines (SIA) was founded on 28 January 1972 and is now one of the most lucrative and successful airlines globally. SIA has received several accolades, including "World's Best Airline", and Fortune has ranked it as number 18 in their list of the 50 World's Most Admired Companies.[18]

According to the SIA FY2019/20 sustainability report, the company owns 203 aircraft combining subsidiary companies (Silk Air, Scoot) and flies to 141 destinations worldwide. SIA has a long record regarding

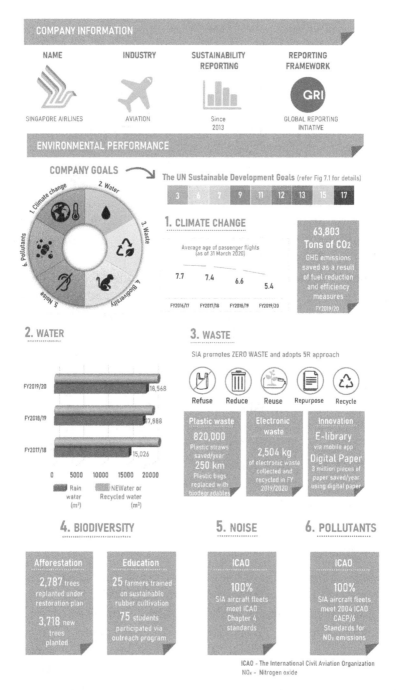

Figure 7.3.   Environmental performance of Singapore Airlines (SIA) for FY 2020.

environmental stewardship dating back to 1992. It has pioneered environmental recognition, such as setting up environmental programs, fostering UN climate change goals, forest conservation, plastic elimination, and so on. Since 2013, SIA report to its stakeholders every year on its sustainability status while continually strengthening its commitment to sustainability principles in its operations.

According to the SIA sustainability report on environmental stewardship, the organization has put in place several long-term and short-term strategies. For example, the company has aimed for plastic straw-free operations by FY2019/20, achieving 15% electricity reduction (office buildings) by FY2020/21 by leveraging renewable sources, and a 30% reduction of waste generation from office buildings by FY2020/21. Figure 7.3 shows the SIA environmental performance report captured from the SIA sustainability report FY2019/20.[2] By 2050, the organization feels compelled to promote *UN climate change action* and *carbon neutrality programs*. The company has reinforced sustainable philosophies in its core business operations by proposing six goals (shown in Figure 7.3) to achieve sustainability. As a result, the organization will successfully optimize its six targets while still achieving the UN SDGs to combat global challenges.

Climate change due to rising global temperatures is in part caused by the ongoing release of greenhouse gases into the atmosphere. The United Nations has advocated corporate action strategies to get global temperatures down by 1.5°C by 2050.[19] As shown in Figure 7.3, the SIA company has continuously upgraded its fleets to energy-efficient, low carbon-emitting flights. The average age of passenger flights is 5.4 years old, making it the world's youngest fleet. Younger planes, in theory, consume fuel more efficiently and release fewer greenhouse gases. SIA evidently supports the UN climate change program as a sustainability thinking organization.

The firm, additionally, has a successful *water* conservation policy. Although SIA heavily relies on the public water board for its business operations, it is leveraging rainwater harvesting and NEWater (recycled water) to meet nearly 1/4 of its water requirements. Also, the company has a well-established *waste* management scheme, which includes electronic and plastic waste. SIA has taken a hard stance against plastic usage and e-waste via leveraging the 5R approach and embracing digital technologies.

Similarly, the company is extensively responsible for other aspects of environmental stewardship, including biodiversity, noise control, and pollution. In conclusion, we can infer from SIA's environmental performance that corporate sustainability thinking is growing, with businesses setting deadlines/targets to reach the UN SDGs by modifying business practices.

7.3.2. *Microsoft Corporation*

Microsoft was established in 1975 by Bill Gates and Paul Allen. The company is one of the leading software and IT service providers in the market. Microsoft has always had a keen concern for social responsibility and has consistently been ranked in 1st position.[20] For example, Sustainalytics recognized Microsoft as an outperformer in 2017 based on SR. Similarly, other rating firms such as Reputation Institute in 2016 and 2017 and Refinitiv in 2021 placed Microsoft in 2nd position for the best CSR.

As a technology powerhouse, Microsoft utilizes technological solutions to inspire and leverage individuals while also preserving the environment. Hence, for its socially conscious actions and inspiring nature to support communities, the technological giant earned several honors and accolades. Detailed social performance of Microsoft captured from CSR for FY2020[21] is shown in Figure 7.4.

Microsoft reports CSR using GRI and SASB standards, and it is classified into three parts: A) Support inclusive economic opportunity, B) Protect fundamental rights, and C) Empower employees. According to the CSR report, the social component has received the most coverage, accompanied by the environmental aspect, and the governance aspect has received the least attention.

A) Inclusive economic opportunity

As a technology business company, Microsoft inaugurated the Global Skills Initiative project to ensure that everyone has access to the technical skills and resources required to achieve high-demand employment in an evolving economy. The program has reached 13 million learners with market readiness level as of 2020 and is expecting to achieve 25 million learners by early 2021.

The Airband Initiative from Microsoft is another genius Microsoft project. Without enough access to the internet, more people would be at the

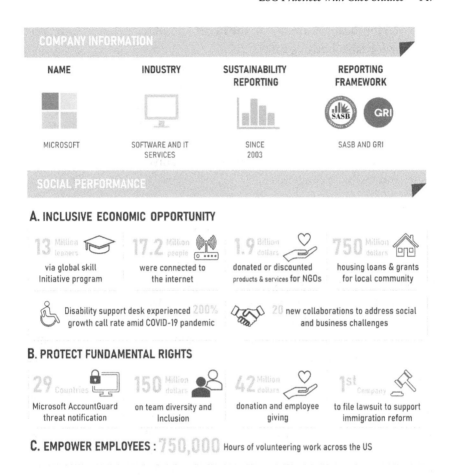

Figure 7.4.   Social performance of Microsoft Corporation for FY 2020.

bottom of the heap, poverty-stricken, unaddressed, and unable to achieve their full potential. The Airband Initiative's ultimate aim is to link people to the internet and change societies, especially in the fields of technology, education, and entrepreneurship. The initiative has reached 17.2 million people so far and is expecting to hit 40 million people by July 2022.

Bill Gates is well-known for his philanthropic efforts. Similarly, Microsoft contributed almost $1.9 billion in subsidized products and services in 2020 to fund 243 thousand charities. Companies are ranked by rating firms such as Refinitiv depending on how much they serve their local communities. Microsoft is indeed a great contributor to the local community. The company has contributed $750 million in loans and grants to enrich the local community in the Puget Sound region of Washington to realize affordable housing units.

Microsoft is well-known for using individuals with disabilities and offering fair work prospects. Similarly, the disabled people technical assisting team experienced a 200% growth call rate amid the Covid-19 pandemic demonstrating a supportive gesture against the disabled community. On the other hand, the company has established 20 new collaborations among NGOs, governments, universities, etc., to address social and business challenges.

B) Protect fundamental rights

To combat cyber threats, Microsoft has started an AccountGuard threat notification service to identify cyberattacks via email. Microsoft shows its appreciation for front-end staff, human rights, and charitable groups by providing them with cyber technology. Today, the program is accessible in 29 countries and covers over two million accounts.

To reduce ethnic discrimination, Microsoft has proposed a target of five years. The organization would spend another $150 million in equity and inclusion programs to raise the number of Black and African American people in senior management in the US by 2025.[22]

In 2020, the company donated via technologies and services and inspired employees via a giving program to contribute nearly $42 million to six humanitarian emergencies. Also, the company has carried out 100+ emergency relief missions in 28 nations with the help of 1,000 employees. Microsoft was even the first corporation to call for an immigration overhaul. In 2017, the organization also lodged a legal objection to the rescission of DACA (Deferred Action for Childhood Arrivals).

C) Empower employees

Microsoft never fails to empower, enrich, and motivate its employees. Via employee enrichment program, over 750,000 hours of volunteer services have been given to US communities representing smooth cohesion between community and employees.

7.3.3. *Samsung Electronics*

Samsung Electronics (formerly known as Samsung Electric Industries) is a subsidiary of the Samsung group, which was formed in 1969. The firm produces several personal and commercial electronic devices, including semiconductors devices, computers, electronic displays, home appliances, medical imaging equipment (X-ray devices), and telecom products such as mobile phones, networking devices, etc.[23]

Samsung Electronics has been actively pursuing sustainability goals since it started to report its first sustainability report in 2008. Refinitiv has placed Samsung Electronics in the first position among 100 other Computers, Phones & Household Electronics companies (data retrieved on 18 March 2021).[24] Similarly, MCSI has mentioned Samsung Electronics as the ESG pioneer with regard to Governance performance.[25]

Samsung Electronics has been working hard to boost its Governance score (as seen in Figure 7.5 captured from Samsung Electronics Sustainability Report 2020[26]) and has defined six main sustainability issue areas that illustrate core Samsung governance qualities: 1) Corporate Governance, 2) Compliance, 3) Risk Management, 4) Stakeholder Engagement, 5) Responsible Business Practice, and 6) Sustainability Value Creation.

Corporate Governance: The company has organized board members comprising management, audit, compensation, governance, independent director recommendation, and related party transactions committee. The diverse board of directors with broad perspectives guarantees that the operational team's strategic decisions remain consistent with the core values and ensure greater independence and openness. Samsung Electronics has a separate governance committee composed of six independent directors to manage sustainability-related topics and issues. The committee ensures that sustainability values are clearly articulated and communicated to stakeholders via CSR reporting.

Compliance: Apart from the internet regulatory framework, almost all corporations should comply with regional laws and regulations. Samsung Electronics, without a doubt, has a good compliance management process consisting of three stages, starting from *prevention* to *monitoring* to *follow-up management*. Compliance is a regulatory framework that one must follow; for example, an employee or any stakeholder participating in the company's activities should undergo a compliance management program that requires basic training (*prevention* stage). The *monitoring* stage

COMPANY INFORMATION

NAME	INDUSTRY	SUSTAINABILITY REPORTING	REPORTING FRAMEWORK
SAMSUNG	📱	📊	SASB · GRI
SAMSUNG	COMPUTERS, PHONES & HOUSEHOLD ELECTRONICS	SINCE 2008	SASB AND GRI

GOVERNANCE PERFORMANCE

CORPORATE GOVERNANCE
> Supervision
> Decision-making functions
> Ensure transparent operations via CSR

COMPLIANCE
Ethical standards and Laws
> Prevention
> Monitoring
> Follow-up management

RISK MANAGEMENT
> CSR risk management committee
> Ensure non-financial risks – climate change, human rights and safety addressed properly

STAKEHOLDER ENGAGEMENT
> Communicate with NGOs, CSR Council and Institutions to gather sustainable information

RESPONSIBLE BUSINESS PRACTICE
> Business principles and in-house ethical management services such as anti-corruption training

SUSTAINBILITY VALUE CREATION
> KPMG True Value method to measure sustainable management effects

Figure 7.5.   Governance performance of Samsung Electronics for FY 2020.

involves ensuring continuous checking against compliance-related issues such as bribery, misbehavior, etc. In the final step, where a compliance-related problem persists, *follow-up management* applies countermeasures and preventive measures by training and education.

Risk Management: Samsung Electronics has established a CSR Risk Management Committee to track the effects of non-financial risk on business performance. The CSR risk management team comprises independent directors and department representatives overseen by the Governance Committee. The team addresses and handles non-financial risks such as climate change, human rights, and safety associated with the organization.

Stakeholder Engagement: Most corporate companies have established channels for engaging their stakeholders. Companies, for example, communicate with customers and shareholders via financial disclosure, economic performance, and other means. Samsung Electronics publishes its CSR performance to NGOs, CSR Committees, and Specialist Organizations every year to gain feedback on the company's long-term sustainable performance and development phase.

Responsible Business Practices: This subject may be accomplished by establishing good corporate practices and ethical principles. In this vein, "Ethical Business Guidelines" are needed for large companies like Samsung Electronics. The guidance aims to ensure that all stakeholders (such as vendors and contractors) adhere to business integrity and fairness policy. The guidelines, on the other side, assist staff in maintaining credibility, avoiding misconduct or fraud, and increasing operational accountability.

Sustainability Value Creation: Since 2016, Samsung Electronics uses the KPMG 'True Value' methodology to assess sustainability activities. The True Value method is a systematic procedure developed by KPMG to calculate the positive and negative impacts of ESG performance. S and G factors are determined by monetary value brought to shareholders and how much it has provided to society. Similarly, the E factor is estimated based on emissions, water usage, waste generation, recycling, etc. The company's True Value has been steadily increasing since 2017, with a minor drop in 2019 due to decreased net income.

7.4. The Importance of ESG from an Investor's Standpoint

So far, we have seen the various facets of ESG reporting. In Chapter 6, we gained a basic understanding of sustainable investment principles and discussed ESG rating companies. This chapter has given in-depth information about how businesses disclose their ESG following various requirements such as GRI, SASB, and others. The conceptual link between firms, rating agencies, and the investment group seems to be quite clear; in a perfect world, businesses announce their ESG results, and investors get attracted.

Institutions (investing firms, e.g., banks, insurance companies) and individuals (non-professionals buying and selling securities via brokerage firms) can engage in investments. Let us understand institutional investors due to their large trading volume and dynamic operations. To begin, we review the academic studies that endorse ESG-driven investments and their conclusions.

Friede *et al.* conducted a detailed analysis aggregating more than 2,200 empirical studies dating back to the 1970s to establish the link between ESG and corporate financial performance. Their report suggested that approximately 90% of the literature signifies the relationship between ESG and financial performance with a positive outcome. The study has recommended that a comprehensive and detailed understanding is required to incorporate ESG parameters into investment processes.[27]

Similarly, a team of experts from Oxford University and Arabesque has investigated ESG investments by consulting over 200 scholarly, business, newspaper, and book outlets. The study observed that nearly 88% of the companies that follow sustainable policies outperform operational efficiency. Also, good sustainable strategies have a significant effect on investment results, according to 80% of respondents.[28] Similarly, several other studies indicate that combining ESG considerations can improve company efficiency and investors' returns.[29,30]

In this direction, private companies such as MCSI,[31] Morgan Stanley,[32] RBC Global Asset Management,[33] CFA Institute,[34] KPMG,[35] and so on offer spectacular perspectives on how institutional investors treat the ESG factor when making investments decisions. Institutional investors are most inclined to participate in firms with business-driven ESG problems, according to these studies. RBC Global Asset Management survey (2018) results show that, on a global scale, 72% of institutional investors are integrating ESG concerns in their investment strategy and decisions, which is an improvement from 66% the year before.

We have already discussed how an investor looks at the ESG factors and the investment strategies to undertake investment decisions in Chapter 6 (refer to section 6.2.3 and Figure 6.4). Currently, there are no widely agreed normative standards for CSR reporting, so institutional investors can be misled when deciding which ESG factors to have in their portfolios. Indeed, so many surveys, reports, and private firms suggest differing optimal situations for investors to forecast the industrial performance based on ESG metrics. Furthermore, the United Nations Principles for Responsible Investment and Organization for Economic Co-operation and Development guidelines include some guidance about what to do when ESG variables are involved. Figure 7.6 offers detailed indicators while evaluating the ESG performance of an organization for institutional investors.[36]

At the institutional investor level, ESG considerations are seen as criteria for managing long-term risks and forecasting new opportunities. One of the most common explanations for introducing ESG into the investing phase is to effectively control main variables that are thought to be a significant risk and return generators.[31] In this sense, ESG considerations may be used to identify businesses that are well run and able to offset challenges, while capitalizing on opportunities arising from environmental and social concerns.

For example, the environmental category seeks to assess how business operations handle global climate change through carbon emissions, and how the organization plans to reduce carbon emissions to in turn reduce carbon tax. From an investment standpoint, this will expose the firm to operating and financial danger; therefore, investors use this indicator to construct portfolios and develop ESG benchmarks to predict how businesses manage longer-term risk. Similarly, other categories such as Social and Governance factors are evaluated based on individual metrics. One of the top reasons for the importance of ESG is that investment professionals consider ESG issues as a way to manage risks and demand board transparency.[34]

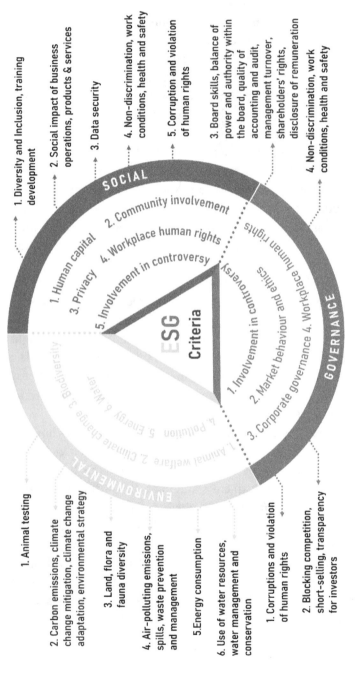

Figure 7.6.   ESG criteria assessed by institutional investors.

Concluding Remarks

Businesses may restructure their existing inefficient business processes by replacing harmful environmental activities, adopting responsible business practices, and fulfilling societal needs, according to the UN SDGs. We have seen the importance of CSR reporting and acknowledged the increasing trend among corporate companies to do so. However, owing to the absence of global regulation enforcing documentation obligations for sustainability studies, the CSR process and implementation remain challenging to grasp.

Nevertheless, this chapter has provided some detailed empirical evidence for how to prepare a sustainability report. Top ESG performing companies (according to Refinitiv) such as Singapore Airlines, Microsoft Corporation, and Samsung Electronics were studied. Although these reporting organizations subscribe to differing reporting standards, their adherence to ESG performance was exceptional.

The chapter concludes with the following key points: 1) It is evident from the case studies that SR significantly increases ESG performance and makes a company more attractive to stakeholders. 2) ESG reporting is gaining momentum among institutional investors on a global scale. 3) Investment professionals consider ESG issues as a conduit to manage long-term financial risks and demand board transparency.

References

1. Sustainability reporting: implementation roadmap | Institute of Singapore Chartered Accountants. https://isca.org.sg/media/2238512/isca-sustainability-report-implementation-roadmap.pdf.
2. Singapore Airlines sustainability report. https://www.singaporeair.com/saar5/pdf/Investor-Relations/Annual-Report/sustainabilityreport1920.pdf.
3. Sharp sustainability report 2020 | Sharp Electronics. https://global.sharp/corporate/eco/report/ssr/pdf/ssr2020_e.pdf.
4. Work of the Statistical Commission pertaining to the 2030 Agenda for Sustainable Development | United Nations. http://ggim.un.org/meetings/2017-4th_Mtg_IAEG-SDG-NY/documents/A_RES_71_313.pdf.
5. Carroll, A. B. A three-dimensional conceptual model of corporate performance. *Acad. Manag. Rev.* **4**, 497–505 (1979).

6. Schwartz, M. & Carroll, A. Coporate social responsibility: three domain approach. *Bus. Ethics Q.* **13**, 503–530 (2003).

7. Friedman, M. The social responsibility of business is to increase its profits. *The New York Times Magazine* (1970).

8. Idowu, S. O., Capaldi, N., Zu, L. & Gupta, A. D. *Encyclopedia of Corporate Social Responsibility*. Springer (2013).

9. Matten, D., Crane, A. & Chapple, W. Behind the mask: revealing the true face of corporate citizenship. *J. Bus. Ethics* **45**, 109–120 (2003).

10. Claydon, J. A new direction for CSR: the shortcomings of previous CSR models and the rationale for a new model. *Soc. Responsibility J.* 7, 405–420 (2011).

11. Nalband, N. A. & Al Kelabi, S. Redesigning Carroll's CSR pyramid model. *J. Adv. Manag. Sci.* **2**, 236–239 (2014).

12. Manes-Rossi, F. *et al.* Ensuring more sustainable reporting in europe using non-financial disclosure — de facto and de jure evidence. *Sustainability* **10**, 1162 (2018).

13. Manes-Rossi, F., Nicol, G. & Argento, D. Non-financial reporting formats in public sector organizations: a structured literature review. *J. Public Budg. Account. Financial Manag.* **32**, 639–669 (2020).

14. Kurniawan, P. S. An implementation of sustainability reporting model in village-owned enterprise and small and medium enterprise: case study in Bali, Indonesia. doi:10.31219/osf.io/6p8uv (2019).

15. Karaman, A. S., Kilic, M. & Uyar, A. Sustainability reporting in the aviation industry: worldwide evidence. *Sustain. Account. Manag. Policy J.* **9**, 362–391 (2018).

16. Bergman, D., Henriksson, F., Taheri, K. & Cunningham, G. The role of sustainability reports in investment analysis. https://www.diva-portal.org/smash/get/diva2:322337/FULLTEXT01.pdf.

17. Gray, R., Owen, D. & Adams, C. *Accounting & Accountability: Changes and Challenges in Corporate Social and Environmental Reporting.* Prentice Hall (1996).

18. Singapore Airlines | Infopedia. https://eresources.nlb.gov.sg/infopedia/articles/SIP_1705_2010-08-10.html.

19. Business ambition for 1.5°C: our only future — United Nations partnerships for SDGs platform | United Nations. https://sustainabledevelopment.un.org/partnership/?p=33482.

20. Spaulding, M., Merchant, K. A. & Hwan, S. Microsoft Corp: CSR Execution. https://msbfile03.usc.edu/digitalmeasures/kmerchan/intellcont/Microsoft%20CSR%20[A218-01]-1.pdf.

21. Microsoft Corporate Social Responsibility Report | Microsoft. https://query. prod.cms.rt.microsoft.com/cms/api/am/binary/RE4JaGo.
22. Microsoft adds to diversity investment, aims to increase number of Black employees | Reuters. https://www.reuters.com/article/us-microsoft-race/ microsoft-adds-to-diversity-investment-aims-to-increase-number-of-black-employees-idINKBN23U2ZM.
23. Samsung Electronics Co Ltd — Company Profile and News | Bloomberg Markets. https://www.bloomberg.com/profile/company/005930:KS.
24. ESG Scores | Refinitiv. https://www.refinitiv.com/en/sustainable-finance/ esg-scores.
25. ESG Ratings Corporate Search Tool | MSCI. https://www.msci.com/our-solutions/esg-investing/esg-ratings/esg-ratings-corporate-search-tool/issuer/ samsung-electronics-co-ltd/IID000000002138664.
26. Samsung Electronics Sustainability Report 2020 | Samsung. https://images. samsung.com/is/content/samsung/p5/uk/aboutsamsung/pdf/Sustainability_ report_2020_en_F.pdf.
27. Friede, G., Busch, T. & Bassen, A. ESG and financial performance: aggregated evidence from more than 2000 empirical studies. *J. Sustain. Financ. Invest.* **5**, 210–233 (2015).
28. Clark, G., Feiner, A. & Viehs, M. From the stockholder to the stakeholder: how sustainability can drive financial outperformance. doi: 10.2139/ ssrn.2508281 (2015).
29. Amir, A. Z. & Serafeim, G. Why and how investors use ESG information: Evidence from a global survey. *Financial Anal. J.* **74**, 87–103 (2018).
30. Inderst, G. & Stewart, F. Incorporating environmental, social and governance (ESG) factors into fixed income investment. doi:10.2139/ssrn.3175830 (2018).
31. Briand, R., Urwin, R. & Chia, C. P. Integrating ESG into the Investment Process: From aspiration to effective implementation. https://www. top1000funds.com/wp-content/uploads/2011/08/Integrating_ESG_into_ the_Investment_Process_Aug_2011.pdf.
32. Heugh, K. & Fox, M. ESG and the sustainability of competitive advantage. https://www.morganstanley.com/im/publication/insights/investment-insights/ii_esgandthesustainabilityofcompetitiveadvantage_en.pdf.
33. Responsible investing accelerates as investment merits gain traction, RBC global asset management survey finds. http://www.rbc.com/newsroom/ news/2018/20181002-gam-investing-rpt.html.
34. Hayat, U. *et al. Environmental, Social, And Governance Issues In Investing: A Guide for Investment Professionals.* CFA Institute (2015).

35. ESG: A view from the top. https://assets.kpmg/content/dam/kpmg/cn/pdf/en/2018/09/esg-a-view-from-the-top.pdf.

36. Integrating ESG factors in the investment decision-making process of institutional investors | OECD Business and Finance Outlook 2020: Sustainable and Resilient Finance | OECD iLibrary. https://www.oecd-ilibrary.org/sites/b854a453-en/index.html?itemId=/content/component/b854a453-en#section-d1e5949.

Exercises

1) How many SDGs has the United Nations established?
    (A) 17
    (B) 18
    (C) 20
    (D) 22

2) Who introduced the corporate social performance of an organization in 1979?
    (A) Friedman
    (B) Ackerman
    (C) Carroll
    (D) Bowen

3) What are the expected outcomes from the environmental aspect of SR?
    (A) Resource efficiency and Transparency
    (B) Resource efficiency and Climate change
    (C) Climate change and Fair procurement
    (D) Climate change and Transparency

4) Which reporting standard is used by commercial real estate owners and asset managers?
    (A) Global Reporting Initiative (GRI)
    (B) Sustainability Accounting Standards Board (SASB)
    (C) GRESB
    (D) All the above

5) What does Singapore Airlines' 'Zero Waste' scheme based on the 5R strategy entail?
    (A) Refuse, Remake, Reuse, Repurpose, Recycle
    (B) Refuse, Reduce, React, Repurpose, Recycle
    (C) Refuse, Reduce, Reuse, Relate, Recycle
    (D) Refuse, Reduce, Reuse, Repurpose, Recycle

6) Which company is highly regarded as socially responsible based on SR?
   (A) Microsoft Corporation
   (B) Singapore Airlines
   (C) Samsung Electronics
   (D) Apple Inc.

7) Why, when seen through an ESG lens, do investors and the general public become increasingly worried about corporate governance?
   A) Because companies are not transparent in their operations
   B) Because companies are making more profit
   C) Because companies are spending more money on capital
   D) Because companies are not disclosing their financial statements

8) What do we learn from a business's sustainability reporting?
   A) Efforts by businesses to solve global challenges whilst increasing profits
   B) Efforts by businesses to solve national conflicts through transparent operations
   C) Efforts by businesses to increase revenues through sustainable sales
   D) Efforts by businesses to solve global challenges by reducing social and environmental impacts through transparent operations

9) What is the CSR risk management strategy of Samsung Electronics?
   (A) Forming a risk management team comprising independent directors and department representatives
   (B) Selling electronics to First World countries through product promotion
   (C) Employee retrenchment in the event of risk findings
   (D) Risk is underestimated and not shared throughout the management team

10) At the institutional investor level, ESG considerations are seen as criteria
   (A) For the sole purpose of optimizing financial returns
   (B) For the sole purpose of managing long-term risks and forecasting new opportunities in businesses
   (C) For the sole purpose of evaluating the success of social harmony
   (D) For the sole purpose of enhancing logical judgments and preventing illicit transactions

CHAPTER EIGHT
SUSTAINABLE BUSINESS MODELS

Introduction

Over the past decade, entrepreneurship is seeing rapid growth with new and innovative technologies that have made the business environment much more flexible and inclusive. This may be attributed to the proliferation of business tools and methods. As a result, business model innovation and the Lean Startup have seen a recent wave in theoretical studies and business practice.

This chapter discusses Osterwalder's fundamental business model canvas (BMC) before delving into the details of Ries' Lean Startup method, with a focus on Minimum Viable Product. Osterwalder's business model focuses on the economic gains, with the environmental and social components getting less consideration. As a result, the chapter recognizes that changing business models factoring in social and environmental concerns is needed to realize a Sustainable Business Model (SBM).

Readers will see for themselves how an SBM adds superior value to customers and firms by meeting social and environmental demands via the way the business is steered. Following that, various definitions from an academic perspective for SBM are discussed, in line with the UN Sustainable Development Goals, to provide a basic understanding of SBM. The chapter further delves into SBMs developed by Osterwalder (triple bottom line business model) and Joyce & Paquin (triple layered BMC), and explains the sustainability aspects of a business model. Finally, we discuss

Sustainable Business Model Innovation (SBMI) and provide a conceptual representation of how to combine SBMI with the Lean Startup method.

8.1. Introduction to Traditional Business Model

Business, the famous term among humankind, starts with a concept or idea and a name, can transact, create values, transform society, and serves the purpose of our existence. Business is a calculated risk that requires a detailed plan, team, operating procedure, working capital, and products or services that meet customer requirements. To put it another way, companies need a business model or framework to succeed.[1]

Despite the reality that there is no standard description of a *business model*, scholars and entrepreneurs agree that it determines how a business works, creates value, and delivers to customers.[2] Magretta wrote an essay for *Harvard Business Review* in 2002 in which she explained that a business model should be a narrative. In other words, the business model should clarify, 'Who is the consumer and what does the customer value most?' and 'What is the fundamental economic rationale that describes how we should give value to consumers at a fair price?'[3]

Osterwalder's BMC (as seen in Figure 8.1) is the most recognized tool/method among entrepreneurs for conceiving and designing business

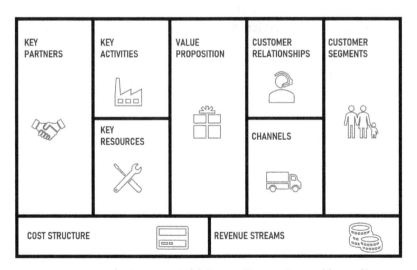

Figure 8.1.   The Business Model Canvas. (Source: Osterwalder *et al.*)

models. The business model was developed by Osterwalder *et al.,* and describes the rationale of how an organization creates, delivers, and captures value. It illustrates the reasoning and facts that justify a value proposition for its consumers, along with viable revenue streams, cost structure, and key partners.[4] This canvas is a one-page tool containing nine blocks for describing a business model at its most fundamental level. In 2008, Richardson introduced an integrated business model (as shown in Figure 8.2) that grouped nine blocks into three parts: the value proposition, the value creation and delivery system, and the value capture system.[5]

8.1.1. *Value Proposition*

This section is at the forefront of constructing a viable BMC. It has three components, as seen in Figure 8.2: A) Customer segments, B) Product/Service with a unique selling point, and C) Customer relationships.

A) Customer segments: Target consumers interested in purchasing the product or service and identify their pain points.
B) Product/Service with a unique selling point: Define the proposed solution. If a solution is available in the marketplace, determine if customers are happy with it, and if not, consider how to enhance it.
C) Customer relationships: This section defines how the company interacts with the customer, for example, providing personal assistance, dedicated customer service, self-service, automated service, etc.

It is always good to start from a customer's perspective before constructing the BMC. Seeing yourself as a customer will help to condense

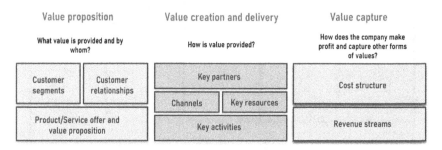

Figure 8.2. The Business Model Framework based on value. (Adapted from: T. Wautelet, Source: Osterwalder & Richardson.)

and express the problem statement clearly. For example, do *I or my friends, family, or community* have any relationship with this problem? How do I or we personally connect to the problem statement? What could be the potential solution? What are competitors doing? What motivates you to do it? Why now? How do others see the problem, what did they miss, and what have you experienced? Why are you uniquely qualified to work on this problem? Answering these questions would provide early justification to identify and establish the connection between your customer segments and products/services.

8.1.2. *Value Creation and Delivery*

This segment outlines the business model's function and explains how a company arranges its operations to generate and provide value to its consumers. As seen in Figure 8.2, this segment has four blocks:

A) Key partners: Defines your relationship with other businesses or entities, for example, your manufacturers, business partners, suppliers, etc. Your partners will support your organization in situations where it would be inefficient for you to manage it alone.

B) Channels: How do you connect with your customers, and how do you deliver your value proposition to your customers? For example, mobile app, websites, etc.

C) Key resources: Key resources refer to the physical, financial, intellectual, or human requirements of the company. Key resources can be owned or rented by the company or acquired from key partners.

D) Key activities: They are critical tasks that an organization must complete to achieve its goals and stay competitive, for example, research and development, sales, manufacturing, or repair and distribution.

8.1.3. *Value Capture*

As seen in Figure 8.2, this section has two components that explain the costs and revenue streams involved.

A) Cost structure: It addresses the costs that a company incurs due to its operations and activities, such as salary, administrative expenses, utilities, procurement, infrastructure, etc.

B) Revenue streams: It discusses how to make profit by delivering a service or a product to consumers, such as commission, software as service, product selling, etc.

8.2. Business Model Integration into the Lean Startup Ecosystem

Thus far, we have seen the widely recognized BMC and studied the nine building blocks with examples. The BMC would be the starting point for an entrepreneur to put business ideas and proposals together to visualize the business outcome tangibly. Now, let us see how to apply this BMC in a Lean Startup environment. For beginners, the Lean Startup is an unconventional, flexible, iterative method to test business hypotheses in a limited time frame, efficiently and cost-effectively.[6] The Lean Startup approach focuses on creating an ongoing connection with customers during the product development cycle, using consumer input regularly, and modifying the product outcome or shifting the scope as necessary.

8.2.1. *The Lean Startup*

Before delving into the nuances of Lean Startup methodology, we shall understand the genesis of the concept. The lean production theory began in the 20th century, and was developed by Toyota to minimize waste by improving production efficiency, ultimately giving birth to the Lean Startup methodology.[7] The idea was to mitigate market and financial risks by prototyping and validating a **Minimum Viable Product (MVP)** for consumers before scaling up the product.[8] Toyota, for example, could not afford to take financial or market chances by taking a long time to produce a product, or expect consumers to purchase it after a long delay, or risk having an obsolete product, and so on. As a result, MVP operates by quickly and cost-effectively planning products, allowing for the quick launch of new features and markets by collaborating with consumers. Subsequently, small businesses and startups have followed the Lean Startup methodology, enabling them to reach new markets without incurring additional expense or risk.

Entrepreneur Eric Ries popularized the notion of Lean Startup.[9] The Lean Startup follows the hypothesis-driven entrepreneurship concept

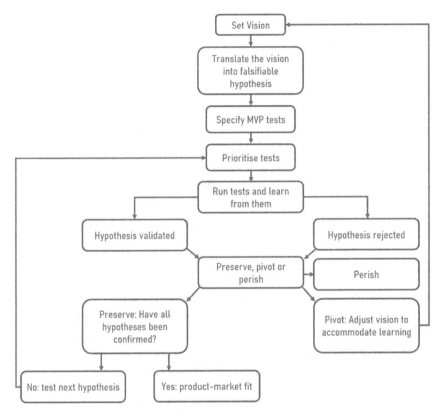

Figure 8.3.   Hypothesis-driven entrepreneurship process steps. (Adapted from Eisenmann *et al.*)

(Figure 8.3) and embraces lean manufacturing principles developed by Toyota. As seen in Figure 8.3, the Lean Startup approach has three essential tasks that repeat over time: Plan, Build & Validate, and Pursue.

In the **Plan** stage, entrepreneurs draw up a business concept or hypothesis by setting a vision on a BMC and evaluating it for usability. The second stage is **Build & Validate**: entrepreneurs seek to falsify the assumptions of their business model. Entrepreneurs and innovators will create an MVP after concluding the initial assumptions. MVP is a prototype of a product with a minimal number of working features and functionalities. The MVP is designed and developed with minimal effort and time, which gives an initial understanding of the product to invalidate hypotheses. The invalidated hypotheses are studied, evaluated, and substituted with new assumptions until enough checks suggest that critical assumptions have been confirmed.[9]

The final stage is **Pursue**: the prototype may undergo modifications based on feedback from potential customers until it reaches a certain degree of market readiness level. In this case, the MVP has a niche in the marketplace, and the customers may buy the fully functional product in the future without hesitation. If the Pursue stage is not attained successfully, the team can pivot the vision to other consumer segments if the hypotheses are proven false or discontinue further developments. The idea is to quickly validate the MVP by engaging customers, pivot if required, and conclude results as soon as possible without wasting time and resources.[10]

8.2.2. *The Lean LaunchPad*

The Lean LaunchPad is an entrepreneurial curriculum exercise developed by serial entrepreneur Steve Blank and venture capitalist Jerry Engel to discover and validate business ideas focused on customer querying and learning.[11] Steve Blank, in 2003, published his book *The Four Steps to the Epiphany* which documents the practice of customer development that laid the foundation for the Lean LaunchPad curriculum. Steve Blank realized the potential of *BMC* developed by Osterwalder (Figure 8.1) and *agile engineering*, and integrated the framework and principles into the Lean LaunchPad program. *(Agile engineering refers to rapid and accurate product development by testing, iterating, and collecting feedback on product design.)*

In section 8.2.1, we looked at how Eric Ries established the Lean Startup approach and the steps involved in creating a good MVP and launching a market-ready product. Eric Ries was a student at Steve Blank's Lean LaunchPad class at Berkeley's Haas School of Business. He was inspired by the Lean LaunchPad program and embraced the ideas into his software development. Pursuing this direction, he eventually published his "The Lean Startup" in 2011, fostering the MVP, iterative release ideas, and the hypothesis-driven entrepreneurship concept (Figure 8.3). Top universities in the world adopt the Lean LaunchPad into their curriculum and promote entrepreneurship via Lean Startup Methodology. This approach acts as a connection between engineering and business school students by forming a team; the team converts lab designs into business plans, tests hypotheses via customer validation, and emerges as entrepreneurs through the successful Lean LaunchPad program.

In conclusion, the Lean LaunchPad is a platform that requires valuable components such as Customer Development, BMC, and Agile Engineering to get to the Lean Startup destination.

8.3. Understanding Sustainable Business Model

So far, we have seen the basics and foundations of the typical business model methods, tools, and process steps. Traditional BMC focuses on scale-up, economic benefits, high returns, profits, and so on.[11] One point to bear in mind is that although the conventional BMC is impressive, it might not be suitable for a long-term sustainable business. We recognize that there are three components of sustainability: environment, society, and economy. If we analyze startups from this lens, we will quickly deduce that businesses that wish to embrace sustainability will need a "new" business model to deliver and capture value.[12]

Looking at the literature on sustainable business models (SBMs), the term continues to be hazy and difficult to understand. The majority of SBM concepts come from academic sources, and scholars can have multiple viewpoints with no or little industrial experience. Most certainly, researchers lay the groundwork for various sustainable business theories; but when it comes to bringing them into effect, such as business formulation focused on academic SBM, these theories and principles do not hold up.[13]

There are many definitions for SBM on the internet and in scholarly papers. We can understand that these definitions are compatible with common sustainability concepts and consistent with incorporating corporate sustainability values into organizational strategy and operations. For instance, Geissdoerfer *et al.*[14] presented a review paper on defining various SBM definitions and identified underlying concepts, and they also translated SBM into working descriptions. Similarly, Morioka *et al.*,[15] Freund *et al.*,[16] and many other researchers have conducted detailed literature surveys to identify suitable working SBMs for industrial settings. Let us see some of the widely adopted academic definitions of SBM.

Schaltegger *et al.* (2016) condensed the definition for SBM from the literature as follows: "*A business model for sustainability helps in describing, analyzing, managing, and communicating (i) a company's sustainable value proposition to its customers and all other stakeholders, (ii) how it creates and delivers this value, and (iii) how it captures economic value while maintaining or regenerating natural, social, and economic capital beyond its organizational boundaries*".[17] Geissdoerfer *et al.* (2016) defined an SBM as a "*simplified representation of the elements (customers, community, shareholders, environment...), the interrelationship between these elements, and the interactions with its stakeholders that an organizational unit uses to create, deliver, capture, and exchange sustainable value*".[18] Bocken *et al.* (2014) wrote in their definition of BMIs for sustainability: "*Innovations that create significant positive and/or significantly reduced negative impacts for the environment and/or society, through changes in the way the organization and its value-network create, deliver value and capture value (i.e., create economic value) or change their value propositions.*"[19]

The core concept of SBM is obvious; academics took influence from traditional business models to describe SBM by adding sustainability concerns. Richardson introduced an integrated business model on top of Osterwalder's conventional business model, as shown in Figure 8.2, and modified the nine-block depiction into three blocks based on value (create value, deliver value, and capture value). Similarly, Morioka *et al.*[15] drew inspiration from Richardson,[5] Bocken *et al.*,[19] and Geissdoerfer *et al.*[18] to propose the SBM framework (as shown in Figure 8.4) by considering a value-based approach in line with the UN Sustainable Development Goals.

Morioka *et al.* have shown a fair understanding of SBM by proposing a framework focused on scholarly knowledge and case studies. The SBM framework has three core elements: value proposition, value creation and delivery, and value capture, as shown in Figure 8.4.

8.3.1. *Value Proposition*

As we all know, in typical business settings, the value proposition is about identifying core business values and finding targeted customers. As a result, products and services are offered to customers primarily to make a profit.

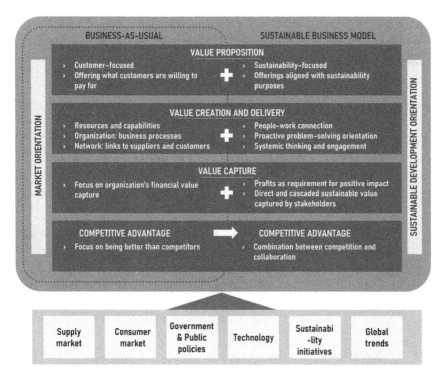

Figure 8.4.   Framework to support SBM implementation of organizations aligned with the UN Sustainable Development Goals. (Adapted from Morioka *et al.*)

In a sustainable business, the value proposition should reflect the sustainable philosophy and purpose of the organization. Furthermore, the organization may accept consumer groups who want to make a positive impact while still being able to pay for the products or services offered by the company.

8.3.2. *Value Creation*

Conventional value creation is discussed in section 8.1.2. In the SBM aspect, *value creation* represents *people-work connection*, *proactive problem-solving*, and *systemic thinking and engagement*. To reflect SBM, the business-as-usual components of Osterwalder's standard BMC are replaced with sustainability variables, as seen in Figure 8.4. We recognize that sustainability is all about linking individuals, the environment, and the economy; in this direction, elements of value creation of SBM are interlinked. In other words, each stakeholder must deliver long-term sustainable results; else, the overall business will suffer.

8.3.3. *Value Capture*

Value capture corresponds to the company's revenue. In the SBM perspective, the non-financial benefits are viewed alongside financial returns. Non-financial benefits may refer to positive social and environmental interactions, business partnerships, information sharing, reliable transactions, etc.

Naturally, the SBM has some logistical difficulties when it comes to implementation. Nevertheless, at present, SBM understanding and application are on the rise. Academic contributions must be acknowledged, as these studies help entrepreneurs understand sustainability considerations better in their business models.

8.4. Development of Sustainable Business Models

Since sustainability is such a broad subject, bringing it into practice may be difficult. Why do we need to embrace SBM? Because we have induced much damage and violated the laws set by nature, for example, marine pollution due to plastic waste disposal. So, how do we restore the situation? The only way out is to limit the ongoing harmfulness (e.g., plastic ban) or innovate alternative ways. Of course, restricting our usage of sophisticated technology will be difficult; therefore, the alternative is to develop business models that foster sustainability.

Realistically, at least in this century, we cannot eliminate the linear consumption model. But we should exploit the current infrastructure, find business prospects, implement technical advances, and recognize innovative SBMs. Sustainability business must encompass social and environmental factors into the business model innovation. Hence, we need to come up with a different set of ideas and perspectives supported by business tools to assist team members in developing a shared strategic business strategy.[20] In this segment, we will look at some of the most creative SBMs.

8.4.1. *Osterwalder — Triple Bottom Line Business Model*

Osterwalder & Pigneur have made valuable contributions to the creation of the BMC with the handbook *Business Model Generation*. The duo subsequently addressed the sustainability aspect by integrating social and environmental factors in the existing BMC, resulting in their proposed triple bottom line business model (Figure 8.5). The triple bottom line business model is an extended version of the original (Figure 8.1) representing two outcomes: (1) social and environmental *costs* (negative impact), and (2) social and environmental **benefits** (positive impact).

In a typical business setting, the company seeks to maximize revenue while simultaneously minimizing financial costs. Similarly, in an SBM concept, the company may focus on social and environmental benefits by reducing costs. Wit & Pylak (2020) used the triple bottom line business model and proposed an SBM for the logistics management of the disposal of toxic waste-containing asbestos. The theoretical work suggested that the waste management companies should include the triple bottom line aspects in their business model to avoid business risk, satisfy stakeholders, and especially comply with the EU 2014a/95 standards.

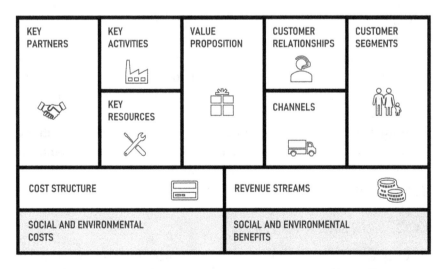

Figure 8.5.   Triple Bottom Line BMC. (Source: Osterwalder *et al.*)

8.4.2. *Joyce & Paquin — The Triple Layered Business Model Canvas*

In 2016, Joyce & Paquin published an article titled "The triple layered business model canvas: A tool to design more sustainable business models" in the *Journal of Cleaner Production*. Since then, the article has received much attention, with nearly 736 citations (as of March 2021). While there are several other SBM articles, we chose this because of its uniqueness, relevance to the Osterwalder business model, and numerous citations. The study introduces the Triple Layer Business Model Canvas (TLBMC) as a practical tool for entrepreneurs to emulate sustainable thinking and develop sustainable businesses by integrating economic, environmental, and social concerns into the existing Osterwalder business model.

Since Osterwalder had already established the economic context for the BMC, Joyce & Paquin created a business model for environmental and social sustainability. Because of this convergence, the triple layered SBM was born. Let us look at the pillars that were considered when designing the environmental and social layers.

8.4.2.1. *Environmental Layer of the TLBMC*

We have discussed how to conduct a Life Cycle Assessment for products/ services in Chapter 5 and presented two case studies (coal-fired power station and solar power) using openLCA software. We have discussed different aspects of performance evaluation of environmental impacts by analyzing the Life Cycle Impact Assessment (LCIA). The LCIA refers to the environmental output performance of a product/service, in which the entire life cycle (material extraction to disposal) is analyzed and converted into measurable outcomes (resource depletion, CO_2 emission, etc.). In this direction, authors inspired by the LCIA approach extracted the features of LCIA components and integrated them with traditional BMC to construct an environmental layer of SBM. We can understand that the environmental layer of the TLBMC was built based on the life cycle approach and Osterwalder BMC, as seen in Figure 8.6.

8.4.2.2. *Social Layer of the TLBMC*

In Chapter 7, we looked at the social performance of Microsoft Company based on the 2020 CSR report (see Figure 7.4) and learned

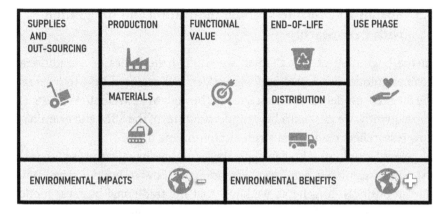

Figure 8.6. Environmental layer of the TLBMC. (Source: Joyce & Paquin.)

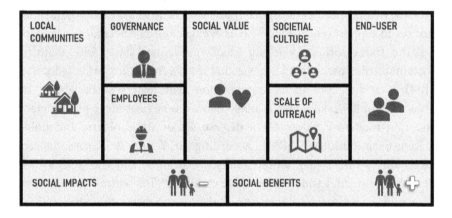

Figure 8.7. Social layer of the TLBMC. (Source: Joyce & Paquin.)

how corporations are involved in promoting social sustainability. Such companies significantly leverage their stakeholders in all aspects and adopt *a stakeholder management approach.* For starters, the stakeholder management approach strives to align the interests of the organization's stakeholders rather than seeking maximum profit for the business. Joyce & Paquin identified this sweet spot, unpacked the vital components of the stakeholder management approach (such as employees, local community, government, shareholders, etc.), and integrated them into a business model to construct the social layer of the SBM, as shown in Figure 8.7.

8.5. Sustainable Business Model Innovation and Integration with Lean Startup

At the beginning of this chapter, we studied the basics of a traditional business model developed by Osterwalder and explored how to leverage the business model via the Lean Startup through MVP (refer to Figure 8.3). Subsequently, we grasped a basic understanding of the SBM and examined how researchers made great strides in improving them.

Now, let us look at how to apply the lessons we have learned so far, with the aim of gaining a better understanding on how to build a sustainable startup business. In general, we know that the traditional business model primarily focuses on financial returns, thus leaving environmental and social aspects behind. But SBMs address these constraints and emulate business settings on a far larger scale by integrating unaddressed sustainability aspects. To start, we may need a conceptual framework or working theory/guidelines that could support our SBM to help us evaluate our business ideas.

The framework or working theory/guidelines starts with defining Sustainable Business Model Innovation (SBMI). According to Geissdoerfer, SBMI is at the core of an organization that fosters sustainability by proactive multi-stakeholder management, the development of monetary and non-monetary values for a diverse set of stakeholders, and holds a long-term outlook.[14] SBMI, according to Young & Reeves, tackles externality vulnerability, sustainability constraints, and the capacity for new environmental and societal value creation.[21] *The central message from these authors is clear; if we integrate all these components and position them in a shared context, we arrive at the UN Sustainable Development Goals (SDGs). In other words, SBMI acts as a tool that ensures SBMs, especially value delivery (refer to Figure 8.4), should reflect the UN SDGs.*

As presented in Figure 8.8, we shall explore how to integrate SBMI into a conventional business ecosystem and decode the process steps involved. The entire process involves four major steps: Design Thinking, Sustainability Integration, Lean Startup, and Growth Hacking.

8.5.1. *Design Thinking*

Design thinking is the method of extracting a problem statement specific to individuals, organizations, or societies. It is an iterative, continuous

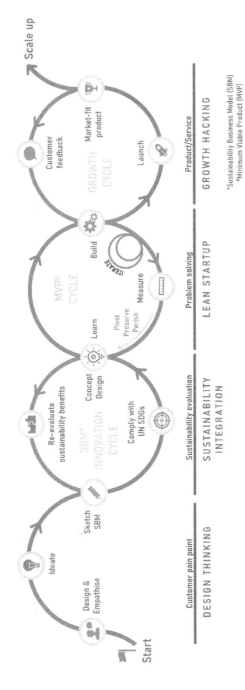

Figure 8.8.   Conceptualization of SBM Innovation Cycle.

reflection, and generates insights towards the problem statement to correct/ provide appropriate solutions.[22] This is the first stage of any business idea, which is sometimes hazy and challenging to comprehend. It begins with the formulation of possibilities and fosters creativity while being agile, broad, and experimental.

8.5.2. SBM Innovation Cycle

SBM innovation cycle starts with sketching an SBM canvas (refer to Figures 8.1, 8.5, 8.6, 8.7). To put it another way, we might conclude that an SBM that seeks to provide sustainable solutions should represent the UN SDGs, as we discovered in section 8.4 (Figure 8.4). Hence the cycle remains passive until the core value proposition addresses sustainability via products/services.

8.5.3. The Lean Startup

The next cycle, the Lean Startup, will begin after the SBM invention cycle. We gained detailed insights about the Lean Startup from section 8.2 (refer to subsection 8.2.1). This stage follows the lean manufacturing principle, which involves designing an MVP that reflects basic functionalities and features that solve the problem statement without spending a lot of time and money.

8.5.4. Growth Hacking

The final stage, growth hacking, is a relatively new idea in the startup environment. The objective of growth hacking tactics is to reach as many consumers as possible with the least amount of money.[23] Sean Ellis, founder and CEO of GrowthHackers, invented the word "growth hacking" in 2010. Once the market readiness level and strategic fit according to the finalized business plan is ready, the beta product is launched to target customer groups to evaluate its performance. Modifications and diversifications are made in response to early-bird customer feedback, and changes are implemented quickly to meet the customer's needs.

Concluding Remarks

Business used to be simple if you look at it from the eyes of nostalgia. However, we lacked a concrete and structured business model theory to evaluate the financial and non-financial benefits. The advent of business techniques such as the BMC and the Lean Startup in the 21st century has changed our fundamental views of doing business. Startup businesses have become common and ubiquitous as a result of the introduction of such business tools.

Students and innovators outside business school settings often lack business foundations, especially in the context of sustainability. This chapter has provided a deeper understanding of the SBM and presented a broad view on developing SBM for emerging entrepreneurs and innovators. The knowledge here gets you started with business planning and teaches you how to use the new business techniques.

We have introduced the Lean Startup methodology, Osterwalder's business model, and SBM innovation cycle, which are useful concepts for entrepreneurs in developing innovative business models and determining the trajectory of sustainability-oriented business venture. Hopefully this chapter will assist newcomers who wish to build any feasible sustainable business ideas from the ground up, all the way to product launch.

References

1. Business Definition. https://www.investopedia.com/terms/b/business.asp.
2. Shafer, S. M., Smith, H. J. & Linder, J. C. The power of business models. *Bus. Horiz.* **48**, 199–207 (2005).
3. Magretta, J. Why business models matter. *Harv. Bus. Rev.* **80**, 86–92 (2002).
4. Osterwalder, A. & Pigneur, Y. *Business Model Generation: A Handbook for Visionaries, Game Changers, and Challengers.* John Wiley & Sons (2010).
5. Richardson, J. The business model: an integrative framework for strategy execution. *Strateg. Chang.* **17**, 133–144 (2008).
6. Blank, S. G. *The Four Steps to the Epiphany: Successful Strategies for Products that Win.* Lulu Enterprises Incorporated (2006).
7. Bortolini, R. F., Nogueira Cortimiglia, M., Danilevicz, A. de M. F. & Ghezzi, A. Lean Startup: a comprehensive historical review. *Manag. Decis.* **online ready** (2018).

8. Mansoori, Y. Enacting the lean startup methodology: The role of vicarious and experiential learning processes. *Int. J. Entrep. Behav. Res.* **23**, 812–838 (2017).

9. Eisenmann, T., Ries, E. & Dillard, S. Hypothesis-driven entrepreneurship: the lean startup. https://edisciplinas.usp.br/pluginfile.php/5048746/mod_resource/content/1/hde.pdf.

10. Blank, S. & Dorf, B. *The Startup Owner's Manual: The Step-by-Step Guide for Building a Great Company.* John Wiley & Sons (2012).

11. Godelnik, R. & Meer, J. van der. Sustainable Business Models in an Entrepreneurial Environment. In: A. Aagaard (ed.), *Sustainable Business Models: Innovation, Implementation and Success*, pp. 239–276, Palgrave Macmillan (2019).

12. Shakeel, J., Mardani, A., Chofreh, A. G., Goni, F. A. & Klemeš, J. J. Anatomy of sustainable business model innovation. *J. Clean. Prod.* **261**, 121201 (2020).

13. Bocken, N., Ingemarsdotter, E. & Gonzalez, D. Designing Sustainable Business Models: Exploring IoT-Enabled Strategies to Drive Sustainable Consumption. In: A. Aagaard (ed.), *Sustainable Business Models: Innovation, Implementation and Success*, pp. 61–88, Palgrave Macmillan (2019).

14. Geissdoerfer, M., Vladimirova, D. & Evans, S. Sustainable business model innovation: A review. *J. Clean. Prod.* **198**, 401–416 (2018).

15. Morioka, S. N., Bolis, I., Evans, S. & Carvalho, M. M. Transforming sustainability challenges into competitive advantage: Multiple case studies kaleidoscope converging into sustainable business models. *J. Clean. Prod.* **167**, 723–738 (2017).

16. Lüdeke-Freund, F. & Dembek, K. Sustainable business model research and practice: Emerging field or passing fancy? *J. Clean. Prod.* **168**, 1668–1678 (2017).

17. Schaltegger, S., Hansen, E. G. & Lüdeke-Freund, F. Business models for sustainability: origins, present research, and future avenues. *Organ. Environ.* **29**, 3–10 (2016).

18. Geissdoerfer, M., Bocken, N. M. P. & Hultink, E. J. Design thinking to enhance the sustainable business modelling process — A workshop based on a value mapping process. *J. Clean. Prod.* **135**, 1218–1232 (2016).

19. Bocken, N. M. P., Short, S. W., Rana, P. & Evans, S. A literature and practice review to develop sustainable business model archetypes. *J. Clean. Prod.* **65**, 42–56 (2014).

20. Saari, U. A. *et al.* Sustainable Business Model Ideation and Development of Early Ideas for Sustainable Business Models: Analyzing a New Tool Facilitating the Ideation Process. In: A. Aagaard (ed.), *Sustainable Business Models:*

Innovation, Implementation and Success, pp. 239–276, Palgrave Macmillan (2019).

21. Young, D. & Reeves, M. The quest for sustainable business model innovation. https://image-src.bcg.com/Images/BCG-The-Quest-for-Sustainable-Business-Model-Innovation-Mar-2020_tcm9-240570.pdf.

22. Kozlowski, A., Searcy, C. & Bardecki, M. The reDesign canvas: Fashion design as a tool for sustainability. *J. Clean. Prod.* **183**, 194–207 (2018).

23. What is growth hacking? A simple definition + how to get started. https://optinmonster.com/glossary/growth-hacking/.

Exercises

1) Who introduced the widely recognized BMC?
   (A) Magretta
   (B) Osterwalder
   (C) Richardson
   (D) Ries
2) What are the three parts of Richardson's integrated business model which are based on Osterwalder's original BMC?
   (A) value proposition, value creation & delivery system, and value capture
   (B) value production, value creation & delivery system, and value capture
   (C) value proposition, value creation & delivery system, and value avoidance
   (D) value proposition, value creation & distribution system, and value capture
3) Who developed the lean production theory and when?
   (A) Samsung in the 20th century
   (B) Motorola in the 19th century
   (C) Toyota in the 20th century
   (D) BMW in the 20th century
4) What does MVP stand for?
   (A) Minimum Value Product
   (B) Maximum Value Purchase
   (C) Maximum Viable Purchase
   (D) Minimum Viable Product
5) Who popularized the notion of "Lean Startup"?
   (A) Magretta
   (B) Osterwalder
   (C) Richardson
   (D) Ries

6) Which concept is attributed to rapid and accurate product development by testing, iterating, and collecting feedback on product design?
   (A) System Engineering
   (B) Agile Engineering
   (C) Materials Engineering
   (D) Computer Engineering
7) What are two parts introduced by Osterwalder in his initial BMC to represent SBM canvas?
   (A) Social & Environmental cost and Social & Environmental benefit
   (B) Social & Economic cost and Social & Economic benefit
   (C) Cultural & Environmental cost and Cultural & Environmental benefit
   (D) Social & Environmental damage and Social & Environmental pressure
8) What are the three layers of Joyce and Paquin's "triple layered business model canvas"?
   (A) Energy, Environmental, and Social layers
   (B) Economic, Environmental, and Cultural layers
   (C) Economic, Environmental, and Social layers
   (D) Economic, Entropy, and Social layers
9) What does SBMI stand for?
   (A) Sustainable Business Multitude Innovation
   (B) Sustainable Business Model Innovation
   (C) Sustainable Business Multitude Inversion
   (D) Sustainable Business Model Initiation
10) Which aspect of the SBMI should reflect the UN SDGs?
   (A) Value delivery
   (B) Value capture
   (C) Value production
   (D) Value proposition

CHAPTER NINE
SUSTAINABLE BUSINESS —
CASE STUDY

Introduction

In the last chapter, we grasped a basic understanding of sustainable businesses and discussed different sustainable business models proposed by researchers elaborating individual (Economic, Environmental and Social) components. This chapter will apply your theoretical understanding of sustainable business to a realistic business case study with a domain emphasis.

We all know very well that plastic is harmful and toxic, not only for humans, but also other living beings and the planet itself. Due to its low cost and ease of fabrication, plastic sneaks into the food packing industry and has become an unimaginable threat. Sustainable food packaging, on the other side, is gaining traction to solve this problem. TRIA, a Singapore-based startup focused on sustainable food packaging utilizing plant-based materials, is one example.

This chapter takes TRIA (www.triafoodware.com) as a business case study and illustrates business models for each component of sustainability. It starts with a general overview of TRIA and its products, NEUTRIA® and Bio24, and explains how TRIA is motivated to foster sustainability via circularity. We take you through analyzing the economic business model of TRIA inspired by Osterwalder's business model canvas. Each section of the model is critically examined and explained in depth.

Environmental and social business variables must be weighed when developing a fully sustainable business model. As a result, Joyce & Paquin's sustainable business model is used to illustrate environmental and social business models with detailed explanations. Using the analysis derived from TRIA's case study, the chapter will enlighten entrepreneurs and researchers to understand complete sustainable business models and ignite entrepreneurship focusing on sustainable products.

9.1. TRIA — Sustainable Foodware Company

TRIA is an award-winning Singapore-based sustainable food packaging firm that was established in 2016. It produces and sells food packaging products to some of Asia's most prominent food service operators.[1] TRIA has gotten to the root of a long-standing problem of disposable product packaging and has come up with sleek, cutting-edge ideas. The company encourages and inspires the food services sector to foster sustainable consumption practices and ultimately become a zero-waste service provider via sustainable packing solutions.

Let us first consider the nature and implications of plastic waste before going into more depth regarding TRIA. Plastic is toxic to all living beings in the ecosystem, including us, as we all recognize. We addressed the effects of plastic pollution and how it impacts the whole environment in Chapter 1 (refer to section 1.3.1), including public well-being, marine pollution, and even climate change. Unfortunately, it has become an inextricable aspect of our lives. We use plastic for many applications, but our emphasis in this segment is on food packaging. It is easy to understand why we use polypropylene and polystyrene (Styrofoam) as food packaging products, when we consider that they are low-cost to manufacture, and take nearly 1,000 years to decompose.

Figure 9.1 shows that during the Covid-19 lockdown, Singapore produced approximately 1,334 tonnes of plastic waste from food packaging and delivery in just two months.[2] Consider the ramifications of these plastic wastes: if we incinerate them, we are, of course, pumping poisonous gases into the atmosphere; if we landfill them, we will run out of space, since they take hundreds of years to break down. Moreover, the act of manufacturing 1,334 tonnes of plastic products itself emits nearly 8,000 tonnes of CO_2 emissions,[3] which contributes to climate change.

COMPANY INFORMATION

NAME	INDUSTRY	LOCATION	REVENUE MODEL
TRIA	Food packing	Singapore	Product selling

PROBLEM STATEMENT

During COVID-19 lockdown, in 2 months, **Singapore** generated

1,334 Tonnes of plastic waste from food packing and delivery **=** **90 Double-decker buses**

~8,000 Tonnes of CO$_2$ emissions

SOLUTION

Replace plastic packing material with biodegradable, plant-derived packing material

Plastic container   ✕   Biodegradable container   ✓

SUSTAINABILITY GOALS

TRIA contributes to the UN Sustainable Development Goals by incorporating Goal 12: RESPONSIBLE CONSUMPTION AND PRODUCTION into its operations.

Figure 9.1.   TRIA — Sustainable foodware company, with a problem statement and a solution. (Source: TRIA, Stopplastics Canada.)

Hence, what is the tangible solution? Entirely ban plastic or innovate new materials. The plastic ban movement is gaining momentum to reduce further catastrophic environmental damages; on the other hand, companies like TRIA have developed advanced materials to substitute plastics, as shown in Figure 9.1. Figure 9.2 depicts a comprehensive operational landscape of TRIA. The firm works on two different technologies/approaches while still addressing sustainability concerns by closing the loop via circularity. Figure 9.2 shows (1) NEUTRIA®, a plant-based bioactive polyester that can be used to substitute disposable plastic product packaging in the supply chain, and (2) Bio24, an organic waste digester that turns food waste into bio-composites in as little as 24 hours.

The firm was inspired by nature and created plant-based composite materials to manufacture NEUTRIA®. As previously said, NEUTRIA® is a line of foodware products, specifically food packaging containers (for both solid and liquid food) that outperform their petroleum-based plastic counterparts while maintaining their functionality.

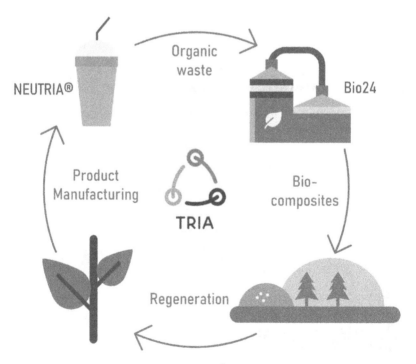

Figure 9.2.   TRIA's supply chain demonstrating sustainability commitment.

The second critical innovation is the Bio24 digester (see Figure 9.2), which degrades used NEUTRIA® and food waste to manufacture organic composites. The Bio24 digester uses the latest state-of-the-art technology that decomposes NEUTRIA® and food waste using chemical-free treatment into bio-composites within 24 hours. The bio-composite is shipped back to farmers for agricultural use. In this way, TRIA aspires to develop environmental ideals in its supply chain by promoting sustainable consumption practices and transforming waste into organic matter that naturally returns to the ecosystem.

Despite the reality that there are several biodegradable food packaging manufacturers across the world, TRIA's principal differentiator is the ability to close the circle. Competitors often concentrate on only replacing plastic packaging with biodegradable alternatives; the majority of it would still either be incinerated or disposed of in landfills, causing detrimental environmental effects. In other words, one aspect of the equation is solved while the other is overlooked.

Incineration, as we all realize, releases carbon into the environment during the combustion process. Leaving biodegradable wastes on land for natural decomposition, on the other hand, requires at least two years for complete degradation. TRIA has elegantly resolved this conundrum by integrating sustainability thinking and leveraging a closed loop business approach. It has partnered with local food waste-collecting agents to collect the used foodware (NEUTRIA® + food waste) from restaurants and hotels and send them to the decomposing facility (Bio24) to achieve the closed-loop principles at the fullest.

9.2. Economic Analysis of Business Model Canvas

TRIA's economic BMC analysis is depicted in Figure 9.3. Economic BMC analysis is inspired by the Osterwalder *et al.*[4] and Richardson model,[5] and further grouped into three main elements namely (1) Value proposition, (2) Value creation and delivery, and (3) Value capture.

9.2.1. *Value Proposition*

As we discussed in the last chapter, this section is at the core of constructing a viable BMC. It discusses what values are delivered via product/service and

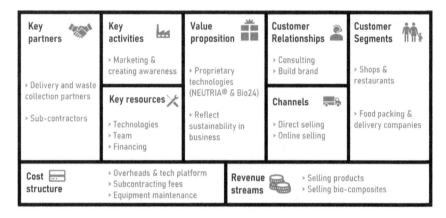

Figure 9.3.   Economic aspect of TRIA's BMC.

to whom. It is also broken down into A) Customer segments, B) Product/ Service with a unique selling point, and C) Customer relationships.

9.2.1.1. *Customer Segments*

We previously noted that businesses should begin with the customer in mind, solving their pain points. The customer's paint point is not stated directly in TRIA. However, vendors are currently pressed to switch to sustainable packaging, who are unwilling to pay for the green premium. Besides, there is a possibility that governments will prohibit the use of plastic, placing restaurants and food distribution services at risk. TRIA has defined consumer pain points and recognized its customer segment, such as restaurants and hotels, food packaging and distribution firms, etc., in light of the circumstance that will occur soon. Food delivery services such as foodpanda, and the general public who prefer takeaway food, may also be considered as customer segments of TRIA.

9.2.1.2. *Product/Service with a Unique Selling Point*

As seen in Figure 9.3 (value proposition), TRIA offers NEUTRIA® foodware products to its customer segments while maintaining an in-house Bio24 food digester. TRIA constructs its core value proposition by leveraging technologies such as plant-derived NEUTRIA® foodware and an efficient

Bio24 organic digester with a turnaround time of 24 hours to decompose food waste and NEUTRIA®. Selling NEUTRIA® to the customers is at the forefront; besides, integrating Bio24 with NEUTRIA® allows TRIA to remain a sustainable leader. Also, TRIA stimulates its customer segments to reflect sustainable practices by using its brands and products.

9.2.1.3. *Customer Relationships*

TRIA reaches out and interacts with customers through brand building and consulting. The trademark/brand identity is an aspect to consider when retaining the product's brand value. TRIA has registered NEUTRIA®; hence, the firm has protected the brand identity and prevented competitors from cloning it. With time, the brand identity will spread across the industry and become recognizable to various consumer segments.

9.2.2. *Value Creation and Delivery*

This section has four blocks: (A) Key partners, (B) Channels, (C) Key resources, and (D) Key activities. The fundamentals are covered in Chapter 8 (refer to section 8.1.2).

9.2.2.1. *Key Partners*

Key partners refer to business relationships with other entities. TRIA has engaged two business entities to succeed: (1) Waste pick-up and delivery partners, and (2) Subcontractors. Bio24 Alliance, which oversees the processing and shipping of food waste to the digester facility, has collaborated with TRIA. Singapore is a small and expensive city-state, thus posing a challenge in setting up a manufacturing plant. TRIA has foreseen this scenario and established a manufacturing facility for NEUTRIA® overseas.

9.2.2.2. *Channels*

Channels refer to how to deliver a product or service to consumers. TRIA has planned to build an online selling platform, as well as engaging consumers over the phone or through direct selling.

9.2.2.3. *Key Resources*

TRIA's key resources are technologies, teams, and financing. The company created the scientific cornerstone of a biodigester with a 24-hour processing time by focusing on research and development. The management team, likewise, is made up of impact-driven executives from various backgrounds and disciplines. The corporation also works with prestigious institutions such as the National University of Singapore regularly. These combined core tools also boosted business visibility and attracted private-sector grants and investment.

9.2.2.4. *Key Activities*

Key activities represent how companies stay competitive and achieve their goals. In TRIA's business model, the main competing products are plastic-based foodware; hence, transforming customer segments into sustainable products is a major leap. TRIA has addressed this issue by including environmental concerns in its business model and encouraging its consumers to shift toward a more sustainable economy. To accomplish this mission, TRIA must create a strong marketing team and increase the awareness of sustainable products. TRIA works with the customers to redesign their packaging portfolio so that it (a) uplifts the brand experience (b) without compromising on the functional requirements.

9.2.3. **Value Capture**

As seen in Figure 9.3, this section has two parts that describe the costs and revenue streams involved.

9.2.3.1. *Cost Structure*

Since TRIA is a foodware product manufacturing company with in-house biodigester facilities, significant funds are allocated to subcontracting (logistics partner, etc.) and equipment maintenance. Additionally, the company incurs operating and overhead expenses.

9.2.3.2. Revenue Streams

TRIA generates sales by selling two types of products: (a) sustainable foodware and (b) bio-composites to farmers. Multiple income sources will hugely increase earnings/profit, and TRIA is playing this game eloquently.

9.3. Environmental Analysis of Business Model Canvas

9.3.1. Functional Unit

Readers are advised to review Chapter 5 (section 5.2) and Chapter 8 (section 8.4.2.1) to get an idea of the functional unit. Let us draw inspiration from Joyce & Paquin's model[6] to determine the functional unit for TRIA's environmental analysis. TRIA's objective is to replace the plastic foodware in the marketplace and promote sustainable products. Now let us connect sustainable products (TRIA's foodware) to carbon emissions and quantify the environmental impacts via Life Cycle Assessment.

To arrive at a quantitative result, especially about carbon emissions, we must make realistic assumptions. For instance, as shown in Figure 9.4, we assume two NEUTRIA® foodware items were used by 1,000 consumers a year. In this situation, we will ascertain the environmental consequences once we have objectively determined the values to compare to the traditional practice (plastic foodware).

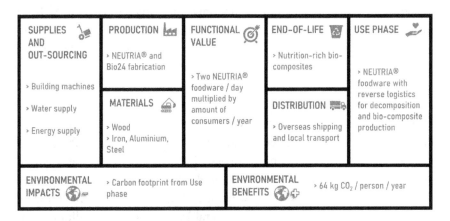

Figure 9.4.   Environmental aspect of TRIA's BMC.

9.3.2. *Use Phase*

Figure 9.2 represents the use phase of TRIA's product. As mentioned, TRIA supplies NEUTRIA® foodware to its customers, collects the NEUTRIA® foodware along with food waste, and sends them to the digestion facility for rapid decomposition. In this whole scenario, TRIA emits carbon when transporting NEUTRIA® to the customer location, and when transporting food waste + NEUTRIA® back to the facility, as well as when using electricity from the grid for digestion, and even when transporting bio-composites to farmers overseas. Naturally, these pollutants are inevitable unless we increase our reliance on clean energy sources.

Due to a lack of data, we do not have reliable carbon emission numbers for TRIA's operations. However, one thing is clear; the environmental harm caused by plastic foodware, such as landfills or incineration, is far greater than the harm caused by transportation of TRIA's foodware.

9.3.3. *End-of-Life*

The term "end-of-life" applies to how consumers treat a product when its use time has finished. Customers, for example, tend to dispose of, reuse, or resell products. Due to increasing environmental concerns, governments are pressuring businesses to track their products and promote proper disposal or recycling of electronic waste, for example, by Extended Producer Responsibility. In this vein, TRIA is not only collecting the NEUTRIA® from the customers, but it also upcycles and decomposes the NEUTRIA® into useful bio-composites at the end of its life cycle, ensuring true sustainability.

9.3.4. *Distribution*

Distribution refers to logistics to deliver the functional value. TRIA's distribution network includes overseas shipping via sea or air freight and a local distribution/collection network. The delivery component would critically inform you of the environmental impacts caused by the logistics/transports. Due to the complex nature of activities and the growing consumer base, estimating environmental losses (e.g., CO_2 pollution) for TRIA at this point is difficult.

9.3.5. *Production*

Production is the process of converting raw or unfinished materials into more valuable outputs. TRIA produces NEUTRIA®, a bioactive polyester resin derived from plants, and Bio24, which also requires electrical, computer, and mechanical components to fabricate. Thus, manufacturing components need resources in the form of gasoline, electricity, and other forms of energy and these manufacturing processes often release pollution into the air. Before commencing a manufacturing operation, it is always a good idea to conduct an impact evaluation through life cycle analysis; this way, pollution minimization strategies can be formulated.

9.3.6. *Materials*

Materials refer to basic raw materials used for building products. Since NEUTRIA® is derived from plants, the raw material is typically wood pulp. Hence manufacturing NEUTRIA® requires wood logs derived from natural sources. Similarly, Bio24 requires iron ore, aluminum, steel, copper, and other natural resources to build. The rationale behind these material evaluations is to ensure the sustainability of our natural resource stock.

9.3.7. *Supplies and Outsourcing*

This segment reflects *Key Partners* in the Economic BMC, illustrating business relationships with other entities. If we investigate via an environmental lens, we could see the nexus between the participating company (TRIA) and environmental sources such as water, electricity, etc. This section facilitates us in evaluating how we derive and use our resources effectively. TRIA, for example, utilizes municipal water and grid power, resulting in lower resource efficiency. As we addressed in Chapter 7, larger companies (such as Singapore Airlines) use rainwater and recycled water to meet 1/4 of their water need. Given the essence and scale of TRIA, we obviously cannot use the same comparison. The main takeaway from this section is to develop an environmental business model that focuses on resource efficiency.

9.3.8. *Environmental Impacts*

We discussed how much it would cost the business to deliver the value proposition in the economic context. Similarly, environmental impacts lead to possible environmental damage that could occur as a result of delivering the functional value. In other words, TRIA delivers NEUTRIA® to the marketplace and subsequently collects it back for post-processing to convert into compost. We mentioned that this process requires energy, and of course, emissions are inevitable. Thus, we need to objectively assess the post-product environmental performance to make sure it outweighs the environmental impacts.

9.3.9. *Environmental Benefits*

We measure the overall outcome of the environmental business model in this section. As shown in Figure 9.4, we assumed that our functional value is 2 NEUTRIA® food containers/day/person/year. Let us understand the potential impact assuming the same scenario in the absence of NEUTRIA®. Consider a situation in which two plastic food containers are used every day, per human, per year. Since each plastic container weighs ~15 g, everyone uses 30 g of plastic each day, or 10.8 kg of plastic each year. During processing, this 10.8 kg of plastic emits almost 64 kg of CO_2. As a result, if we use NEUTRIA®, we can save 64 kg of CO_2 footprint.

9.4. Social Analysis of Business Model Canvas

9.4.1. *Social Value*

We have seen how TRIA benefits its customers by incorporating sustainable values into its economic business model. Similarly, TRIA improves individual lives by using NEUTRIA® as a foodware material. In the environmental BMC, we stated that an individual would need 10.8 kg of plastic/year, resulting in an indirect contribution of 64 kg of CO_2. TRIA takes advantage of this fact and encourages people to use plastic-free products, thus changing people's minds toward sustainability.

The second social value from the social BMC of TRIA (Figure 9.5) is to develop long-term relationships with farmers by providing nutrition-rich

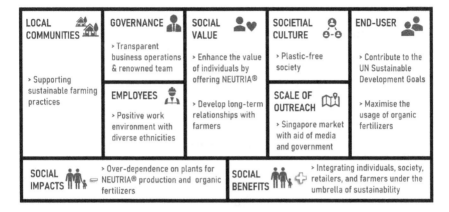

Figure 9.5.   Social aspect of TRIA's BMC.

composites from the Bio24 digester. This way, TRIA ensures that it contributes to society sustainably by integrating its stakeholders (farmers) in its operation.

9.4.2. *End-users*

This segment reflects end-users' personalities, social concerns, and awareness and discusses how the company's value proposition benefits the end user's quality of life. Most of the individuals in Singapore, for example, have environmental concerns and recognize the UN SDGs. Individuals acknowledge the impact of plastic pollution and work towards a plastic-free environment out of self-interest, believing that greater quality of life is worth the effort. Secondly, farmers are switching from inorganic fertilizers to natural alternatives such as bio-composites. Holistically, TRIA thus satisfies individuals' and farmers' needs with its modus operandi.

9.4.3. *Societal Culture*

Different societies may have different standards of values and beliefs; this segment acknowledges the potential impact of the product served to the community and positively transforming society towards sustainable thinking. Converting society to a plastic-free environment is a significant undertaking. Regardless, in the context of Singapore, piloting TRIA's product to replace plastic foodware is possible owing to size and ease of implementation. Other countries are urged to follow suit soon, transforming their societies into plastic-free nations.

9.4.4. *Scale of Outreach*

The scale of outreach reflects the long-term partnership that the organization has established with its partners and communities. This may indicate how the firm has expanded its reach beyond its home nation and how the product/solution has influenced the global market. Additionally, it signifies how the organization has impacted/contributed to the surrounding community's cultural, ethical, and political characteristics. TRIA is an early-stage venture that competes with low-cost plastic foodware while still aiming to persuade the local community, in this case Singapore, to use sustainable packaging. As a consequence, TRIA is up against a big obstacle. Nevertheless, TRIA has cemented its position in Singapore with the aid of local media and government funding, and it may one day enter the global market.

9.4.5. *Governance*

In Chapter 6, we learned about the value of Governance in an organization, and in Chapter 7, we illustrated Samsung Electronics as a case study for Governance. Investors and shareholders believe that businesses should be transparent and accountable for their actions. To do this, the management committee should embody sustainability philosophies, include a wide range of backgrounds and perspectives, have unbiased auditing appointed to the board, and be trustworthy. TRIA is steered by industry leaders and distinguished professors from the National University of Singapore and INSEAD.

9.4.6. *Employees*

Employees are an essential part of every business that wants to succeed. As seen from the sustainability lens, an organization's success is decided by its interaction with employees, safe work environment, welfare, race, and gender equality. Additionally, how a company leverages its employees by allowing them to contribute to society, advance their careers, and so forth, are crucial to retaining them. These conditions are primarily applicable to big organizations, although several startup firms are using these criteria to improve their organizational performance at an early level. TRIA has embraced diversity and created a welcoming job place for people of various ethnicities and backgrounds.

9.4.7 *Local Communities*

In Chapter 7, we have seen how Microsoft Corporation contributes to the local community by assisting residents in meeting their housing needs. Naturally, larger companies like Microsoft are financially stable and wealthy, and donating to the local community through grants/incentives/products/services is not unusual. When we apply this to startup firms, it becomes challenging to pursue, especially at the early stage. Regardless, sustainability startups should incorporate and envision this section alongside financial profits in their business models. In TRIA's business model, of course, we could see that TRIA is supporting sustainable farming practice by supplying bio-composites, empowering farmers through incentivizing programs, and indirectly benefiting local communities.

9.4.8. *Social Impacts*

This portion is straightforward to interpret while considering the economic and environmental dimensions of the business model. As we know, NEUTRIA® is made from plants. Thus, there could be a shortage of plants for large-scale manufacturing, or it could lead to farmers being forced to cultivate the plants for NEUTRIA® resulting in less room for other crop production. Another possibility is that by encouraging farmers to use bio-composites, TRIA may inadvertently raise the price of agricultural goods (for example, fruits). TRIA could also be unable to provide bio-composites to large-scale farmers.

9.4.9. *Social Benefits*

Any company aiming for social responsibility should strive for this section as its final goal. We have thoroughly examined TRIA's business model in terms of the social dimension. TRIA's social business analysis demonstrates that the organization is not only raising sustainability concerns; it also integrates its partners (individuals, society, consumers, and farmers) within the sustainability umbrella.

Concluding Remarks

Plastic, one of the best inventions by humans, is at the same time inextricably harmful to its creator and other living beings on the planet. Raw materials used to manufacture plastic bags are derived from natural materials such as crude oil or gas that took millions of years to form. One of the inevitable applications of plastic is food packing due to ease of fabrication and low cost.

We have highlighted the adverse effects of plastic pollution in the first chapter of this book. In addition, we have found out in this chapter that the manufacture of 10.8 kg of plastic releases almost 64 kg of CO_2. We must accept that sustainable food packaging is the only lifeline to solve this disadvantageous condition. In this vein, TRIA, a sustainable food packaging startup headquartered in Singapore, has developed cutting-edge technology to combat plastic waste by offering plant-based sustainable packaging solutions.

In this chapter, we used the Joyce & Paquin model to explain TRIA's sustainable business model in terms of sustainability, and critically evaluated the Economic, Environmental, and Social dimensions. The chapter's core message is that every sustainable startup should examine each aspect of sustainability individually and test them using illustrated business model frameworks.

This chapter will provide guidance and perspectives before writing the business strategy for any entrepreneurs who choose to establish a sustainable business. Along with the standard economic business model, it is recommended to conduct Life Cycle Assessment and Life Cycle Cost Analysis to accomplish the business model for environmental and social aspects.

References

1. Sustainable & Innovative Foodware | TRIA. https://triafoodware.com/.
2. Singapore households generated additional 1,334 tonnes of plastic waste during circuit breaker: Study | TODAY. https://www.todayonline.com/singapore/singapore-households-generated-additional-1334-tonnes-plastic-waste-during-circuit-breaker.
3. Carbon footprint of plastic | Stop Plastics. https://stopplastics.ca/carbon-footprint-plastic.
4. Osterwalder, A. & Pigneur, Y. *Business Model Generation: A Handbook for Visionaries, Game Changers, and Challengers.* John Wiley & Sons (2010).
5. Richardson, J. The business model: An integrative framework for strategy execution. *Strateg. Chang.* **17**, 133–144 (2008).
6. Joyce, A. & Paquin, R. L. The triple layered business model canvas: A tool to design more sustainable business models. *J. Clean. Prod.* **135**, 1474–1486 (2016).
7. Benoît, C. & Mazijn, B. Guidelines for social life cycle assessment of products. https://www.lifecycleinitiative.org/wp-content/uploads/2012/12/2009%20-%20Guidelines%20for%20sLCA%20-%20EN.pdf.

Exercises

1) Why does plastic find a way into the food packaging industry?
   (A) Because of the biocompatibility of food packing material
   (B) Because of low cost and ease of fabrication
   (C) Because of the molecular property of plastics
   (D) None of the above
2) What alternative material may be used to fabricate packaging that is not single-use plastic?
   A) Plant-based bioactive polypropylene
   B) Plant-based bioactive polyester
   C) Coal-based bioactive polyester
   D) Coal-based bioactive polypropylene
3) What treatment process is used by the Bio24 digester to transform food waste into bio-composites?
   (A) Chemical mixture
   (B) Toxic agents
   (C) Virulent treatment
   (D) Chemical-free

4) TRIA's customer segments are
   (A) Shops and Universities
   (B) Shops and Restaurants
   (C) Schools and Hotels
   (D) Schools and Hostels

5) Why has TRIA registered NEUTRIA®?
   (A) To sell more products
   (B) To showcase the company's profile
   (C) To protect brand identity and avoid cloning
   (D) To earn money

6) How does TRIA generate sales?
   (A) By selling sustainable foodware and bio-composites
   (B) By selling application software
   (C) By selling users' information to the restaurants
   (D) By selling its Bio24 digester

7) Define *Extended Producer Responsibility*:
   A)   Producers collect post-consumer waste for treatment or disposal
   B)   With the assistance of the government, consumers dispose of waste
   C)   The government disposes of wastes with the assistance of consumers
   D)   Producers and consumers dispose of their own waste on-site

8) What is TRIA's objective?
   (A) Support emerging businesses
   (B) Replace aluminum containers with plastic food packing material
   (C) Halt restaurant businesses due to plastic pollution
   (D) Replace plastic foodware with sustainable food packing material

9) What are the social values of TRIA's social business model?
   (A) Enhance the individual value and develop long-term relationships with farmers
   (B) Support local community through fundraising
   (C) Contribute to the poor
   (D) Provide jobs for minorities

10) What is the societal culture of TRIA's social business model?
   (A) Plastic-free farms
   (B) Plastic-free planet
   (C) Plastic-free oceans
   (D) Plastic-free society

CHAPTER TEN
SUSTAINABILITY — OPPORTUNITIES AND PROSPECTS

Introduction

This chapter starts with outlining the connection between engineering, business, and people through a sustainability lens. Historically, technological advancements have fueled human progress via business settings but lack sustainability thinking along the way. For instance, consider advancements fueled by fossil fuels and how these advancements have catalyzed detrimental effects on humanity and the environment, culminating in monstrous consequences such as climate change. To address these challenges, engineering must incorporate sustainability thinking, using tools such as Life Cycle Assessment and coordinating with sustainable businesses that communicate Corporate Social Responsibility (CSR). The context in which these sustainable engineering and corporate practices interact with social aspects is discussed.

The chapter also walks the reader through five fields (Climate change, Ecosystem & Resource, Waste management, Food, and Energy) that, in our opinion, require immediate attention from academics and business communities. For instance, climate change is our most important concern, as recommended by the UN, due to ongoing greenhouse gas emissions that have harmful consequences for humanity, the environment, and other living things. Many nations have pledged to support carbon-neutral programs by leveraging sustainable practices in all aspects. We propose and outline in detail different areas and prospects to explore from the academic and business standpoints for each field, providing insights to scientific communities and entrepreneurs to conduct sustainable research and business.

Finally, a roadmap to zero carbon emissions by 2100 is suggested, focusing on four critical areas: food production and consumption, transportation, energy and infrastructure, and conservation and policy.

10.1. Sustainability Interactions

So far, we have looked at and learned about sustainability, sustainable development, ESG, sustainable business model, and its realistic implementation. Now, let us examine some of the underlying factors and the critical things to remember to grasp sustainability from the author's viewpoint. As seen in Figure 10.1, we begin by understanding how engineering interacts with other fields such as business and people in the context of sustainability.

10.1.1. *Engineering*

Engineering and technology are at the center of all advancements. Manufacturing industries, transportation, commercial and residential buildings all rely heavily on engineering growth. Energy and materials, for instance, oils, coal, uranium, gold, copper, iron, and so on derived from the environment are used to progress engineering. As a result of these advances, we are depleting natural resources and polluting the environment by emitting greenhouse gas emissions and nuclear radiation.

We may deduce that engineering progress and advancements raise living standards, promote economic prosperity, and boost social improvements. In the first chapter, we explored the issues induced by the Linear Economy model. We looked at alternate ways to address the challenges in the second chapter, and we concluded that Circular Economy might be the answer. Unfortunately, we discovered that the social perspective was lacking, so we began researching sustainability

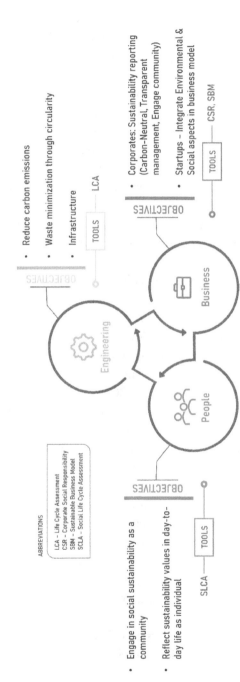

Figure 10.1.   Conceptual illustration of sustainability interactions between engineering, business, and people.

ideas and developments. Our fourth and fifth chapters gave some outlook on engineering dimensions of sustainability, and showed readers that sustainability and engineering have a close connection.

Now let us see the importance and principal requirements of practicing engineering in line with sustainability. Indeed, we are aware that technological advancements, such as industrialization, are at the root of these catastrophic detrimental effects on our ecosystem. These advancements, on the other side, are motivated by our desires, as seen in Figure 10.1. In other words, we are the enablers of engineering development and seekers of sustainable solutions. In this direction, let us think, ideate, and forecast what factors should be considered in the future to promote sustainable engineering. To support this argument, Marc Rosen proposed five areas in which engineering and sustainability should coexist.[1]

Natural resources are undeniably scarce, especially non-renewable resources such as fossil fuels, which are extremely important. Hence, we must maximize renewable energy resources, but of course, that situation may lead to material scarcity. The idea is simultaneously applying sustainable principles across multiple domains to address global challenges by leveraging sustainable engineering. For example, to combat climate changes, we are motivated to reduce CO_2 by avoiding fossil fuel burning. To meet our current energy demands, we may need to construct additional wind turbines or solar panels, although this will result in the extraction of rare earth metals. We can address this concern by perhaps leveraging recycling or materials circularity, but the social implications (e.g., exploiting people in low-income countries) must be factored in.

According to the UN's climate change initiative, 110 countries have pledged to achieve carbon neutrality by 2050.[2] While this multinational coalition resolution is a big step forward, the UN claims that technology is on our side. Achieving carbon neutrality is entirely coming out from fossil fuels and leveraging renewable resources. According to an IEA study,[3] renewable energy sources account for only 3% of global energy demand despite having a lower environmental effect, especially low air pollution. Also, the energy conversion efficiency of renewable sources such as photovoltaic, thermoelectric, piezoelectric is getting better, resulting in a significant gain-to-cost ratio.[4]

With the advancement of sustainable engineering practices, we are on our way to being a zero-carbon economy.[5] For example, electric vehicles and buses, net-zero energy buildings, and other innovative technologies such as carbon capture and energy storage using novel batteries and supercapacitors were developed by our research group, headed by **Professor Seeram Ramakrishna at the National University of Singapore**. Hydrogen has the potential to be a future energy source for electricity and transportation. It represents close to zero-carbon if derived from renewable energies, or via carbon capture fostering sustainable energy if we address storage and cost factors.

We can, of course, measure sustainable performance with the help of commercially available software tools for evaluating the current situation and forecasting the future. In Chapter 5, for example, we looked at coal and solar-powered energy-generating plants and their environmental effects. Thus, before any action, we can use these engineering tools to predict potential scenarios and model a sustainable ecosystem considering the available resources without compromising future needs.

10.1.2. *Business*

We covered sustainable business models in Chapter 8, and saw a case study in Chapter 9 from a sustainable startup context. Also, we studied Environmental, Social, and Governance (ESG) reporting in Chapter 7 from corporate companies. Now let us understand how sustainability and businesses are related to form sustainable businesses and how it interacts with engineering and social aspects of sustainability.

From an engineering standpoint, defining sustainability is somewhat straightforward. For example, as seen in Figure 10.1, one of the primary goals is to reduce carbon emissions; one way to do that is to substitute non-renewable energy sources with renewable alternatives. From a corporate viewpoint, sustainability involves framing long-term business decisions in a balanced scenario, taking environmental and social factors into account alongside financial benefits. Nowadays, businesses, such as Apple Inc., aim to achieve carbon neutrality across their entire operations, production supply chain, and product life cycle by 2030. Apple's global business activities are now carbon-neutral, and this recent pledge ensures that by 2030, any Apple product sold would have a net-zero climate impact.[6]

Similarly, Microsoft Corporation[7] is one of the global pioneers in terms of how businesses interact with society. We have outlined how Microsoft leverages local and global communities and empowers its employees (refer to section 7.3.2). The message from these corporations is clear; there is an increasing trend in combining environmental and social issues alongside financial benefits and explicit signs that businesses want to be carbon-neutral.

These corporate companies convey their sustainability performance via CSR or ESG reporting. CSR facilitates companies in improving their strategic positions by tying sustainability and business strategies together. It entails turning the problem into business strategy terminologies such as organizational performance, value creation, strategic path, and market expansion. According to Gergely Tóth, CSR reporting should represent a commitment to sustainability, which includes carbon footprint reduction, sustainable consumption and energy efficiency, encouraging environmentally friendly actions, and ensuring that societal ideals are reflected.[8]

We have highlighted how to generate a sustainable business model canvas considering the social and environmental factors and outlined how to launch a successful sustainable startup in Chapter 8. Any startup should always start with identifying customer problems; in this case, customers are society. Once we have identified the customer's problem, we must determine a feasible and long-term solution. We can use the business model tools established in Chapters 8 and 9 to formulate the stakeholders, pain points, engineering solutions, and social and environmental benefits. In this way, social and engineering aspects are connected to work in tandem to support sustainable businesses and help companies become more competitive.

10.1.3. *People*

Why do we need to foster engineering or business sustainability? Because we do not stifle our desire to move forward, our need to advance and progress. Thus, as individuals, we must incorporate all facets of sustainability into our daily lives. We have already established the linkage between CSR and human well-being by focusing on different indicators such as employee welfare, community engagement, protecting fundamental human rights, and so on (refer to section 7.3.2). In addition, in Chapters 8 and 9, we developed the Social Business Model Canvas via the case study of a startup business.

As shown in Figure 10.1, let us view this section in two aspects:

(1) Engage in social sustainability as a community
(2) Reflect sustainability values in day-to-day life as individual

Social sustainability is an integral part of the business that brings people together and helps them flourish as a community, resulting in higher incomes. It is evident that most multinational businesses incorporate ethical considerations into their business models, adhere to business principles, and promote social welfare. Within their workforce families, businesses campaign for human rights, racial equity, cultural ideals, and equitable employment opportunities.[9] Besides, private organizations encourage employees to donate to charitable projects or provide humanitarian assistance, demonstrating seamless harmony between society and the employees.[10] Also, businesses embrace local communities and contribute to their well-being by delivering technology, education, water, and sanitation services that embody sustainable social values and positive contributions.

We, the people, are embedded in a complex network of social interactions and interdependence. We would not be discussing sustainability if human evolution, population explosion, and industrialization had never happened, which brings us to the fact that humans are at the forefront of both positive and negative consequences. Regardless of poverty, political shifts, languages, cultures, or geography, we must all focus on one thing: are we on the correct path to achieving sustainability?

To answer this question, we as an individual must step out of the sustainability circle and perceive how we interact with nature and society. At this point, we could say, most of the individuals across the planet do not realize what sustainability means. For example, although people in developed countries may consider sustainability, they use more than three times the amount of energy and resources as people in developing countries.[11] On the other hand, people from developing countries do not comprehend sustainability; thus, environmental and social effects such as pollution, biodiversity loss, conflicts, and discrimination get amplified.

Global leaders and the UN[12] recognize these negative consequences and have continually provided direction by elevating corporate and economic stature and outlining social sustainability principles. We, as the people, should embrace sustainable principles and use sustainable engineering practices to reduce the harmful effects that place stress on the environment and our society.

10.1.4. *Remarks*

The conceptual structure outlined in Figure 10.1 incorporates the most critical relations that characterize engineering, business, and social elements. The objectives, interdependence, relationships, and tools associated with each component are readily evident and reflect usability that aids in achieving sustainable results. In summary, since each component is interconnected and impact-driven, it is appropriate to leverage individual components concurrently.

10.2. Opportunities in Sustainability

As shown in Figure 10.2, we have selected five fields on which researchers and entrepreneurs could focus their efforts immediately. For instance, climate change is our most important concern, having a dramatic effect on our business and economy. Our existing infrastructure, such as electricity generation, must adapt to minimize emissions, incorporate green technology, and reduce dependency on non-renewable energy sources for energy generation. As our development is contingent upon natural resources, resource depletion such as deforestation has a detrimental impact on the ecosystem; therefore, sustainable consumption practices are stressed. Once we use resources, we produce waste, so we have placed a high premium on fostering sustainable waste management, especially for electronic waste. Food is our next area of action for sustainability; our current food production strategies are questionable and ignore sustainable practices. Therefore, we scrutinize our food consumption practices and present areas to improve. Lastly, our energy resources are largely based on fossil fuels, and we are aware of the negative consequences of burning fossil

Figure 10.2.   Sustainability landscape and opportunities.

fuels for electricity generation; thus, our modern energy infrastructure and areas for sustainable integration are addressed.

10.2.1. *Climate Change*

Our planet is unquestionably warming. Without immediate and aggressive efforts to reduce carbon pollution, global temperatures will shoot up, and the number of severe weather incidents will increase significantly. By 2100, experts estimate that the global temperature would have risen by nearly 5.0°C if existing carbon emissions continue unabated, posing a devastating threat to humans and the biosphere.[13] The UN Paris Climate Agreement, which aims to keep global warming far below 2°C, ideally 1.5°C, in the second half of the 21st century is on the horizon but falling backwards.[14]

The World Economic Forum has outlined the carbon emissions status of many countries; small countries such as Bhutan and Suriname have already achieved Net Zero Carbon status, with several more following suit.[15] As seen in Figure 10.3, let us view the carbon emissions from the context

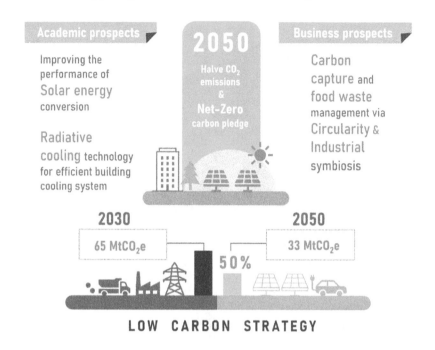

LOW CARBON STRATEGY

Figure 10.3.   Singapore's action towards a low-carbon economy reflecting academic and business prospects.

of Singapore. The country's maximum CO_2 emissions will be 65 $MtCO_2$ around 2030, but it will seek to halve emissions to 33 $MtCO_2e$ by 2050 to achieve net-zero emissions as quickly as possible in the second half of the century.[16]

10.2.1.1. *Academic Prospects*

While Singapore is advancing towards a zero-carbon economy, we can anticipate numerous prospects for innovation in the research spectrum. For example, at the manufacturing level, photovoltaic solar cell technology made from gallium arsenide has achieved a maximum energy conversion efficiency of 24.1%. Similarly, emerging technologies such as dye-sensitized TiO_2, thin-film Si, organic, perovskite, and quantum dots exhibiting promising energy conversion efficiency and easy fabrication techniques are being refined at the laboratory level.[17]

Since Singapore is a small city-state with many high-rise buildings and sunshine year-round, innovations are pushed towards efficient building cooling and management. In this direction, thin-film technologies have been developed to reflect the sunshine and maintain building temperature without spending much energy using advanced engineering materials.[18] Research to combat global warming using renewable energy sources are also expected in these areas.

10.2.1.2. *Business Prospects*

There are several business opportunities for addressing sustainability in Singapore, and the following suggested concepts may be implemented in other countries as well. For instance, the organic food packaging we discussed in the last chapter is a classic illustration of a sustainable business model. Our end goal is to reduce our carbon footprint; carbon capture and sequestration is the best-suited method naturally.

There is growing interest in this area, and companies such as Global Thermostat, CO_2 Solutions, Carbon Engineering, and Climeworks focus on capturing and storing carbon using state-of-the-art technologies.[19] If we apply the same principles in the Singapore context, we could address two main issues simultaneously. Food waste is a big issue worldwide, not only in Singapore; innovations for converting food waste into nano-engineered materials capable of capturing carbon are also on the horizon. Using circularity and industrial symbiosis, we may use these innovations to build a sustainable business aimed at carbon capture and food waste management.

10.2.2. *Ecosystem and Resources*

An ecosystem is a living society made up of animals, plants, and microorganisms that communicate with the non-living environment. We, as humans, rely on ecosystems for essential needs such as food, water, and shelter.[20] A sustainable ecosystem is capable of functioning and regenerating at maximum potential even after resources are extracted for human use. According to Smith, ecosystem sustainability will dramatically deteriorate because of human actions such as inefficient resource management, increased resource extraction, and continuous waste disposal leading to polluting the environment and affecting human health.[21]

As previously stated, the ecosystem satisfies human needs through services such as food, materials and resources, and settlement land; therefore, humans bear a significant obligation to retain integrity while interacting with the ecosystem. Forests are our primary source of resources; we contribute to deforestation by harvesting our resources, which increases CO_2 emissions and reduces oxygen supply. These are cascading effects of deforestation, hence we view deforestation as a pressing issue that requires immediate academic and business focus. A graphical illustration of the deforestation scenario is provided in Figure 10.4.

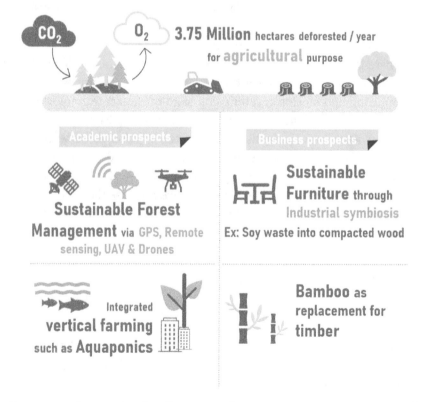

Figure 10.4.   Opportunities for afforestation reflecting academic and business prospects.

10.2.2.1. *Academic Prospects*

From the academic perspective, deforestation is tackled by sustainable forest management (SFM) practices. SFM begins by preserving existing forests while satisfying human needs, and creating new forest areas by planting new trees. Mathematical modeling,[22] as well as cutting-edge technologies such as LIDAR, GPS connectivity, remote sensing, Unmanned Aerial Vehicles, and Airborne Laser Scanning have already been developed.[23] Integrating these technologies with SFM can provide insights into deforestation and allow for the implementation of preventative measures.

Agriculture is another significant element in deforestation. Every year, the vast landscape, which covers 3.75 million hectares, is converted for agricultural purposes.[24] Urban farming, or vertical farming, is gaining traction to provide organic alternatives of fruits and vegetables to urban citizens. Aeroponic, Aquaponic, and Hydroponic Vertical Farms are examples of integrated sustainable farming, and potential research directions can improve the efficiency of these practices.[25]

10.2.2.2. *Business Prospects*

Since forestry materials such as wood and timber drive furniture industries, there is room for innovative business models. For instance, waste produced by soy processing plants could be repurposed to manufacture sustainable furniture. As previously stated, industrial symbiosis is a critical component of sustainability.

Many creative business models that promote afforestation exist, such as Dendra[25] programs that use drone seeding technologies, Esosia,[26] an online search platform that produces revenue for tree planting, and so on. However, our emphasis is on sustainability and circularity; because the furniture industry has been using slower-growing timber, we can use bamboo to replace timber furniture since it is fast-growing, reliable, durable, and long-lasting. Such innovations are already happening in southeast Asia, but the reach is limited as bamboo only grows in the tropical regions of Asia. Once we have production innovations for lightweight furniture that incorporate compacted bamboo dust and sustainable logistics in place, we would be able to exploit bamboo for global applications.

10.2.3. *Waste Management*

Why do we produce waste? Waste occurs as a consequence of insufficient planning. Waste generation is so widespread that it is almost ubiquitous on the globe, including outer space. We have clearly outlined the adverse effects of the linear production model in the first chapter, highlighting the current situation and future scenario representing waste generation by food, construction, and transport industries. The evidence and future scenario under business-as-usual conditions were alarming to us, and hopefully to you as well. Businesses and industries constantly struggle to curb waste generation, despite authorities imposing legislations and researchers throwing ideas and technologies to support waste management.

Conventionally our current waste management strategy starts with waste generation, collection, and disposal (landfill or incineration).[27] This condition is satisfactory and not hazardous when urban solid waste such as food and household waste is considered. On the other hand, electronic waste (e-waste) is increasing daily, and the hazards associated with it are immense; therefore, let us consider waste management in terms of e-waste.

According to the UN's Global E-waste Monitor 2020, a total of 53.6 million metric tonnes (Mt) of e-waste was produced worldwide in 2019, up 21% in only five years. Furthermore, according to the same survey, global e-waste could reach 74 Mt by 2030,[28] indicating massive challenges ahead. We may need to embrace new technologies and innovative business models to overcome these disasters and further integrate sustainable practices into our waste management as shown in Figure 10.5.

10.2.3.1. *Academic Prospects*

Academics are already investigating future directions and opportunities in line with e-waste management. Although lithium-ion batteries are popular among mobile phone and electric vehicle manufacturers due to their high energy storage capacity, they are not environmentally friendly, emitting poisonous fumes into the air when recycled.[29] Environmentally safe batteries, such as lithium-sulfur[30] and magnesium batteries[31], are, on the other hand, gaining popularity for large-scale energy storage applications

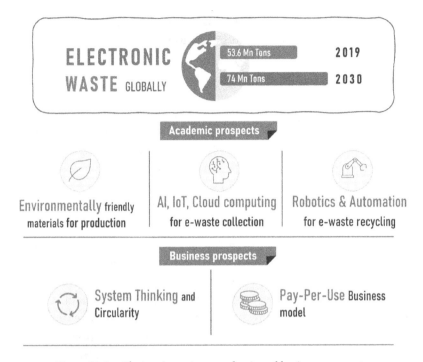

Figure 10.5. Electronic waste — academic and business prospects.

with long-term sustainability concerns. We may use novel technology in this way to reduce harmful e-waste in the first place.

It is difficult to imagine a future without electronic devices, but we can eventually tackle e-waste by suitably handling and maintaining it. Our conventional e-waste disposal system is inefficient due to a lack of awareness, especially in developing countries. Providing e-waste knowledge among communities and enabling them with technologies could potentially improve the efficiency of the e-waste management process. For instance, the Internet of Things (IoT)-enabled smart bin e-waste collection boxes[32] and AI-based e-waste collection,[33] as well as a mobile app powered by cloud computing technology, may be used in the e-waste collection phase.

The final step, disposal, or recycling provides significant opportunities for material recovery. Developing nations accept the job to generate income but expose themselves to severe health issues in the recycling process.[34]

Recycling and materials recovery using robots and automation may be the potential long-term solution in this direction.

10.2.3.2. *Business Prospects*

When it comes to e-waste management, several businesses have also begun to embrace sustainable business practices. Under the supervision of the National Environmental Agency of Singapore,[35] Starhub, Singtel, and other telecom firms in Singapore have begun introducing an Extended Producer Responsibility (EPR) scheme for e-waste management.

But our current e-waste management needs further elevation via sustainable startup business models that integrate a system thinking approach. Traditional electronic devices and components, for example, are laborious and costly to refurbish; as a result, consumers are more likely to purchase new electronic products, creating little space for product circularity.[36] New business models should consider system thinking; adhere to the circular economy principle and provide a disassembly facility that enables each part to be replaced as soon as a malfunction is detected. This improves the product re-cycling and life cycle of electronic products and components.[37]

Pay-per-use model: Tesla and Renault have started leasing batteries on a pay-per-use basis to electric vehicle operators. These batteries are recycled to store electricity produced from renewable energy sources, greatly extending their life spans. Batteries will be disassembled towards the end of their useful life, and their usable components will be used to manufacture new ones. Similarly, consumer products such as cameras, computers, and cell phones may use the pay-per-use model to minimize e-waste via sustainable market practices.[38]

10.2.4. *Food*

Since food is such an intrinsic part of human existence, we intuitively understand the negative consequences of food scarcity. In Chapter 1, we have outlined our existing food production model, explained what the implications are while producing our food and how we waste our food while processing, and highlighted what could be the future scenario in 2050.

Given the dire condition, the United Nations Sustainable Development Goals (SDGs) also stressed the importance of setting national objectives for reducing global carbon footprint via sustainable production and consumption.[39] The UN SDG 12 (Responsible Consumption and Production) encourages us to achieve our global food *production* by reducing our dependence on fossil fuels, emitting low carbon, limiting chemical fertilizers, and effectively using natural resources (land, water). Furthermore, sustainable *consumption* entails minimizing food waste during processing and handling and consuming responsibly without wasting food.

Sustainable food production is described as a way of producing environmentally friendly food while conserving non-renewable energy and natural resources, is cost-effective, is sustainable for farmers, societies, and customers, and does not impede the needs of future generations.[40] Of course, considering the rising population and the need to satisfy global food demand, it is fairly difficult to catch up on food production through sustainable practices. But science and business communities never cease their quest for sustainable food production and consumption, as shown in Figure 10.6.

10.2.4.1. *Academic Prospects*

A quick Google search for Sustainable Food Production and Consumption yields a comprehensive map of current academic studies and proposals. The global research community is still searching for innovative approaches to satisfy global food demand while adhering to sustainability values.

Sustainable Food Production: (1) Agriculture emits huge greenhouse gas emissions; thus, the research community should leverage renewable sources. (2) High-yield crops through gene modification and nanoengineering and artificial meats through tissue engineering should be developed.[41] (3) Artificial fertilizer replacements include synthetic biology, reconfigurable photosynthesis, ecological biocontrol, and bio-compost made from food waste circularity.[41] (4) Urban & vertical farming (Aeroponic, Aquaponic, and Hydroponic) combine land-based organic

Figure 10.6.   Sustainable food production and consumption — academic and business prospects.

and landless food production as the replacements for land reclamation for agriculture.[42] (5) Efficient rainwater harvesting, drone technologies for visual mapping, IoT sensors, and cloud computing for humidity and temperature management are all supporting technologies.

Sustainable Food Consumption: In 2020, nearly 1.1 and 0.55 billion tonnes of food waste were generated during processing and consumption phases, respectively, reflecting our inefficient food handling and poor consumption practices.[43] (1) We must leverage efficient solar-powered food and meat storage techniques.[44] (2) As urban food waste is unavoidable, we must exploit food circularity to generate bio-composites through food digesters.

10.2.4.2. *Business Prospects*

Business ideas depend on regional problems. For instance, in India, power outages are common, putting farmers under pressure. Hence, social entrepreneurs may utilize sustainable business model innovation to lease high-efficient solar panels and electrical components during the food production stage and portable solar-powered and biogas units derived from cow dung during the preservation stage.

Food waste collection and conversion into bio-composites already exist, so we should take advantage of the business model and integrate it with sustainable earthworm production to improve soil fertility. In the city context, we may innovate the business model by creating value from food waste such as leftover food collection via mobile apps and converting into bio-composites, and cloud computation for food sharing. Additionally, bioorganic materials using nanostructure technology have been developed; hence, we could use these concepts for sustainable food packing.

In the end, circularity thinking must be adopted by sustainable business models such as restoring nutrients to the ecosystem, effective food handling, and processing in both urban and rural areas.

10.2.5. *Energy*

We will continue to use fossil fuels for at least until the middle of the 22nd century as our main energy source. Our road to carbon neutrality, on the other hand, is just on the horizon. Our initiatives toward renewable energies continue to rise, presenting both opportunities and challenges. While we have succeeded in converting clean energy sources such as solar, wind, geothermal, and ocean power to electricity, we do need to address energy conversion efficiency and environmental impacts.

Scientific advancements, especially material science in energy generation and storage, present significant opportunities and shed light on our renewable future. Many academic groups are making progress in green energy, with industrial solar panels, for example, achieving energy efficiency of around 24.1%.[17] Also, innovative business ideas in renewable energies are gaining traction at an incredible rate. Figure 10.7 depicts the future opportunities in the cleantech area in the context of academic and business settings.

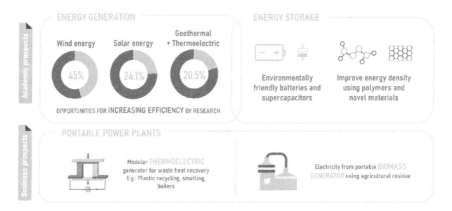

Figure 10.7.   Aspects of sustainable energy — academic and business prospects.

10.2.5.1. *Academic Prospects*

Energy generation: Theoretically, wind energy could achieve a high energy conversion efficiency of 59.6%,[45] whereas our existing realistic system only achieves 30–45%,[46] indicating that there is potential for improvement by using the best aerodynamic model and reducing wind noise.[47] Solar energy conversion technology currently achieves a conversion efficiency of 24.1% in realistic environments, and its potential for development was addressed in section 10.2.1.1. Geothermal energy has ample scope, though often limited by geographical constraints. Nevertheless, when combined with solid-state thermoelectric systems, it achieves a substantial energy conversion performance of 20.5%.[48] Indeed, other technologies such as fuel cells, biomass, hydrolysis, and so on need attention as well. Wind, hydro, geothermal, and solar, on the other hand, seem to be well adapted for large-scale installations, and research studies should concentrate on optimizing system performance in practice.

Energy storage: For applications in transport and electronic products, rechargeable batteries, especially lithium-ion batteries, have become the dominant technology. Unfortunately, lithium-ion batteries are not environmentally friendly, and alternative materials such as lithium-sulfur, lithium-magnesium, etc., are gaining popularity. Integrating the next-generation environmentally friendly batteries with supercapacitors could open up new areas, especially in the electric vehicle market. For large-scale energy storage applications requiring high energy density, rapid charging capability, and long life, novel materials such as carbon nanotubes and other polymers can pave the way for future research.[49,50]

10.2.5.2. *Business Prospects*

There are many business opportunities, especially in the context of energy generation and storage, in developing countries. Given our commitment to sustainable business, one field of opportunity is the use of thermoelectric generators. Developing countries like India, Indonesia, and the region of Southeast Asia, for example, produce enough heat from plastic processing and recycling to drive thermoelectric generators. They represent less energy conversion efficiency, but when integrated with solar panels they open a world of possibilities.

Biomass energy conversion is often underestimated, but anaerobic portable biomass systems could open new opportunities in developing countries. The supply of inexpensive fossil fuels like gasoline or diesel might be more attractive considering the cost of biomass energy production. However, prices and global demand of crude oil could force a shift away from fossil fuels and toward biofuels in the future. Biomass energy is, of course, feasible in rural countries seeking to achieve long-term sustainability while protecting the environment.

10.3. Roadmap for a Zero-carbon Planet

Figure 10.8 depicts a list of scopes and fields that must be pursued immediately to achieve a zero-carbon planet. Fortunately, we have emerging technologies and sustainable business practices by our side in this battle. As we stated in the first chapter of this book, our pressing concern is the growing population that contributes to increased resource consumption, waste generation, emissions, biodiversity loss, and so on. We should model our world in such a way that our continued life is assured, while preserving harmony with nature and other living things. To realize the sustainable condition, especially in the context of carbon emissions, we must address and act on these five areas presented in Figure 10.8.

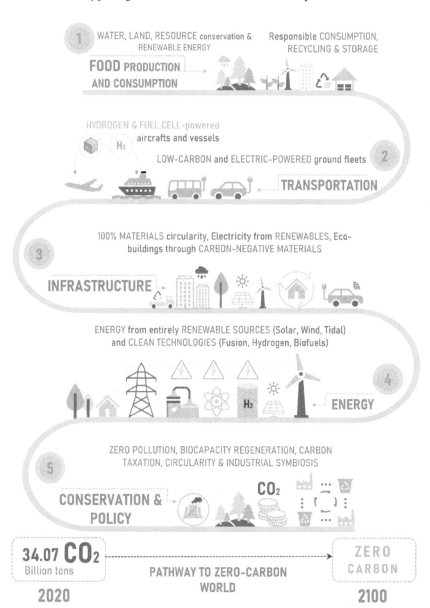

Figure 10.8.   Scopes defining roadmap for a zero-carbon planet.

Sustainable food production and consumption: We should incorporate sustainability principles in all aspects of food, such as production, storage, distribution, consumption, and recycling. As the roadmap depicted in Figure 10.8 indicates, we must ensure sustainability through resource conservation by leveraging vertical farming, for example, and food production through renewable energies. Additionally, sustainable consumption should be maintained, especially in urban areas where food is wasted at a higher rate, and sustainable food recycling should be practiced in all nations.

Sustainable transportation: Moving towards zero-emitting fleets is our grand plan. Leveraging clean energy technologies such as hydrogen, fuel cells, renewable sources could transform our transportation industries. Many companies, such as Tesla, have already unveiled electric cars, and Airbus, for example, has presented its vision for manufacturing hydrogen-powered aircraft. Of course, we cannot get rid of fossil fuels in our transportation until we have extracted the last drop of oil; our zero-emission goal is quite a long way off, so we will have to depend on our technology to get us there and follow it actively.

Sustainable infrastructure: Buildings are another source of carbon emission. Buildings worldwide have also begun to incorporate sustainability principles into their material extraction, construction, and demolition processes. However, we are not yet fully prepared to eradicate carbon emissions; developing nations need an immediate shift in their approach, especially when building new infrastructures. Developed countries should take the lead by promoting material circularity, eco-green design, and carbon-negative products in constructing zero-energy buildings, and share the technology know-how to get other countries to follow suit.

Sustainable energy: Clean energy innovations such as solar, wind, hydrogen, tidal, and fuel cells are increasingly gaining traction. The positive news is that costs are decreasing, and more people are adopting renewable technologies. Energizing our planet with renewable technology is a significant jump, but we have already demonstrated that the technologies work in real life settings. Our renewable technology will grow and evolve as a powerhouse in the coming decades, assisting us in reducing emissions.

Conservation and policy: New policies towards resource conservation, carbon taxation, incentivizing clean technologies, green infrastructure, waste management, and sustainable startups, as well as novel business ideas such as industrial symbiosis, carbon trading, circularity, urban farming, recycling, and sharing businesses should be embraced immediately. There are many conservation policies already in place, but we should create universal standards by educating and integrating business and engineering practices, so that we may cultivate a situation where all stakeholders participate towards a zero-carbon planet.

The ideas proposed here are subjected to improvement and depend on many factors such as political shifts, economy, resources, global crisis, businesses, academic performance, and so on. But to combat global challenges, we must remain steadfast and embrace sustainable practices, especially in the direction of a carbon-free world for the betterment of future generations.

Concluding Remarks

Responding to global challenges requires collective efforts from people, governments, academics, and entrepreneurs. By now, we are all conscious of the ongoing global problems that need urgent action in all facets of technology, social collaboration, and business initiatives. The transition from traditional economic growth, which largely fueled the linear economy, to sustainable development necessitates a strong link between people, engineering, and business, as we stated at the beginning of this chapter. This new set of initiatives improves upon traditional business models, fostering sustainable growth by promoting new business practices that embrace social welfares, preserve the environment, cultivate sustainable attitudes, and eventually ensure that our future generation is safe and secure.

We identified five fields in which academics and business communities could concentrate immediately. Sustainability needs increased understanding at the university level; universities and educators must incorporate sustainability, especially in the areas of social welfare, environmental conservation, and economic progress. Although technological innovations are not inherently revolutionary, they are often necessary for progress in our world characterized by a diverse set of players, politics and economic fabrications, market forces, trends, and legislation. To understand this context, technologies and business studies must continually relate to sustainability. On the other hand, new business models must adhere to sustainability principles and circular thinking, combining environmental and social aspects with financial gains.

Academic and business prospects that we proposed in this chapter may lack complete sustainable thinking due to our primitive linkage between engineering and business fields. But we hoped to have familiarized readers with the basic ideas. Extending our objectives towards resource efficiency, environmental friendliness, energy savings, social welfare, and fighting inequalities are what we need to embrace regardless of policies or political climates. Ultimately, the onus is on us to adapt to a lifestyle that integrates peace with nature and all species, and work towards a zero-carbon planet by leveraging science, technologies, businesses, policies, and social harmony beyond borders.

References

1. Rosen, M. A. Engineering sustainability: A technical approach to sustainability. *Sustainability* **4**, 2270–2292 (2012).
2. Carbon neutrality by 2050: the world's most urgent mission | United Nations Secretary-General. https://www.un.org/sg/en/content/sg/articles/2020-12-11/carbon-neutrality-2050-theworld's-most-urgent-mission.
3. Renewables — Global Energy Review 2020 — Analysis | IEA. https://www.iea.org/reports/global-energy-review-2020/renewables.
4. Ramadoss, T. S. & Ramakrishna, S. Human Vibration Energy Harvester with PZT. In: B. Raj, M. van der Voorde & Y. Mahajan (eds.), *Nanotechnology for Energy Sustainability*, pp. 649–678, John Wiley & Sons (2017).
5. Dodds, R. & Venables, R. Engineering for sustainable development: Guiding principles. https://www.raeng.org.uk/publications/reports/engineering-for-sustainable-development.
6. Apple commits to be 100 percent carbon neutral for its supply chain and products by 2030 | Apple (SG). https://www.apple.com/sg/newsroom/2020/07/apple-commits-to-be-100-percent-carbon-neutral-for-its-supply-chain-and-products-by-2030/.
7. Spaulding, M., Merchant, K. A. & Hwan, S. Microsoft Corp: CSR Execution. https://msbfile03.usc.edu/digitalmeasures/kmerchan/intellcont/Microsoft%20CSR%20[A218-01]-1.pdf.

8. Tóth, G. Circular economy and its comparison with 14 other business sustainability movements. *Resources* **8**, 159 (2019).

9. Azapagic, A. & Perdan, S. Indicators of sustainable development for industry: A general framework. *Trans IChemE* **78**, 243–261 (2000).

10. Microsoft corporate social responsibility report | Microsoft. https://query.prod.cms.rt.microsoft.com/cms/api/am/binary/RE4JaGo.

11. Rethinking finance in a circular economy. https://www.ingwb.com/media/1149417/ing-rethinking-finance-in-a-circular-economy-may-2015.pdf.

12. Social Sustainability | UN Global Compact. https://www.unglobalcompact.org/what-is-gc/our-work/social.

13. Tollefson, J. How hot will be earth by 2100? *Nature* **520**, 444–446 (2020).

14. 1.5 degrees Celsius: The sad truth about our boldest climate change target | Vox. https://www.vox.com/energy-and-environment/2020/1/3/21045263/climate-change-1-5-degrees-celsius-target-ipcc.

15. Here's a list of countries committed to a net-zero emissions goal | World Economic Forum. https://www.weforum.org/agenda/2019/07/the-growing-list-of-countries-committing-to-a-net-zero-emissions-goal.

16. Singapore's enhanced nationally determined contribution and long-term low-emissions development strategy. https://www.nccs.gov.sg/media/press-release/singapores-enhanced-nationally-determined-contribution-and-long-term-low-emissions-development-strategy.

17. Polman, A., Knight, M., Garnett, E. C., Ehrler, B. & Sinke, W. C. Photovoltaic materials: Present efficiencies and future challenges. *Science* **352**, aad4424 (2016).

18. Chen, L. *et al.* Sub-ambient radiative cooling and its application in buildings. *Build. Simul.* **13**, 1165–1189 (2020).

19. 7 companies to watch in carbon capture and storage | Greenbiz. https://www.greenbiz.com/article/7-companies-watch-carbon-capture-and-storage.

20. Alcamo, J. *et al. Ecosystems and Human Well-Being.* Island Press (2003).

21. Clarke, G. L. *Elements of Ecology.* John Wiley & Sons (1954).

22. Arshad, Z., Robaina, M., Shahbaz, M. & Veloso, A. B. The effects of deforestation and urbanization on sustainable growth in Asian countries. *Environ. Sci. Pollut. Res.* **27**, 10065–10086 (2020).

23. Mozgeris, G. & Balenovic, I. Operationalization of remote sensing solutions for sustainable forest management. *Remote Sens.* **13**, 572 (2021).

24. Drivers of deforestation | Our World in Data. https://ourworldindata.org/drivers-of-deforestation.

25. Birkby, J. Vertical farming issues. https://attra.ncat.org/product/vertical-farming/.

26. What is Ecosia? — The search engine that plants trees. https://info.ecosia.org/.

27. Seadon, J. K. Sustainable waste management systems. *J. Clean. Prod.* **18**, 1639–1651 (2010).

28. Forti, V., Baldé, C. P., Kuehr, R. & Bel, G. The Global E-waste Monitor 2020. https://www.itu.int/en/ITU-D/Environment/Documents/Toolbox/GEM_2020_def.pdf.

29. Science for Environment Policy Future Brief: Towards the battery of the future. https://ec.europa.eu/environment/integration/research/newsalert/pdf/towards_the_battery_of_the_future_FB20_en.pdf.

30. Shaibani, M. *et al.* Expansion-tolerant architectures for stable cycling of ultrahigh-loading sulfur cathodes in lithium-sulfur batteries. *Sci. Adv.* **6**, eaay2757 (2020).

31. Orikasa, Y. *et al.* High energy density rechargeable magnesium battery using earth-abundant and non-toxic elements. *Sci. Rep.* **4**, 1–6 (2014).

32. Kang, K. D., Kang, H., Ilankoon, I. M. S. K. & Chong, C. Y. Electronic waste collection systems using Internet of Things (IoT): Household electronic waste management in Malaysia. *J. Clean. Prod.* **252**, 119801 (2020).

33. Nowakowski, P., Szwarc, K. & Boryczka, U. Combining an artificial intelligence algorithm and a novel vehicle for sustainable e-waste collection. *Sci. Total Environ.* **730**, 138726 (2020).

34. Wilson, D. C., Velis, C. A. & Rodic, L. Integrated sustainable waste management in developing countries. *Proc. Inst. Civ. Eng. Waste Resour. Manag.* **166**, 52–68 (2013).

35. Extended Producer Responsibility (EPR) System for E-waste Management System | NEA. https://www.nea.gov.sg/our-services/waste-management/3r-programmes-and-resources/e-waste-management/extended-producer-responsibility-(epr)-system-for-e-waste-management-system.

36. Ghoreishi, M. & Happonen, A. Key enablers for deploying artificial intelligence for circular economy embracing sustainable product design: Three case studies. *AIP Conf. Proc.* **2233**, 050008 (2020).

37. Selvan Ramadoss, T., Alam, H. & Seeram, R. Artificial Intelligence and Internet of Things enabled Circular economy. *Int. J. Eng. Sci.* **7**, 55–63 (2018).

38. Avci, B., Girotra, K. & Netessine, S. Electric vehicles with a battery switching station: Adoption and environmental impact. *Manage. Sci.* **61**, 772–794 (2015).

39. #Envision2030 Goal 12: Responsible Consumption and Production | United Nations Enable. https://www.un.org/development/desa/disabilities/envision2030-goal12.html.

40. Senker, P. Foresight: The future of food and farming, final project report. *Prometheus* **29**, 309–324 (2011).

41. Herrero, M. *et al.* Innovation can accelerate the transition towards a sustainable food system. *Nat. Food* **1**, 266–272 (2020).

42. Kalantari, F., Tahir, O. M., Joni, R. A. & Fatemi, E. Opportunities and challenges in sustainability of vertical farming: A review. *J. Landsc. Ecol. Republic* **11**, 35–60 (2018).

43. Food and the circular economy. https://www.ellenmacarthurfoundation.org/explore/food-cities-the-circular-economy.

44. Lingayat, A. B., Chandramohan, V. P., Raju, V. R. K. & Meda, V. A review on indirect type solar dryers for agricultural crops — Dryer setup, its performance, energy storage and important highlights. *Appl. Energy* **258**, 114005 (2020).

45. Goldstein, L. A proposal and a theoretical analysis of a novel concept of a tilted-axis wind turbine. *Energy* **84**, 247–254 (2015).

46. How do wind turbines work? | Good Energy. https://www.goodenergy.co.uk/how-do-wind-turbines-work/.

47. Cao, J. F., Zhu, W. J., Shen, W. Z., Sørensen, J. N. & Sun, Z. Y. Optimizing wind energy conversion efficiency with respect to noise: A study on multi-criteria wind farm layout design. *Renew. Energy* **159**, 468–485 (2020).

48. Assareh, E., Alirahmi, S. M. & Ahmadi, P. A Sustainable model for the integration of solar and geothermal energy boosted with thermoelectric generators (TEGs) for electricity, cooling and desalination purpose. *Geothermics* **92**, 102042 (2021).

49. Pendashteh, A., Palma, J., Anderson, M., Vilatela, J. J. & Marcilla, R. Doping of self-standing CNT fibers: promising flexible air-cathodes for high-energy-density structural Zn-air batteries. *ACS Appl. Energy Mater.* **1**, 2434–2439 (2018).

50. Lee, H. *et al.* High-energy density Li-O2 battery with a polymer electrolyte-coated CNT electrode via the layer-by-layer method. *ACS Appl. Mater. Interfaces* **12**, 17385–17395 (2020).

Exercises

1) What are the three fields that must be merged to achieve sustainable interaction?
   - (A) Engineering, People, Policy
   - (B) Engineering, People, Planet
   - (C) Engineering, People, Business
   - (D) Engineering, People, Countries

2) How do corporations show their commitment to sustainable business practices?
   (A) By implementing a carbon-neutral business strategy
   (B) By interacting with communities and adhering to ethical standards
   (C) By doing business in an open and transparent manner
   (D) All the above

3) Which one of the following is not an example of industrial symbiosis?
   (A) Waste generated by soy-processing facilities may be used to create environmentally friendly furniture
   (B) Waste produced by construction and demolition used to pave roads
   (C) Waste from atomic power plants can be used to recycle water
   (D) None of the above

4) What is the aim of nearly 3.75 million hectares of land transformed per year?
   (A) Building and construction
   (B) Agriculture
   (C) Mining
   (D) None of the above

5) Which kind of waste is expected to hit 74 million tonnes by 2030?
   (A) Food waste
   (B) Plastic waste
   (C) Electronic waste
   (D) Chemical waste

6) Why are lithium-ion batteries not environmentally friendly?
   (A) Emits toxic fumes while recycling
   (B) Because of the presence of radiative anode and cathode
   (C) Due to its weight
   (D) All the above

7) Aeroponics is an example of:
   (A) Desert farming
   (B) Ocean farming
   (C) Space farming
   (D) Urban farming

8) What conservation initiatives and policies are necessary to attain a carbon-neutral world?
   (A) Resource conservation
   (B) Carbon taxation
   (C) Incentivizing clean technologies
   (D) All the above

9) What could be the energy sources for future planes?
    (A) Jet fuels and Solar cells
    (B) Solar cells and Batteries
    (C) Hydrogen and Fuel cells
    (D) Hydrogen and Solar cells
10) Which technology generates electricity from waste heat?
    (A) Thermoelectric
    (B) Photovoltaic
    (C) Electromagnetic
    (D) All the above

ANSWERS TO EXERCISES

Chapter 1

A C C D A B C D A D

Chapter 2

A A C C A C D A C A

Chapter 3

A D A C A B C A D A

Chapter 4

A C A D A B C D C A

Chapter 5

B C A D B B C B B A

Chapter 6

C A C A B C D D A B

Chapter 7

A C B C D A A D A B

Chapter 8

B A C D D B A C B A

Chapter 9

B B D B C A A D A D

Chapter 10

C D C B C A D D C A

INDEX

CPSIA information can be obtained
at www.ICGtesting.com
Printed in the USA
JSHW030511290822
29823JS00004B/124

9 789811 243165